Principles and
of
Grief Counseli

Howard R. Winokuer, PhD, is the founder of the Winokuer Center for Counseling and Healing in Charlotte, North Carolina, where he maintains a full-time clinical practice. He completed his PhD in 1999 at Mississippi State University, where he developed the first course in Grief Counseling Skills. As the founder of TO LIFE, a not-for-profit educational and counseling organization, he was the associate producer of seven PBS specials and helped pilot one of the first teen suicide prevention programs in the Southeast. He has taught numerous courses and been a guest lecturer at many colleges and universities, including New York University, Rochester University, the University of North Alabama, Queens University, Appalachian State University, and The University of North Carolina.

Dr. Winokuer has conducted workshops and seminars throughout the United States as well as in nine foreign countries, including programs for St. Christopher's Hospice and St. George's Medical Center, London, England; The National Assistance Board, Barbados; and the United States Embassy at The Hague, Netherlands. He wrote a bimonthly column in *The Concord Tribune* entitled "Understanding Grief" and hosted a regular radio show on WEGO entitled *Life Talk*. He was a consultant to WBTV, the local CBS affiliate in Charlotte, NC, after the tragedy of September 11, and has been the mental health "professional on call" for Fox TV's news show *The Edge*. He has recently appeared on the radio show *Healing the Grieving Heart* and has been interviewed by the *ACA Journal* and *Counseling Today*, as well as in the *Staten Island Advance*, the *Houston Chronicle*, *The Charlotte Observer*, the *Detroit Free Press*, and the *Chicago Tribune*. He also led an international delegation of funeral directors to Russia and Holland to study death and funeral practices in those countries.

Dr. Winokuer has been actively involved in the field of dying, death, and bereavement since 1979. He has presented workshops and seminars to many organizations, including the National Funeral Directors Association, The University of North Carolina's Department of Neurological Surgery, the Tennessee Health Care Association, and the Presbyterian Hospital. He also developed the crisis management plan for the Cabarrus County School System. He has been an active member of the Association for Death Education and Counseling (ADEC) for almost three decades and has served in numerous leadership positions. In his almost 30 years of membership, he has chaired the national public relations committee, co-chaired the 2000 and 2003 national conference, served on the Board of Directors, co-chaired the 2011 international conference that ADEC co-hosted with the International Conference on Grief and Bereavement in Contemporary Society, was the president of ADEC, and was one of the co-editors for the recently released book *Grief and Bereavement in Contemporary Society: Bridging Research and Practice* (2011).

Darcy L. Harris, PhD, FT, is a professor in the Department of Interdisciplinary Programs at King's University College at the University of Western Ontario, London, Ontario, Canada, where she is the coordinator of the Thanatology Program. She also maintains a private clinical practice with a focus on issues related to change, loss, and transition. She serves as a consultant for the Southern Ontario Fertility Treatment Program, and she is a community consultant for victims of traumatic loss. She also serves on the ethics committee and the quality care committee at St. Joseph's Health Centre in London, Ontario.

Dr. Harris planned and developed the undergraduate degree program in Thanatology at King's University College, which provides students from around the world with the opportunity to study about death, dying, and bereavement. She has implemented coursework in Thanatology in the specific interest areas of critical theory, social justice, and the exploration of grief after nondeath losses. She is also adjunct faculty in the College of Graduate Studies at the University of Western Ontario and is on the board of directors for ADEC.

Dr. Harris has written extensively and frequently provides presentations on topics related to death, grief, and loss in contemporary society. Topical areas include the social context of grief in Western society, women's experiences of reproductive losses, and shame and social stigma in death and grief. She has recently released a book that explores nondeath and nonfinite loss entitled *Counting Our Losses: Reflecting on Change, Loss, and Transition in Everyday Life,* and she is the co-editor of another recently released book entitled *Grief and Bereavement in Contemporary Society: Bridging Research and Practice.*

Principles and Practice
of
Grief Counseling

HOWARD R. WINOKUER, PhD

DARCY L. HARRIS, PhD, FT

SPRINGER PUBLISHING COMPANY

NEW YORK

Springer Publishing Company, LLC
11 West 42nd Street
New York, NY 10036
www.springerpub.com

Acquisitions Editor: Sheri W. Sussman
Composition: S4Carlisle Publishing Services

ISBN: 978-0-8261-0872-2
E-book ISBN: 978-0-8261-0873-9

12 13 14/ 5 4 3 2 1

The author and the publisher of this Work have made every effort to use sources believed to be reliable to provide information that is accurate and compatible with the standards generally accepted at the time of publication. The author and publisher shall not be liable for any special, consequential, or exemplary damages resulting, in whole or in part, from the readers' use of, or reliance on, the information contained in this book. The publisher has no responsibility for the persistence or accuracy of URLs for external or third-party Internet Web sites referred to in this publication and does not guarantee that any content on such Web sites is, or will remain, accurate or appropriate.

Library of Congress Cataloging-in-Publication Data
Winokuer, Howard Robin.
  Principles and practice of grief counseling/Howard R. Winokuer, Darcy Harris. —1st ed.
    p. cm.
  ISBN-13: 978-0-8261-0872-2
  ISBN-10: 0-8261-0872-5
1. Grief.   2. Grief therapy.   3. Loss (Psychology)   I. Harris, Darcy.   II. Title.
  BF575.G7W596 2012
  155.9′37—dc23

2011049075

Printed in the United States of America by Hamilton Printing

I would like to dedicate this book to all my students, colleagues, clients, and friends who have influenced my life both personally and professionally. I would also like to dedicate this book to Dr. Darcy Harris, my co-author, with whom it has been a joy, privilege, and honor to work.

— H.R.W.

For Brad and Lauren.

— D.L.H.

Contents

Preface

This book grew out of our need to have a text for the university-based courses that each of us teaches to students who are interested in furthering their knowledge and skills in grief counseling and support. We found that there are many good texts that explore research and theory in counseling psychology, and many other books that expound upon grief and bereavement theory and research. However, we have been unable to find a book that combined both the practical aspects of counseling with the current research and theory related to grief and bereavement. After years of piecing together articles, course reading packets, and chapters selected from different texts, we decided to design a book that would explore both the practical knowledge and skills that are available in counseling psychology with some of the current research and theory in the area of loss, grief, and bereavement. Both of us have been practitioners in this area for over 30 years, and we have drawn upon our own clinical work to "flesh out" things that we think would be most helpful to clinicians who wish to effectively work with bereaved individuals.

We are often asked by clinicians who specialize in other areas of counseling, "How can you do this kind of work all the time?" We also smile at our students' surprised faces when they see that we are not (always) dressed in black, morbid, and void of humor, as the expectations of someone who would work around individuals who are dying or bereaved are often stereotyped in this way. We try to convey to our students our passion for this area, and the rewards that we find in our practice with bereaved individuals. We realize that every day is precious. Our clients continually remind us that life is a gift, and that our time is limited—so we make the most of it. We firmly believe that working with individuals who are dying and bereaved makes us live our lives more consciously, fully, and with a greater appreciation. In our work with bereaved individuals, we have had the privilege of sharing very personal time with people who are hurting, vulnerable, and broken. However, we have also had the opportunity to see how these same individuals draw upon their strengths and innate resilience and reenter the world with a stronger sense of themselves and of the gifts that life has to offer.

We view the practice of grief counseling as a unique sphere of practice, which is another reason why we wanted to write this book. Although counseling in general is meant to address issues that occur in everyday life, and loss is certainly a universal experience, we wanted to be able to focus upon grief as both a painful but adaptive process, with some unique features that separate it out from other types of issues that are addressed in general counseling practice. We will expand upon this idea later on, but we want to state at the beginning that we believe a key aspect of grief counseling is that it does not focus upon what is wrong, but rather upon what is right about the process the bereaved individual experiences, and our emphasis is upon how we can facilitate the healthy unfolding of this adaptive process rather than upon its containment.

One other unique feature of this book is the discussion of grief as a response to losses that are death related and nondeath related, tangible, and intangible in their description. An individual does not have to lose a loved one to death in order to grieve; grief can occur after a loved one with advanced dementia is placed in a long-term care facility, with the ending of an intimate relationship, with the loss of hopes and dreams, and with the loss of self that may accompany life-altering events. Grief is viewed as an adaptive response to experiences that challenge our assumptions about how the world should work, and how we view ourselves and others within that world. Although we devote an entire chapter to this topic, this broader view of grief will be woven through all the material that is presented in the various chapters.

Because we make no assumptions about the background of the reader, we start with the basics of counseling and the therapeutic relationship. In Chapters 1 and 2, we explore the purposes that counseling may serve and the unique aspects and challenges that may occur in counseling individuals who have experienced significant losses. We then move into some basic material about current theories of grief and bereavement and how these understandings apply to clinical practice in Chapter 3. We then focus on issues that are salient to setting up the therapeutic relationship with clients, and specific counseling practices that we believe are relevant to working with bereaved individuals. We devote an entire chapter (4) to the cultivation of presence within the context of the counseling relationship, using this material to form the foundation from which grief counseling should occur. In no other form of counseling is the value of presence more relevant or timely; counselors who focus on trying to problem solve and "fix" things with their clients may find working with bereaved clients to be an exercise in frustration and futility. We believe it crucial for grief counselors to understand and embrace the gift of presence as the primary therapeutic stance in working with bereaved individuals. In Chapter 5, we explore the basics of counseling practice and the foundation of basic counseling skills.

In Chapter 6, we begin to integrate counseling theory and practice directly with grief and bereavement theory. In this chapter, we explore some of the "nitty gritty" expectations of the counseling process with bereaved clients. We then expand upon definitions and understandings of loss and grief in Chapter 7 by discussing grief that may be present but which may often be unrecognized or wrongly diagnosed because it is not related to a death per se. We included a chapter (8) on working with strong emotions because many clinicians find working with clients who are experiencing such intensity to be intimidating or difficult, and their focus is often upon containment of emotions rather than upon using strong emotional content to deepen the client's process. In this same chapter, we discuss concepts such as emotional intelligence and specific ways that strong emotions can provide valuable grist for the mill in clients' process (and the counselor's self-awareness).

The last five chapters of the book look at specific practice issues in grief counseling. In Chapter 9, we help to set out parameters for knowing when a client's process has gone awry, and when additional resources and referrals are indicated in complicated grief scenarios. Chapter 10 provides an overview of some of the therapeutic techniques and tools that we have found to be effective in working with bereaved individuals, adding to the clinicians' "tool kit" some possible resources that may be helpful with specific types of clients and situations. In Chapter 11, we explore ethical issues that may be particularly relevant to grief counseling, and we make recommendations for how grief counselors can ensure that they are practicing in ways that are competent and ethically sound. Chapter 12 identifies some of the common pitfalls that can affect grief counselors, and how the unique features of individuals who are drawn to this type of work can actually make the counselor more vulnerable to experiences such as burnout and secondary traumatization. Finally, we use the last chapter to expound on some of the current issues and controversies that have arisen in our field recently, so that individuals who wish to specialize in the area of grief counseling can critically reflect upon their practice and be aware of some of the common pitfalls that might hinder them in practicing to the best of their ability. We include a section at the end of each chapter to allow the reader an opportunity to better absorb and reflect on the content with directed questions and exercises and a glossary of important terms.

It is our hope that you will find this book both practical in its clinical content and stimulating in its theoretical underpinnings and philosophy. We find our work with bereaved individuals challenging at times, but also highly rewarding both professionally and personally. It is our desire that you learn some things that you might not have thought of before, and that you might feel better equipped to offer your healing presence to bereaved individuals as a result of reading some of the material from this book. We also hope that you find, as we do, that this work is an opportunity to appreciate the strength, innate resilience, and capacity of human beings. Finally, we hope that you find an affirmation of the gifts that are present in your ability to care about others as we encounter fellow travelers in our life's journey.

Acknowledgments

For both of us, the decision to become a counselor and then to write a book about counseling represents the culmination of many life experiences and relationships with people who encouraged, supported, and entrusted each of us in many ways.

Dr. Harris would like to express her gratitude to the individuals in her life who supported her during her own times of upheaval and loss, and who encouraged her to use the strength she found at these times to embrace the concept of the wounded healer. She would also like to specifically express her thanks to the mentors and colleagues who have offered her inspiration and have served as models to her practice: Anne Cummings, Margaret Rossiter, Marg McGill, Derek Scott, Gary Smith, Ralph Howlett, and Paul Liebau.

Dr. Winokuer would like to express his thanks to his mentors Robert Rieke, Mary Thomas Burke, Jonnie McLeod, Joe Ray Underwood, and Craig Cashwell, who guided him through the education process, and Billie Thomas, his friend and colleague who has been there through both the good times and the bad.

Both of us would like to express deep appreciation to our clients, who granted us the privilege of sharing such deeply personal and vulnerable times with us. We feel honored by the trust that you have placed in each of us. In addition, we dedicate this book to the students who seek to learn more about this process and themselves in our grief counseling classes. It is a great joy to share this vocation with others who are traveling on the same path.

This work constantly reminds us of the profound connection that we share with each other and of the common thread of human experience that binds us together in this world. It is with this awareness that we feel both humility and excitement in sharing this book with our readers.

CHAPTER 1

Basics About Counseling

Most of the time, we find our own way through the difficult times in our lives without the need for a professional to assist us. Life is full of ups and downs, and we usually learn to adjust to change, cope with difficulties, and develop our own sense of resilience along the way. There are times, however, when some of our life experiences throw us into a place of great upheaval, severely taxing our abilities and overwhelming our coping abilities. Many of the experiences that challenge us at this level involve painful and significant losses that force us to deeply question ourselves, others, and the world. It is at these times that we may choose to seek the assistance of a counselor. In this chapter, we will explore what counseling is and examine some of the more common misconceptions about it. We will also look at the therapeutic relationship that develops between the counselor and the client in the counseling setting, different contexts in which counseling may occur, and then briefly discuss the goals of grief counseling.

WHAT IS COUNSELING?

In its simplest form, counseling is about two people sitting down in privacy, with one of these individuals listening intently and responding helpfully to the other person who is expressing his or her concerns about problems in living (Feltham, 2010). The field of counseling psychology arose out of grassroots movements of the 1960s as a response to what were viewed as heavy-handed, elitist therapies that focused upon the weaknesses and foibles of the client and that were seen as perpetuating client dependence and disempowerment.

Counseling is seen as a means to address life concerns and issues related to daily living, not as a means to dissect an individual's deep psychic secrets and family dysfunctions. The philosophy of counseling is basically that human beings possess innate strengths and resilience that can be drawn upon during times of struggle and crisis. Counseling offers the opportunity to help identify these areas of strength within individuals. The counseling process provides an avenue for the empowerment of individuals to draw from these resources in order to work through difficult situations. Goals of counseling may include the following:

- assisting clients to gain insight and perspective on their situation, behavior, emotions, and relationships;
- providing a safe place for clients to express feelings and clarify their thoughts;
- providing a context for the clients' experience within a broader perspective (i.e., within a family context, social and political structures, or existential viewpoint);
- enhancing the development of clients' skills in dealing with painful and distressing situations;
- empowering clients to become their own best advocates; and
- facilitating clients' process of finding and making meaning in their life experiences.

Counseling is an experience, a relationship, and a process. The counseling process is highly dynamic and interactional between the client and the counselor, with the central focus upon the client's needs and experiences. Counseling does not involve having an expert analyze the client and fix him or her. In the counseling relationship, the counselor and the client work together as a team to help the client to understand his or her experiences and to develop awareness of what he or she can do to work through the current issue.

It is important at this juncture to distinguish between counseling and therapy. Counselors typically assist people with issues and problems of everyday life that are causing angst and difficulty. Counselors typically engage with clients who are basically functional but who are struggling with an issue that is having a significant impact upon their life. Counseling is usually short-term or limited in the time that the client needs this assistance. In contrast, therapy involves in-depth work with clients, aimed at long-standing struggles and unresolved deeper issues that may require longer, ongoing supportive work. In therapy, clients usually work on restructuring core aspects of themselves. In counseling, clients focus on reframing everyday life events and identifying the strengths and resources that they need draw upon to work through these events.

MISCONCEPTIONS ABOUT COUNSELING

Popular media and culture perpetuate a negative view of counseling by frequently portraying a client who is loosely identified as "neurotic," sitting in an office with a gloating professional who acts like a condescending parent figure, talking to the client in a way that is belittling and demeaning. In addition, call-in radio and television shows that feature a guest psychologist or "doctor" of some sort who tells people how to solve their problems in 10 minutes or less for the sake of entertainment do not give a very accurate representation of the counseling process. Many people probably have a very unrealistic and stereotypical view of counseling as a result of these types of portrayals. In this section, we will try to dispel some of the more common misconceptions about counseling.

Misconception # 1: Only Individuals Who Are Weak Seek Counseling

Many people think that going to a counselor is a sign that something is wrong with them or that seeking professional assistance is an indication of weakness. This commonly held thought is predicated on the belief that people seek professional help because they are somehow inadequate or needy. This misconception is most likely an extension of our society's value placed upon stoicism and rugged independence, which rewards us for denying and hiding our emotions at times of vulnerability, rather than supporting our healthy need to reach out to our communities and healers when we need to do so. Public expressions of the more vulnerable emotions, such as sadness or anxiety, do not necessarily result in offers of support; rather, their disclosure seems to serve as an invitation for criticism and judgment, along with lowered social status (Harris, 2009).

Our society places a great deal of expectation on us to be "above" emotion and to "overcome" our humanness, and counseling is often associated with emotions that are socially stigmatized. Therefore, seeking counseling is seen as something that "weak" people do because they cannot control their feelings or they are too weak to manage them according to social expectations. Seeing a counselor is not about whether one is weak, but rather, it is more closely associated with our human need to reach out for support when our ability to accommodate something that has happened is deeply challenged. We are social creatures who tend to live in community with others, and yet there is a strong dichotomy in regard to needing to be close to others while not allowing others to see us when we are not strong and independent. Professional counselors understand the courage it takes for a client to be willing to confront his or her problems head on and to expose such vulnerability in order to work through these difficult times.

Misconception #2: The Counselor Is the Expert

Another misconception about counseling focuses on the role of the counselor as the expert. Certainly, professional counselors have usually undergone a great deal of training, and they often have graduate level degrees in their field. The natural assumption is that the counselor is in a position of being the expert, and the client comes to the counselor to find answers to problems by drawing from the counselor's expertise. We distinguish between the expertise of the counselor in the *process of counseling* and the expertise of the client in his or her *life and choices*. The client knows his or her values, beliefs, and life experiences better than anyone else, and the role of the counselor is not to give advice or figure out what the client *should* do. Instead, the counselor acts as a facilitator to help the client to find his or her own answers, solutions, and choices. We strongly believe that each person has his or her own best answers deep inside, and that the role of the counselor is not to solve the client's problems, but rather to help that person find what he or she needs to work through the painful times and problematic areas.

Misconception #3: People Who Need Counseling Are Basically Emotionally Unstable

Another misconception about the counseling process is that a person must be crazy or unstable if he or she is seeking help from a counselor. It is true that when someone is going through a difficult time, especially an acute grief reaction, there is a wide range of emotional responses that can be associated with that loss (Worden, 2009). Those emotions are often described by bereaved individuals as being similar to riding a "roller coaster," with feelings changing rapidly and varying widely, and the sense of being out of control is often highly distressing. Such feelings have led many of our clients to ask questions such as "Am I normal?" and "Am I going crazy?"

We often reassure these clients that although they are normal, the disequilibrium that they are experiencing can be the stuff of "crazymaking!" It is not because people are going crazy or that something is wrong with them that they seek counseling, but rather, it is because they are experiencing a significant challenge (i.e., a death, divorce, grief, a personal trauma, and unresolved childhood issues), and they need to have a safe place to sort these things out with someone who can walk alongside them in an empathetic, yet objective way.

Misconception #4: People Who Have Good Friends Do Not Need a Counselor

Many individuals would say that they could get the same support from having a discussion with close friends or family members as from speaking with a counselor, and it is true that most of us have friends and family members whom we rely upon for support during difficult times. However, sometimes these same individuals are also personally involved in these same difficult situations, or they are directly affected by them. As a result, these individuals may have their own opinions or strong feelings that may hinder our ability to openly share our difficulties or to seek their counsel.

In actuality, a counselor can provide a listening ear and trained support that a friend might not be able to provide. Lewis Aron describes the special type of listening in which counselors engage,

> That is what we offer: We listen to people in depth, over an extended period of time and with great intensity. We listen to what they say and to what they don't say; to what they say in words and to what they say through their bodies and enactments. And we listen to them by listening to ourselves, to our minds, our reveries, and our own bodily reactions. We listen to their life stories and to the story that they live with us in the room; their past, their present, and future. We listen to what they already know or can see about themselves, and we listen to what they can't see in themselves. We listen to ourselves listening. (Safran, 2009, p. 116)

This specific type of listening is unique to counseling and unlike other types of interaction. Unlike a relationship with a friend, relative, colleague, or another caring human being, counselors do not just listen—they provide a means for clients to hear themselves more clearly, and, hopefully, come to some awareness of what is causing them to feel the way that they feel. Although friends might have wonderful listening skills and a desire to help, there is often a problem with friends acting as a counselor because it is so very difficult to see a friend who is hurting, and the desire to "fix" or "rescue" may interfere with the client's ability to solve the problem or issue for himself or herself. Suffice it to say that most of our clients have good friends and family members available to them, but they usually find that the unique relationship with the counselor offers something important that these other relationships cannot during certain difficulties.

Misconception # 5: Focusing on Problems Will Make Them Worse

The last misconception that we would like to address is the belief that we should just forget about our problems and move on in life. Although we readily agree that not everyone will find counseling helpful, especially if they are not prone to talking openly with others about the more personal aspects of their lives, it is a concern that there is so much social pressure for people to ignore their feelings and act as if everything is fine when it is not. Unfortunately, this scenario is what commonly occurs, and in many instances, the problem festers and resides in the background, drawing energy away and resurfacing in unwanted ways throughout one's life.

It is true that in counseling we tend to focus on clients' feelings and their expression rather than supporting their suppression, which is more socially acceptable. However, focusing on feelings and actively working with strong emotions will not cause a client to lose control and have a "mental breakdown." Delving deeply into the difficult emotions that clients bring to the session does not cause depression or encourage the client to "wallow" in pain and self-pity. The contrary often seems to occur, as many of our clients will tell us that they feel lighter and more connected with themselves and others after they have been able to identify and share their feelings with someone who supported them in this way.

As a counselor, it is important to be aware of these common misconceptions and how they may influence your clients. Many people are very fearful of pursuing counseling mainly because of these misunderstandings about the purpose and process of counseling. However, if they were to understand what the counseling process is really about, they might view the process differently.

THE THERAPEUTIC RELATIONSHIP

Developing a range of skills and techniques is very important and useful in working with clients. However, no intervention is more important than first establishing the relationship upon which the therapeutic encounter is founded (Goldfried & Davila, 2005; Lambert & Barley, 2001). The relationship between a counselor and a client is both like and unlike any other kind of relationship. What makes this relationship unique? The following list gives an overview of what is unique about what we call the *therapeutic alliance* with a client:

- The relationship exists to meet the needs of the client; the client's needs and agenda are the primary focus.
- Although the counselor possesses training and experience that are unique to the process, there is recognition that the client is the true expert, as only the client has had direct experience with his or her life, and only the client knows what is best for himself or herself.
- The relationship is a real relationship; counselors will have real feelings about the process and the client, and clients' feelings and stories will most likely have an impact upon the counselor. Because the relationship is a real relationship, issues of personality and goodness of fit may have an effect on the success of the therapy. It is important for counselors to recognize that they may not work well with everyone and for clients to realize that finding a counselor who is a "good fit" is as important as finding a counselor with appropriate training and credentials.
- The relationship has specific, described boundaries that are in place to protect *both* the client and the counselor.
- The relationship exists within a framework of defined ethical practices for counseling.
- The relationship is not a friendship, nor a parental relationship, nor a teacher–student relationship, although certain aspects of each of these types of relationships may, at times, be present within the therapeutic alliance.
- The relationship is built upon a model of respect and empowerment; the counselor follows the lead of the client and builds upon the inherent strengths that are present in the client.

The basic conditions for counseling were defined in person-centered therapy by Rogers (1995) as *accurate empathy, unconditional positive regard,* and *congruence. Accurate empathy* refers to the ability of the counselor to enter the client's inner world of private personal meanings and feelings "as if" it were that of the counselor, but without ever losing the "as if" quality. Entering the world of the client in this way conveys a deep sense of the message "I am with you completely." *Unconditional positive regard* is the stance of the counselor to the client, indicating an attitude that, despite one's failings and faults, the counselor relates to the client with deep respect, value, and without any conditions. It is not that the counselor "sugarcoats" problematic areas in the client's life and way of being or that the counselor ignores negative or unskillful tendencies that are apparent, but the counselor chooses to focus on trusting in the innate tendency of human beings to grow and develop when given the right conditions for this to occur.

Finally, *congruence* is a little more complex in its description within the therapeutic alliance. Basically, when a counselor is congruent, she or he is aware of his or her own thoughts and feelings within the encounter with the client and shares these real thoughts and feelings with the client. A related term to congruence is genuineness, in which the counselor is not merely just fulfilling a role within the therapeutic relationship, but is actively engaged as a *real* person in that relationship, and shares thoughts, feelings, and reflections with the client that are based within the counselor's personal experience with the client and not just from theoretical knowledge and a diagnostic lens (Geller & Greenberg, 2002; Yalom, 2002). In this book, we will repeatedly go back to these conditions as the foundation of the counseling relationship, with an understanding that the concept of engaged presence is the prerequisite to the counselor being able to offer these necessary conditions to the client.

GRIEF COUNSELING

Now that we have discussed what counseling is and is not, it would probably be helpful to discuss the specific subset of counseling practice that focuses on grief and bereavement. In her book *Necessary Losses,* Judith Viorst (1987) stated that loss is something that we cannot avoid and that loss experiences can be both difficult and transformative. Our lives are often shaped and shattered by the experience of various losses over time. The death of a loved one can certainly be one of the most crippling events that we encounter. As we live in a society where we expect to live a long, healthy life, and there is little exposure to death on a regular basis, most people do not have the opportunity to develop a repertoire of responses to death prior to being plunged head first into a major loss experience. We also do not have many good role models for how to walk the path of grief in a way that allows for much variation, other than the typical social messages that offer empty platitudes and reward bereaved individuals for being busy, distracted, and for "getting over it" as soon as possible. A counselor who understands the basic tenets of good counseling practice and who also has expertise in the grieving process can provide a highly specialized form of support to an individual who is struggling with a significant loss (Worden, 2009).

Individual Counseling

Perhaps the most common venue for grief counseling, individual counseling can provide the support and guidance to help a bereaved individual navigate through significant loss experiences. Clinicians who are trained in the unique aspects of grief counseling can help a person better understand this experience and place it into a sense of perspective in regard to normalcy and expectations. Grief counseling might also help the client to identify and develop effective tools to cope at this very time. In addition, the grief counselor is often the safe person who can hear about things that are difficult for the client to tell others within his or her friendship network and family circle. Grief counseling is directly related to general counseling, as loss and grief are universal and everyday experiences, and counseling is aimed at helping individuals to get through times in everyday life that are especially challenging or difficult.

Marriage/Couple Counseling

When two individuals who share an intimate relationship experience a significant loss, there are often challenges to the couple in the form of disparities in grieving style. The most common scenario for couple counseling is after the death of a child (Rosenblatt, 2000). The death of a child is one of the most difficult losses that can be experienced; it is expected that we will inevitably bury our parents, and there is a 50–50 chance that we will have to bury a spouse, partner, or significant other. However, it is not the natural order for parents to have to bury a child. It is not unusual, even in healthy marriages, for conflicts to occur. Partners who are already in a great deal of pain after the loss of a child often do not have the energy to resolve conflicts with the other partner. There is also the compounding issue of differences in grieving style that often surfaces during this painful time (Doka & Martin, 2010). As a result, it is common to hear partners grieve the loss not only of their child, but also of each other because of the deep, paralyzing grief that each experiences, and the disparities in how that grief is manifest. In this scenario, couple counseling can provide the grieving couple with an understanding of their grief and the tools to explore where they are stuck in their grief. As a result, they may be able to learn new behaviors and skills to break out of the destructive cycle of blame and isolation that can cause a great deal of damage to the relationship between them.

Family Counseling

Although there is the expectation that family members will grieve together and provide support to one another, the reality is that dissimilar or incongruent grief often occurs and causes conflicts within the family system (Cook & Oltjenbruns, 1998; Gilbert, 1996). People who experience a mutual loss within a family may be the least able to support each other, as the relational dynamic with each other and the deceased person may impede the ability to find common grief pathways. Loss of a family member disrupts the family system, and the family must reorganize after the loss. Family members may also be depleted after a long period of caregiving, and there may be a lack of available energy to deal with the underlying family dynamics and stresses that have built up over time and often come to the surface after a family member dies. Counselors who are trained in family therapy and who also understand the complexities of grief within these family systems may be able to bridge the gaps in the family system that has been torn by caregiving burdens, losses, and dyssynchronous grief.

GOALS OF COUNSELING

The purpose of grief counseling is to help individuals work through the feelings, thoughts, and memories associated with the loss of a loved one in a way that is congruent with the bereaved individual's personality, preferences, values, and goals. Understanding the goals of grief counseling can help clinicians to work more effectively with clients. Although most people associate grief counselors with assisting individuals who are grieving the loss of a loved one, the scope of grief counseling encompasses supporting individuals through all kinds of change, transitions, and losses. As you look through these goals, think of how they may also apply to losses that may not be related to death, such as the ending of a relationship, the loss of employment, or the loss of functionality or health.

The following are some of the goals of grief counseling:

- providing the bereaved a safe place to share their experiences and feelings;
- helping the bereaved to live without the person who died and to make decisions alone;
- helping the bereaved to honor the continuing bond with the deceased person while moving forward into life again at some point in the future;

- providing support and time to focus on grieving in a safe environment;
- recognizing the importance of occasions such as birthdays and anniversaries and supporting the client through these dates and special times;
- providing education about normal grieving and the normal variations in grieving among individuals;
- assisting clients to integrate the loss into their assumptive world, or to rebuild that world after a significant loss;
- helping the bereaved to understand his or her methods of coping;
- engaging clients to recognize their innate strengths in coping and adapting to significant loss experiences;
- identifying coping problems the bereaved may have and making recommendations for more professionals and resources in the community; and
- empowering the client in approaching life and others after experiencing a life-changing loss.

We have written this book in a way that, hopefully, provides you with a solid foundation in counseling and grief theory, interspersed with practical suggestions for your work with bereaved individuals. At its core, grief counseling is good counseling practice that is also embedded with the current research, theory, and clinical wisdom from those who have spent years in research and practice with bereaved individuals. We hope that the contents of this book will help you to be a better informed and reflective practitioner with clients who have experienced significant, life-altering losses.

Glossary of Terms

Accurate empathy   the ability of the counselor to enter the client's inner world of private, personal meanings and feelings "as if" it were that of the counselor, but without ever losing the "as if" quality.

Congruence   when a counselor is congruent, he or she is aware of his or her own thoughts and feelings within the encounter with the client and shares these real thoughts and feelings with the client.

Core conditions of counseling   established by Rogers in person-centered counseling; these are the three conditions that must be in place for the therapeutic alliance to occur. They are accurate empathy, congruence, and unconditional positive regard.

Counseling   professional support that has defined boundaries with the intent of assisting individuals to effectively work through everyday life issues that cause difficulty or distress.

Therapeutic alliance   the unique relationship with a client that is focused solely upon the client's needs, whereby the client feels safe, supported, and understood by the counselor.

Therapy   in-depth professional work with clients, aimed at long-standing struggles and unresolved deeper issues that may require long-term supportive work. In therapy, clients usually work on restructuring core aspects of themselves.

Unconditional positive regard   the stance of the counselor to the client, indicating an attitude that despite one's failings and faults, the counselor relates to the client with deep respect and value, and without any conditions.

Questions for Reflection

1. Brainstorm about some of the media personalities and popular depictions of counselors that come to your mind. How are the counselors portrayed in these depictions?

   How do you think these portrayals influence the profession of counseling and the view of the general public about counselors and those who seek counseling? Based on the information in this chapter, how is the actual counseling process different from these portrayals?

2. In this chapter, we discuss how counseling is different from receiving support from friends or family members. What do you think are the specific differences between the support from a counselor and other types of support?

3. After reading this chapter, has your thinking about what counseling offers changed from what it was previously? If so, in what ways?

4. If you were to provide grief counseling to bereaved individuals, what do you think would be your biggest challenge personally?

References

Cook, A. S., & Oltjenbruns, K. A. (1998). *Dying and grieving: Life span and family perspectives*. Fort Worth, TX: Harcourt Brace.

Doka, K. J., & Martin, T. L. (2010). *Grieving beyond gender: Understanding the ways men and women mourn*. New York, NY: Routledge.

Feltham, C. (2010). *Critical thinking in counselling and psychotherapy*. London, UK: Sage Publications.

Geller, S., & Greenberg, L. (2002). Therapeutic presence: Therapists experience of presence in the psychotherapy encounter in psychotherapy. *Person Centered & Experiential Psychotherapies, 1*, 71–86.

Gilbert, K. R. (1996). "We've had the same loss, why don't we have the same grief?" Loss and differential grief in families. *Death Studies, 20*(3), 269–283.

Goldfried, M. R., & Davila, J. (2005). The role of relationship and technique in thera-peutic change. *Psychotherapy: Theory, Research, Practice, Training, 42*(4), 421–430.

Harris, D. L. (2009). Oppression of the bereaved: A critical analysis of grief in Western society. *Omega, 60*(3), 241–253.

Lambert, M. J., & Barley, D. E. (2001). Research summary on the therapeutic rela-tionship and psychotherapy outcome. *Psychotherapy: Theory, Research, Practice, Training, 38*(4), 357–361.

Rosenblatt, P. C. (2000). *Help your marriage survive the death of a child*. Philadelphia, PA: Temple.

Safran, J. (2009). Interview with Lewis Aron. *Journal of Psychoanalytic Psychology, 26,* 97–116.

Viorst, J. (1987). *Necessary losses: The loves, illusions, dependencies, and impossible expecta-tions that all of us have to give up in order to grow*. New York, NY: Simon & Schuster.

Worden, J. W. (2009). *Grief counseling and grief therapy* (4th ed.). New York, NY: Springer Publishing Company.

Yalom, I. (2002). *The gift of therapy*. New York, NY: HarperCollins.

CHAPTER 2

Unique Aspects of Grief Counseling

L oss, change, and death are all universal human experiences, and each one of us will become intimately acquainted with the grieving process at many points throughout our lives. Most individuals who are trained in psychology and other counseling-related professions typically have an understanding of the therapy process after significant life events occur. However, we venture further in this chapter to explore what makes grief counseling a unique form of therapeutic support and how the practice of grief counseling may differ from counseling for other types of issues.

One of the most important aspects of grief that differentiates it from other issues that clients bring into the counseling relationship is that the grieving process itself is an adaptive response and not a form of pathology. Grief is the normal, natural response to loss. Grief is not something that we strive to "overcome" or from which there is "recovery," as one might recover from an addiction or an illness. Counselors who work with bereaved individuals understand that although the grieving process may involve a tremendous amount of pain and adjustment, the goal of grief counseling is to facilitate the unfolding of the healthy and adaptive aspects of the process as it is manifested within each client, trusting that this unfolding will eventually help the bereaved individual to re-enter life in a way that is meaningful.

GRIEF AND THE ASSUMPTIVE WORLD

At a basic level, our expectations about how the world works begin to be formed from birth through the development of the attachment relationships of the infant and young child. Bowlby (1969, 1973) posited that early-life attachment experiences lead individuals to form "working models" of the self and of the world. We essentially learn whether the world is a safe or a threatening place from these working models. Bowlby's theory of attachment also suggested that significant losses can threaten these working models, resulting in a need to rebuild or restructure one's working models to fit the postloss world. Building upon Bowlby's work, Parkes (1975) extended the concept of the "internal working model" to that of the "assumptive world," which, he stated, was " . . . a strongly held set of assumptions about the world and the self, which is confidently maintained and used as a means of recognizing, planning, and acting," (p. 132) and that it is " . . . the only world we know, and it includes everything we know or think we know. It includes our interpretation of the past and our expectations of the future, our plans and our prejudices" (1971, p. 103).

Parkes (1971) stated that the assumptions that individuals form about how the world works are based upon their previous life experiences and attachments. He also emphasized that experiencing a significant loss can threaten one's assumptive world. Recent research that links attachment style to the way an individual navigates the grieving process after a significant loss would also support the role of early experiences with attachment figures as a template for how experiences are interpreted and integrated in later life (Stroebe, 2002). In her extensive work that explored the construct of the assumptive world in the context of traumatic experiences, Janoff-Bulman (1992) stated that expectations about how the world should work are established earlier than language in children and that assumptions about the world are a result of the generalization and application of childhood experiences into adulthood. Forming a belief that the world is safe is related to the sense of "basic trust" described by Erikson's (1968) model of human development.

Although attachment theory was originally founded in the psychoanalytic tradition of psychology and the discussion here draws heavily upon attachment as a means of understanding how assumptions are developed, the broader context of the assumptive world goes far beyond the realm of psychological theory or cognition. Janoff-Bulman (1992) identified three major categories of assumptions. The first category is the belief that the world is benevolent—that there is more good than bad in the world and that people are generally trustworthy. The second category is that the world is meaningful—that good and bad events are distributed in the world in a fair and controllable manner. The category of meaningfulness emphasizes the ideas of justice and control over certain aspects of life. Most individuals tend to believe that misfortune is not haphazard and arbitrary and that there is a person-outcome contingency attached to negative life events. At a basic level, negative events are generally viewed as punishment and positive events are rewards. Janoff-Bulman (1992) stated that this assumption is,

> . . . that we can directly control what happens to us through our own behavior. If we engage in appropriate behaviors, we will be protected from negative events and if we engage in appropriate behaviors, good things will happen to us. (p. 10)

The third category is that the self is worthy and has value. Janoff-Bulman stated that these three categories of beliefs can be called world assumptions, and together they make up an individual's assumptive world.

Why are we discussing the development of our assumptive world? Because significant losses often assault those assumptions we have formed about the world from when we were very young. We learn that people can harm, even murder, those whom we love. We learn that our view of the world as a safe and predictable place, where good things come to those who work hard and where all human beings have value and worth, may not be what we actually encounter in our experiences later in life. Somehow, we then have to reconcile the world that we now know to exist with the world that we believed to exist, and the grieving process helps us to rebuild our assumptive world so that we can feel safe and functional again in this new awareness and experience of the world that differs greatly from our previously held beliefs about how that world should work. The revised assumptive world allows us to attach meaning to our experiences and provides us, once again, with a sense of safety about the world. Rather than being a symptom of a disorder, grief is a multifaceted adaptive response to the disorder and disorganization that can occur after our lives have been upturned by a significant loss. Instead of attempting to inhibit grief, we believe that grief needs to be allowed to unfold without hindrance so that the loss experience can be assimilated into one's existing assumptive world, or the assumptive world can be rebuilt in a way that makes sense of the loss that has occurred.

COMING TO TERMS WITH CHANGE AND LOSS

There are many misconceptions about what is involved in grief counseling and the way that therapeutic support works with bereaved individuals. It is not uncommon for a grief counselor to receive a call from an individual who thinks a family member needs grief counseling because they are not "over" the grief or progressing through the grief as they should. The common misunderstanding is that grief counseling will "fix" the person or return them to their prior level of functioning. Some of these kinds of expectations placed upon bereaved individuals are rooted in social norms that reward productivity, stoicism, and materialism, and we will discuss the role of social pressures on bereaved individuals in a later chapter. As it is impossible to reverse time and to control events that are out of our control, we cannot "fix" what has happened, that is, we cannot bring back the deceased person to relieve the separation distress of the bereaved individual. We also do not focus on helping bereaved individuals to feel better necessarily, as we understand the process of rebuilding one's world after a significant loss is naturally going to involve a painful time when the many layers associated with loss must be addressed, and the resulting readjustment that occurs can be a very difficult process.

We crave predictability and stability in our lives. In fact, most of us operate on the assumption that we have a lot of control over the events in our lives and one of the basic assumptions espoused by Janoff-Bulman (1992) indicates that most people in Western society believe that if you work hard, you will be rewarded. In our clinical work, we frequently see individuals who experience profound anxiety because they can no longer live under the illusion that things can remain constant and unchanging, and this realization usually occurs as a result of the experience of a significant loss in their lives. Even though we attempt to function as if there is certainty and stability in everyday life, the world around us and even our bodies serve as metaphors for the normalcy of loss, change, and transition. The seasons change. Living things are born, grow, reproduce, and die. Many of the cells that exist in our bodies today were not present a year ago and may not be present in our bodies in a month from now. This moment is gone and replaced by another moment in time. We cannot stop the changing nature of life, just as we cannot stop time in its place or change the course of events, although this topic has frequently been the subject of fantasy.

Weenolsen (1988) spoke of our innate resistance to change and of our belief that things can remain the same as the "fundamental illusion," functioning to allow us to feel safe and solid in the world. However, our clinging to this image causes us great difficulty when the illusion cannot be maintained, such as when a major loss event does indeed occur or when we come to the realization that we have very little control over ourselves and the people, places, and things that matter very much to us. For many of the bereaved individuals who seek counseling, the realizations that (a) we really have very little control over the events in our lives, (b) there is very little predictability and stability in the world, and (c) we will never be the same again from the foundation of the work that occurs in the counseling process.

UNDERSTANDING BEREAVEMENT THEORY
IN COUNSELING PRACTICE

It is very important for counselors who wish to effectively support bereaved individuals to have a working knowledge of current theories of bereavement. The literature in thanatology is relatively new in comparison with other fields of study, and most of the current thinking in grief counseling is grounded in ways of thinking about grief, loss, adjustment, and coping that have been reported and published within the last 20 years. We will spend an entire chapter exploring some of the current research in bereavement, current bereavement theories, and ways of working therapeutically with bereaved individuals, but at this point it is important to recognize that there is a separate and unique body of literature in this area that has direct application to grief counseling.

One important aspect of the study of bereavement that we keep in mind is that grief is not just a psychological issue that is experienced by the grieving individual in isolation. Grief can be experienced and expressed in many ways, which includes thoughts, feelings, and emotions; however, it can also be experienced physically through bodily symptoms, socially through changes in interpersonal dynamics and expectations for the bereaved individual, spiritually as a quest for meaning or as existential suffering, economically through changes in financial status and expenses incurred after a loss, and practically through the changes that occur in one's day-to-day routine as a result of a loss. Thus, we look at literature in many fields of study for an understanding of the grief process in all of its many facets and complexities.

Another unique aspect of grief counseling is an understanding of the complexity of the experience and the factors that shape an individual's response to loss. For example, when there is a loss within a family system, each individual family member will experience grief, depending upon his or her relationship to the deceased person and other family members, the age and developmental stage of the family members, who provided the caregiving if needed, and the grieving styles of the members (Gilbert, 1996). Individuals tend to grieve in ways that are congruent with their age and developmental stage, according to their personalities and attachment styles (Doka & Martin, 2010; Stroebe, 2002), in the context of social rules and expectations (Doka, 2002; Harris, 2009–2010), with the influence of other factors and concurrent stressors at that time (Worden, 2009). Thus, grief counselors need to have a good understanding of how many different areas intersect in this one experience. For example, exploring only the feelings associated with a loss without understanding the social underpinnings and the impact of the concurrent stressors that shape these feelings would provide an inaccurate and overly simplistic account of the client's full experience.

Understanding current bereavement theory and research allows the counselor to appreciate the normative aspects of grief that may inadvertently be labeled as pathological or abnormal by someone who does not have this awareness. For example, the dominant view of grief until recently was the "grief work" hypothesis (Stroebe, 2002), which stated that individuals must do the "work" of grief by talking about their loss and their feelings, and if a bereaved person did not do this, it was assumed that something was wrong with that individual. The grief work model also posited that the goal of grief was to help the bereaved individual to "let go" of their loved one in order to move forward in life. However, in the mid-1990s, research with diverse groups of bereaved individuals demonstrated that while many individuals do, indeed, talk about their loss and their feelings as part of the grief response, many others did not have this same need, and these individuals seemed to cope just as well afterwards. In addition, the *continuing bonds theory*, derived from research by Klass, Silverman, and Nickman (1996), demonstrated the normalcy of bereaved individuals continuing a relationship with the deceased. These researchers found that the ability to find a way to remain connected to the deceased individual often helped bereaved individuals to move forward in their lives after a loss.

WHO BENEFITS FROM GRIEF COUNSELING?

Most grief counselors assume that their work with bereaved individuals is effective. However, recent research into the efficacy of grief counseling provides more detailed information about who would benefit from and who might actually be harmed by grief counseling. Studies by Kato and Mann (1999) and Allumbaugh and Hoyt (1999) inferred that professional bereavement support did not provide significant benefit to the bereaved participants. It is probably important to take a step back and to ponder the basic premise of many interventions for bereaved individuals. As we have stated earlier in this chapter that grief is a normal and adaptive process, we need to consider why professional intervention may be needed by bereaved individuals to assist an adaptive process that is at work. Indeed, Stroebe, Hansson, Stroebe, and Schut (2001) observed that the general tendency for many bereaved individuals is to improve with or without professional intervention. In addition, Kato and Mann's (1999) study revealed that many of the bereaved participants would have had a better outcome if they had been assigned to the control (nontreatment) group rather than to the treatment group. In another

study, Jordan (2000) reported that for some bereaved individuals, professional intervention may actually do more harm than good.

In response to these findings, researchers in the area of bereavement
have made some comments and suggested a few guidelines that would be
applicable to clinical practice in grief counseling. It is generally agreed that
most bereaved individuals can adapt to the loss that has occurred with the
support of their families and friends and do not require professional intervention. Making the assumption that all bereaved individuals need professional assistance would be inconsistent with the awareness of grief as an
adaptive process. It may be the case that although the grieving process is
normative and adaptive, if one's grief does not fit into a socially acceptable
or recognized pattern, the bereaved individual may be perceived as abnormal and referred for treatment, when in fact, the social norms that judge the
expression of grief in such limited terms may be the issue, and not some
dysfunction within the individual. Wolfelt (2005) suggested a model of
"companioning" with the bereaved, emphasizing the relational component
of therapeutic support, which may be especially helpful if a bereaved individual does not have other supports available to "walk alongside" him or
her during the acute grieving process.

In their review of bereavement efficacy studies, Jordan and Neimeyer
(2003) stated,

> . . . generic interventions, targeted toward the general population of the bereaved,
> are likely to be unnecessary and largely unproductive. Instead, interventions that
> are tailored to the problems of mourners in high-risk categories (e.g., bereaved
> mothers, suicide survivors, etc.), or showing unremitting or increasing lev-
> els of distress after a reasonable period of time are likely to be more beneficial.
> (pp. 778–779)

Parkes (2002) and Stroebe and Schut (2001) identified specific at-risk popu-
lations that may benefit most from grief counseling. These groups include
older men who lose spouses, mothers who lose children, and survivors of
sudden or violent losses with traumatic features. Other high-risk individuals may be those with preexisting psychological disturbances such as depression, substance abuse, posttraumatic stress disorder, and a history of
psychosis. In addition, individuals with high levels of distress early in their
bereavement experience are more likely to benefit from professional intervention. Larson and Hoyt (2007) suggested that some of the research about
the efficacy of grief counseling (and the lack of positive effects that have been
found in many of the studies with bereaved individuals) may be a result of
how participants are recruited versus how clients actually seek counseling
for assistance when they feel they need additional help. These researchers

state that there is a big difference between individuals who respond to calls for participation in studies and bereaved individuals who contact a counselor for assistance with a grief-related issue.

IMPLICATIONS FOR GRIEF COUNSELORS

Once you start into a clinical practice specializing in grief counseling, you will no doubt have clients with a diverse range of losses who also have very different ways of grieving, coping, and adapting to loss. Probably the most important aspect of your work will be your ability to "walk alongside" your clients as they share their experiences with you. It is important that you be able to normalize reactions that may be viewed as abnormal by social norms that are unrealistic and that you be able to recognize when a client is in a high-risk category and in need of additional support. A knowledge of current bereavement theory and research will help you in this process. Being informed and aware of good counseling practice is also essential to providing a safe place for your clients to journey through their grieving process in a way that allows for the integration of the loss experience into their lives in a way that is healing.

Glossary of Terms

Assumptive world   fundamental beliefs that an individual holds regarding how the world works and how others and one's self are viewed. The assumptive world is thought to provide individuals with a sense of safety and security in everyday life situations.

Attachment   the formation of significant and stable connections with significant people in an individual's life. This process begins in early infancy as the child bonds with one or more primary caregivers and later extends to other significant relationships through the life span. Attachment is thought to be an instinctual construct with the purpose of ensuring safety and survival.

"Fundamental illusion"   the belief that things will always remain the same; maintaining this illusion serves the purpose of allowing people to feel safe and solid in the world.

"Grief work" hypothesis   view of grief that individuals must do the "work" of grief by talking about their loss and their feelings, and if a bereaved person did not do this, it was assumed that something was wrong with that individual. Also indicates that the goal of grief is to help the bereaved individual to "let go" of their loved one in order to move forward in life.

Questions for Reflection

1. If grief is an adaptive and healthy process, why do you think we have such a great deal of difficulty acknowledging grief both personally and socially?

2. Think about the section on the assumptive world. What are some of the assumptions that you can identify personally that guide you in your life? What are some of the ways that your assumptions have been challenged by experiences that you have had in your life?

3. If, as the chapter states, change and transition are truly constant companions in life, why do most people have difficulty adjusting to change and loss in their lives?

4. You are a grief counselor and you receive a call from a woman who wants her father to come to see you for counseling after the death of his wife (her mother). She reports that she is concerned that her father does not seem to be grieving at all, and she thinks that he needs to talk with someone. How would you respond to her request?

5. Perform a search on the Internet with one of the well-known search engines, with the key words of "grief counseling," "grief recovery," and "helping bereaved individuals." Read over some of the material that is presented in these links. How many of them still extol the grief work theory of bereavement? What audience do you think each site is trying to target? Based upon your reading of this chapter, do you think there is any potentially harmful content on the sites for bereaved individuals?

References

Allumbaugh, D. L., & Hoyt, W. T. (1999). Effectiveness of grief therapy: A meta-analysis. *Journal of Counseling Psychology, 46*(3), 370–380.

Bowlby, J. (1969). *Attachment and loss: Attachment* (Vol. 1). London, UK: Hogarth.

Bowlby, J. (1973). *Attachment and loss: Separation* (Vol. 2). New York, NY: Basic Books.

Doka, K. J. (2002). *Disenfranchised grief: New directions, challenges, and strategies for practice.* Champaign, IL: Research Press.

Doka, K. J., & Martin, T. L. (2010). *Grieving beyond gender: Understanding the ways that men and women mourn.* New York, NY: Routledge.

Erikson, E. H. (1968). *Identity: Youth and crisis.* New York, NY: Norton.

Gilbert, K. R. (1996). "We've had the same loss, why don't we have the same grief?" Loss and differential grief in families. *Death Studies, 20*(3), 269–283.

Harris, D. (2009–2010). Oppression of the bereaved: A critical analysis of grief in Western society. *Omega, 60*(3), 241–253.

Janoff-Bulman, R. (1992). *Shattered assumptions: Towards a new psychology of trauma.* New York, NY: Free Press.

Jordan, J. R. (2000). Research that matters: Bridging the gap between research and practice in thanatology. *Death Studies, 24,* 457–468.

Jordan, J. R., & Neimeyer, R. A. (2003). Does grief counseling work? *Death Studies, 27,* 765–786.

Kato, P. M., & Mann, T. (1999). A synthesis of psychological interventions for the bereaved. *Clinical Psychology Review, 19,* 275–296.

Klass, D., Silverman, P. R., & Nickman, S. L. (1996). *Continuing bonds: New understandings of grief.* New York, NY: Routledge.

Larson, D. G., & Hoyt, W. T. (2007). What has become of grief counseling? An evaluation of the empirical foundations of the new pessimism. *Professional Psychology: Research and Practice, 38,* 347–355.

Parkes, C. M. (1971). Psycho-social transitions: A field for study. *Social Science & Medicine, 5,* 101–115.

Parkes, C. M. (1975). What becomes of redundant world models? A contribution to the study of adaptation to change. *British Journal of Medical Psychology, 48,* 131–137.

Parkes, C. M. (2002). Grief: Lessons from the past, visions for the future. *Death Studies, 26*(5), 367–385.

Stroebe, M. S. (2002). Paving the way: From early attachment theory to contemporary bereavement research. *Mortality, 7*(2), 127–138.

Stroebe, M. S., Hansson, R. O., Stroebe, W., & Schut, H. (2001). Future directions for bereavement research. In M. S. Stroebe, R. O. Hansson, W. Stroebe, & H. Schut (Eds.), *Handbook of bereavement research: Consequences, coping, and care* (pp. 741–766). Washington, DC: American Psychological Association.

Stroebe, M. S., & Schut, H. (2001). Models of coping with bereavement: A review. In M. S. Stroebe, R. O. Hansson, W. Stroebe, & H. Schut (Eds.), *Handbook of bereavement research: Consequences, coping, and care* (pp. 375–404). Washington, DC: American Psychological Association.

Weenolsen, P. (1988). *Transcendence of loss over the life span.* New York, NY: Hemisphere.

Wolfelt, A. (2005). *Companioning the bereaved: A soulful guide for caregivers.* San Jose, CA: Companion Press.

Worden, J. W. (2009). *Grief counseling and grief therapy* (4th ed.). New York, NY: Springer Publishing Company.

CHAPTER 3

Theories and Orientation
to Bereavement

*I*n this chapter, we will briefly look at models and theories of bereavement that help us to understand the grieving process a little better. Models and theories serve as descriptors for us and for our clients. They help us to "map out" what may occur after a significant loss in someone's life. They may also give us a framework for knowledge and insight into the various ways that people experience grief and adapt to loss or as to how bereavement professionals have observed grief responses in their clients. Research-based theories and models may ground our clinical practice in empirical knowledge, and descriptive models may give us practical insights from the anecdotal accounts of other clinicians who do similar work. It is important to keep in mind that no one theory or model can fully encompass all of the manifestations, expressions, and experiences of grief and loss. However, becoming well-versed in these descriptions may be of benefit to both the counselor and the client.

Before we embark on our exploration of various theories and models of bereavement, it is important to keep some thoughts in mind. First, although loss and grief are universal experiences, shared by all human beings, the grieving process is highly diverse and variable between individuals. Second, grief is more than an emotional response. Many individuals experience grief in ways that are dominated not by their emotions but by cognitive processes, somatic (bodily) changes, and/or changes in their social circles and patterns. In addition, a person who is grieving a loss exists within a broader social and cultural context, and we do a great disservice to individuals by assuming that they exist as separate entities from these spheres of existence. Finally, we tend to think in terms of adapting to losses and integrating these experiences into our assumptive world rather than focusing on "recovery" from grief or "overcoming" a loss.

DEFINITIONS AND ANALOGIES

For the purposes of this book and our study of bereavement, *loss* is defined as the real or perceived deprivation of something that is deemed meaningful. A loss can be death related or nondeath related. A loss experience is one in which a return to some aspect of life that we have cherished or valued is no longer possible. *Grief* is defined simply as the normal and natural reaction to loss. However, the use of the word "normal" implies that there is a defined expectation of what normal grief should look like, and that is far from true. Although grief is a universal experience that is shared by all human beings, the actual grief response in each individual is unique, and the expression of grief can vary greatly from one person to another. Many factors, such as personality traits, the presence of concurrent stressors and previous losses, the nature of the losses, and the social expectations that are present, will have a great deal of influence in shaping the course of grief for an individual, and we will discuss these in later chapters.

Sometimes, it is helpful to share analogies with bereaved clients to help point out the highly individual and unique nature of grief, especially when these individuals are being told by others that somehow their grief response is abnormal!

- The grief response can be compared to snowflakes, where we can look at the flakes and identify them as "snow," but when you look closer, the crystalline structure of each individual flake is unique, and there are an infinite number of patterns that can be found.
- The grief response is like a fingerprint, as all human beings have fingerprints, with each person identified by a unique pattern that is unlike that of anyone else.
- A significant loss can be seen like a deep wound that will heal with proper care and attention. After a deep wound heals, there is usually a scar in its place, so, although the "wound" is healed, the skin is never the same as it was before. (Another aspect of this analogy is that scar tissue tends to be thicker and stronger than the skin surrounding it.)

ATTACHMENT AND THE GRIEF RESPONSE

As we discussed earlier, a key aspect of bereavement theory is the concept of attachment. In humans, attachment is based on one of our most deeply rooted needs for safety and security (Bowlby, 1969, 1973). Attachment bonds are deeper than relational bonds, and they exist at a level in the human experience that is usually not in a person's conscious awareness (Parkes & Weiss, 1983). When we speak of attachment in this context, we mean something more than a relational bond. Attachment relationships are linked to our primary, instinctual need to be close to significant others in order to feel safe and to feel a sense of "anchoring" in our world. In infants, the attachment system is formed around the primary caregiver who is present to meet the basic needs of the infant and who responds to the infant's cries and beginning attempts at social interaction. Later, we form attachments to individuals who tend to be closest to us or to whom there is significance identified for us. It is important to note that the presence of attachment in a relationship is not necessarily dependent upon the quality of the relationship or the personality or temperament of the individuals involved in the attachment bond.

Attachment in humans was first described by John Bowlby, a psychoanalytically trained psychiatrist who worked with young children in postwar England. In his position at the Tavistock Clinic, he observed children who had been separated from their parents (their primary attachment figures), and he made note of some commonalities in the responses of these children, which he termed "separation distress." Bowlby was also influenced by the work of Hinde (1982), who, like Harlow (1961), studied the effects of infant–mother bonding in rhesus monkeys. Bowlby noted that in both researchers' work, there were comparable behaviors demonstrated between primates that were separated from their mothers and human infants who were separated from their human mothers. He termed these consistent behaviors as "attachment behaviors" and suggested that these behaviors functioned to ensure that the primary caregiver stayed in proximity to the needy, helpless infant in both species (Cassidy, 1999).

Bowlby later postulated that attachment between infants and their mothers is an ethologically based[1] construct that serves to ensure the protection and survival of the infant. Thus, attachment theory was initially born as a merging of the psychoanalytic school of thinking and ethology, the study of animal behavior. Attachment was defined as an instinctually mediated response of an infant to its mother, and this response is delineated in the infant's developing mind through object representation and maintained through the attachment behaviors (Bretherton, 1992). Bowlby's later work became an eclectic model that incorporated elements of psychoanalysis,

---

[1] Ethology is concerned with the adaptive, or survival, value of behavior and its evolutionary history. It emphasizes the genetic and biological roots of development; thus, attachment is seen as an instinctual drive in humans and most mammals (Hinde, 1992).

ethology, experimental psychology, learning theory, and family systems to describe the psychological and emotional development of the child.

Colin Murray Parkes, a psychiatrist based in London, England, worked at the Tavistock Clinic under John Bowlby. He postulated that the attachment behaviors observed in infants upon separation from their mothers were the same behaviors that grieving individuals display upon the loss of a loved one through death (Parkes & Weiss, 1983). Parkes (1996) conducted extensive longitudinal research with older widows, documenting their behaviors, thoughts, and feelings after the death of their spouses. He found common behaviors between the separated infants in Bowlby's research and the widows in his own studies. Examples of these common behaviors were searching, pining, and protest upon the disappearance of the attachment figure. Weiss (1975) explored attachment behaviors in the situation of divorce and obtained similar findings.

In addition to comparisons between the separation of infants from their mothers and the separation of adults from attachment figures through death, further studies examined the attachment behaviors of adults in various relationships. The role of attachment in adult relationships has now been explored in longitudinal studies (Berman & Sperling, 1994). Sroufe, Egeland, and Kreutzer (1990) documented stable patterns of attachment behavior in children up to age 10. Kobak and Hazan (1991) examined the identification of adult attachment styles with specific interactions in married couples. Their data suggest that there are significant correlations between attachment security and marital quality. Hazan and Shaver (1987) examined the role of attachment style in adult intimate relationships. They hypothesized that adults demonstrate the same types of attachment style in their relationships with other adults that were originally present when these adults were much younger. Thus, they stated that adult coping strategies and behaviors in intimate relationships were governed by attachment style as determined by childhood attachment experiences.

The "take home" message for this discussion is an understanding that:

- Grief is part of an instinctually based response that is based in our attachment system, which typically exists outside of our conscious awareness unless it is threatened.
- The loss of an attachment figure will be experienced as a threat to most individuals.
- An attachment relationship is one that is significant, but the attachment bond itself is not necessarily dependent upon the quality of the relationship. Infants form attachments to mothers who are not

attentive; however, the *quality* of the attachment bond that is formed is certainly affected by the interaction between the two individuals.
- Attachment relationships are present throughout life and do not only involve parental figures from early life and development.

THE DUAL PROCESS MODEL OF GRIEF

Recent research by Stroebe (2002) and Stroebe, Schut, and Stroebe (2005) has combined the work of all of the researchers in the area of attachment to acknowledge (a) the role of attachment in grief and bereavement, (b) the presence of consistency in adult attachment styles related to childhood attachment style, and (c) the specific coping strategies and appropriate expectations and interventions for grieving adults based upon identified attachment patterns. These authors proposed the *dual process model* of bereavement, which allows for an understanding of diverse responses to separation and loss by examining the underlying attachment issues that are present in grieving individuals. The dual process model (see Figure 3.1) posits that bereaved individuals will spend time in acute, active grief over the loss (called loss orientation)

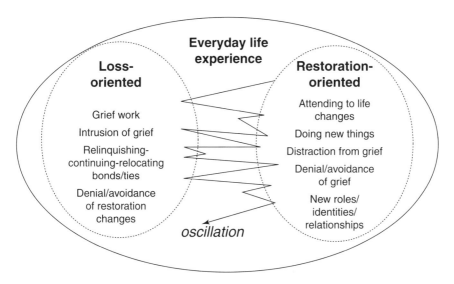

FIGURE 3.1
The Dual Process Model.
(Used with permission from "Attachment in Coping with Bereavement:
A Theoretical Integration" by M. Stroebe, H. Schut, and W. Stroebe, 2005, *Review
of General Psychology, 9*, pp. 48–66.)

and its implications, and they will *also* spend time tending to their everyday life and returning to the world of the living that distracts them from their grief (called restoration orientation).

According to Stroebe et al. (2005), individuals identified as basically secure in their attachment style will demonstrate a more balanced approach to emotion regulation in grief and will tend to "oscillate" more evenly between loss orientation (overt grief) and restoration orientation (daily functionality and activities of daily living). Individuals who display avoidant attachment patterns will tend to focus more upon restoration orientation and will restrict their expressions of distress and avoid seeking support. Individuals whose attachment style is anxious-ambivalent will tend to focus more upon loss orientation, and they are more likely to become preoccupied with their grief through rumination about the deceased individual. Individuals who tend to display patterns of disorganized attachment tend to present in ways that are similar to individuals who have suffered from traumatic experiences and have difficulty integrating their experiences into a relational context. The conclusion of these authors is that attachment style influences the course, intensity, and pattern of grieving after the death of an attachment figure.

The use of attachment theory with its terminology, background, and associated predictions offers some interesting possibilities. For instance, when the concept of attachment theory as an ethological construct is applied to the grieving process, there is an implication that the grieving process itself is an adaptive mechanism that also functions to ensure the survival of the individual after the loss of a significant attachment figure. Grief as we know it may thus be a response that is instinctually programmed into us as a result of natural selection. If this statement is true, then the grieving process itself must be allowed to unfold without hindrance for the assistance in adaptation that grief may afford to the bereaved individual. The grieving response would also be seen as separate from the quality of the relationship to the deceased individual and as more of an extension of the attachment pattern of the remaining bereaved survivor, although certainly the quality of the relationship would likely have an impact upon the grief process.

TWO-TRACK MODEL AND THE CONTINUING BONDS THEORY

In his research and clinical work with bereaved parents in Chicago, and later in Israel, Rubin (1991–1992, 1999) purported that the response to loss can be more effectively assessed when the behavioral–psychological functioning of an individual and the internalized relationship to the deceased are *both* considered. This model addresses grief from a multidimensional lens, exploring both (a) the bereaved individuals' ability to function and navigate the world after a significant loss (track I) and (b) the tendency of bereaved individuals to continue in an ongoing and meaningful, but intangible, relationship with a deceased individual over long periods, and even indefinitely (track II) (Rubin, Malkinson, & Witzum, 2011). Rubin strongly urges clinicians working with bereaved individuals to identify which "track" appears to be more problematic or prominent for the bereaved person and to focus on that aspect of the grief in the support that is offered. For example, if a widow describes a great deal of stress as a result of the financial matters that were associated with her husband's estate, the counselor would serve her more readily by focusing on these issues (track I) rather than engaging in therapeutic work that is focused more on the memories and feelings associated with her deceased husband at that time (track II).

When first describing the two-track model of bereavement, Rubin emphasized that the relationship with the deceased person often remains a focal point for the rest of the lifetime of the bereaved individual. In tandem with this model, Klass, Silverman, and Nickman (1996) described what they termed the bereaved's *continuing bond* with the deceased individual. It was clear from the data presented in these authors' research that the bereaved maintain a link with the deceased that leads to the construction of a new relationship with him or her. This relationship continues and changes over time, typically providing the bereaved with comfort and solace. Most mourners struggle with their need to find a place for the deceased in their lives and are often embarrassed to talk about their ongoing relationship with a person who has died, afraid of being perceived as having something wrong with them. The idea of a continuing, ongoing relationship with a deceased individual was a very novel proposition after so much of popular thought (based on Freud's writings) had been focused on the need to let go of the deceased loved one in order to move forward in life. The work of these researchers actually demonstrated that individuals who were more highly functional and had adapted better after a significant loss were those who were able to maintain a sense of connection (a continuing bond) with their deceased loved one. Obviously, there will be some complications to this process, as when the relationship with the deceased was difficult or complicated (see Field & Wogrin, 2011), or if the bereaved individual is displaying symptoms of prolonged grief disorder rather than developing an adaptive continuing bond with the deceased individual (see Prigerson et al., 2009), which are discussed in more detail later on.

The continuing bonds theory has very important implications for grief counselors. First is that bereaved individuals may be well-served to find ways to reconnect to their deceased loved one in ways that are meaningful. In the course of clinical practice, you will hear myriad stories of how bereaved individuals "connect" with their deceased loved ones— through having conversations with them, journaling to them, dreaming about them, feeling a sense of guidance from them or a sense of their presence with them in an abiding way, or finding "signs" that they believe are from the deceased individual to them. We have had clients tell us about hearing significant songs on the radio at opportune times, birds appearing on their porch, patterns in carpeting, electronic devices that seemed to turn on by themselves, dream encounters and symbols seen in dreams, hearing a voice, feeling a brush of air, finding something that was lost a long time ago in an obvious place, and numerous other ways that are experienced by bereaved individuals as a form of connection with their deceased loved one. The implication here is clear, as Morrie instructs Mitch in *Tuesdays with Morrie*: "Death may end a life, but not a relationship" (Albom, 1997, p. 174). It is very important as counselors to normalize this aspect of grief and to recognize its significance for the bereaved individual's process.

In our clinical practices, we often notice that bereaved individuals seek support at a time when they have lost the physical and tangible presence of their loved one and have not yet been able to establish a link to their deceased loved one in an intangible way. There are obviously many other factors that contribute to a decision to seek support after a significant loss, but this is one area where we actively work with clients to assure them of the normalcy of their experiences and to let them know that they may need to find a way to "hold on" to their loved one in order to "move on."

This is a good time to bring up the controversy that surrounds what is known as the "grief work hypothesis." This belief about grief was that it was necessary for bereaved individuals to talk about their loss and to express emotions in order to work through their grief, and that once painful emotions were worked through, a person could resolve his or her feelings of grief (Stroebe et al., 2005). We now realize that not everyone grieves through feeling and expressing emotion and, in fact, insisting that someone grieve in this way when it is not their propensity may induce more harm than good. The grief work hypothesis also posited that the goal of grief work was to eventually let go of the deceased person and relinquish the relationship to that person in order to move forward in life. We now know from the discussion above that this "letting go" is not supported as necessarily the way many bereaved individuals typically do move forward in their lives after losing a loved one.

STAGES, PHASES, AND TASKS

If you were to ask the average person in casual conversation about grief and what it looks like, you would most likely be quoted the stages of grief, as set out by Elisabeth Kübler-Ross (1969) in her book *On Death and Dying*. This book was a seminal piece of work that openly addressed the needs and feelings of dying individuals in a society that had become increasingly death-denying. In her book, Kübler-Ross identified five stages in facing death and in being confronted with a significant loss: (a) denial, (b) anger, (c) bargaining, (d) depression, and (e) acceptance. Earlier proponents of this model suggested the stages occurred in a more stepwise and linear fashion. However, Kübler-Ross later stated that these stages were more like descriptors rather than proscriptions and that an individual could fluctuate from one to another readily. Although these stages have been heartily embraced in popular (and academic) thinking, it is important to recognize the fact that the five stages were never empirically proven to occur in dying or bereaved individuals (Maciejewski, Zhang, Block, & Prigerson, 2007). The primary usefulness of this theory has been exactly what it did— provide a springboard for beginning discussions about this topic in a society that was generally avoidant and thus relatively uneducated about death and grief.

There are also many theories of bereavement that suggest bereaved individuals go through "phases" in the grieving process. Bowlby (1982) described the "processes of mourning," in which he listed first yearning and searching, then disorganization and despair, followed by reorganization. Parkes (1996) later expanded upon these phases by adding a phase of numbness at the beginning of grief. Sanders (1999) proposed her five phases of the grief process as (a) shock, (b) awareness of loss, (c) conservation/withdrawal, (d) healing, and (e) renewal. Rando (1993) put forth her description of the process of the "six Rs" of bereavement as (1) recognize the loss, (2) react to what has happened, (3) recollect and review memories associated with the loss, (4) relinquish the world as it once was, (5) readjust to life after the loss, and (6) reinvest and re-enter the world. It is apparent that there are many ways of describing the grief process, and many different perspectives from which these descriptions are drawn.

Worden (2009) and Worden and Winokuer (2011) developed a task-based model of grief, in which the grieving process is compared to the developmental tasks that individuals must master in order to move forward in life. These tasks are as follows:

1. Acknowledge the reality of the loss.
   The mourner needs to cease denying that the death has occurred and come to believe that the loved person is truly dead and cannot return to life. The mourner needs to examine and assess the true nature of the loss and neither minimize nor exaggerate it.
2. Process the pain of grief.
   Sadness, despondency, anger, fatigue, and distress are all normal responses to the death of a loved person; people should be encouraged to experience these feelings in appropriate and supported ways, so that they do not carry them throughout their lives.
3. Adjust to a world in which the deceased person is missing.
   A full awareness of the loss of all of the roles performed by the deceased in the life of the mourner may take some time to realize. Challenges to grow are presented to the mourner as he or she assumes new roles and begins to redefine himself or herself, often by learning new coping skills or by refocusing attention on other people and activities.
4. To find an enduring connection with the deceased in the midst of embarking on a new life.
   It is important for the bereaved individual to find an appropriate place for the deceased person to occupy in a spiritual or nontangible sense. This task involves creating and sustaining an appropriate relationship with the deceased based on an ongoing emotional connection and memory, so that person will never be wholly lost to them. This task was revised by Worden (2009) over the earlier versions of his model, and it is now very similar to the process that is described in the continuing bonds theory discussed earlier.

Each description of phases, stages, and tasks may point to important aspects of the grieving process and may provide some realistic expectations for bereaved individuals, provided the phases and stages are not seen as necessary scripts for all bereaved individuals, nor as a "map" of how grief *should* be for everyone. However, the downside of these models is that they do tend to be seen as placing the grieving process in a linear flow (even if not intended by the model's originators), and there seems to be an emphasis on the sameness of the grief experience by all bereaved individuals, rather than an appreciation of the diversity that is present within grief. It is very important to remember that no individual's grief experience will neatly fit into a single prescribed model, as there is much uniqueness in how losses are perceived and also in how grief is expressed and worked through. We will talk more about personal responses to loss later.

MEANING RECONSTRUCTION AND GROWTH

The experience of a significant loss will often pose a strong challenge to an individual's sense of equilibrium. Coping, healing, and accommodation after such experiences are part of a greater process that individuals undertake in an effort to "relearn" their world (Attig, 1996) in light of confrontation with a reality that does not match one's expectations or assumptions. As we discussed in an earlier section, how we see the world (and our lives) as meaningful is based upon the assumptions we have formulated about the world from our earlier life experiences and interactions. A significant loss can shatter the assumptions about how the world should be, and we can experience a high degree of distress when we cannot make sense of what has happened or when we no longer feel a sense of safety or equilibrium in our lives.

Challenges to one's assumptive world are usually met through the processes of *assimilation* (where events are interpreted through the lens of the assumptive world satisfactorily) or *accommodation* (where assumptions are gradually revised somewhat in order to explain a new set of experiences). However, there are times when something may happen that defies belief or overwhelms one's ability to integrate the experience with any known way of how the world should work. The phrase "loss of the assumptive world" is used when a negative life event has challenged one's basic assumptions about the world in a way that these assumptions no longer make sense, and there is no acceptable alternate way of seeing the world that will reconcile previously held assumptions and beliefs with a new reality that does not fit these assumptions (Attig, 1996; Janoff-Bulman, 1992; Parkes, 1971). Preexisting assumptions that are no longer viable in describing the world and one's inner working models or schemata must somehow be reworked in order for the person to feel safe in the world again, but this process can be very difficult. Janoff-Bulman (1992) used the term "shattered assumptions" to describe when a negative life event overwhelms an individual's core assumptions so completely that reconciliation of reality with one's existing assumptive world is not possible.

Tedeschi and Calhoun (2004) spoke of "seismic life events" that "violate" an individual's schemas about how the world should work. It is important to note in this discussion that the individual's subjective appraisal process is very important. How one interprets and perceives an event determines the significance of its impact upon the assumptive world. Meaning-making is the focus of many authors who explore responses to trauma, loss, and negative life events. Making sense of an event involves a process of attempts to reconcile the occurrence of the event with one's working models of the assumptive world (Davis & Nolen-Hoeksema, 2001). Frankl (1963), a concentration camp survivor and the developer of logotherapy, asserted that one can survive all forms of harm and harshness by finding meaning and purpose through what one has experienced. By choosing to reflect upon the possibility of something positive occurring after the negative life event, individuals may be able to assign meaning to their experience, which helps to rebuild the foundation for one's assumptive world that is positive again. Janoff-Bulman (2004) described the existential issues that must also be addressed and assigned meaning after experiencing a critical event. Survivors are not just interested in why an event happened, but also why it happened *to them* in particular. She cites Sartre (1966) in her discussion of existential issues, stating that individuals must create their own meanings through deliberate choice in the face of meaninglessness. She concluded that we may not be able to prevent misfortune, but we have the ability to create lives of value in the wake of misfortune.

Searching for meaning after significant loss appears to be an almost universal phenomenon and an important part of the grieving process (Davis, 2001; Miles & Crandall, 1983; Parkes & Weiss, 1983; Wheeler, 2001). The trauma, shock, and anguish of a major loss assault an individual's fundamental assumptions about the world. Meaning-making can result from reinterpretation of negative events as opportunities to learn new lessons about one's self or life in general, as a means of helping others, or contributing to society in some way that is related to the experience that occurred (such as the formation of an advocacy group or efforts to help others in similar situations). Perhaps this description offers an explanation as to why many bereaved individuals undertake the founding of trusts, advocacy organizations, and public awareness groups. Mothers Against Drunk Drivers is one example of how bereaved parents made meaning by educating the public and advocating stricter enforcement of laws related to driving under the influence of substances after they experienced the loss of their children from accidents that involved drinking and driving.

Neimeyer (2001) and Neimeyer et al. (2002) discussed the social constructivist view of meaning-making through the use of narrative reframing in individuals who have experienced significant losses. Neimeyer's (2001) description of the "master narrative," which is an "understanding of one's life and experiences, along with meanings attached to these" (p. 263), is very similar to earlier descriptions of the assumptive world by other writers. He stated that significant losses disrupt taken-for-granted narratives and strain the assumptions that once sustained them. Individuals must find ways to make meaning of the life events that have been disruptive by a "reweaving" process that incorporates the new experiences into the existing narrative of one's life so that it is once again coherent and sustaining.

Searching for meaning in what seems to be a meaningless event is how human beings attempt to reestablish a sense of order and security in the world and to minimize the high degree of vulnerability that occurs after basic assumptions are shattered. Davis, Nolen-Hoeksema, and Larson (1998) focused on two aspects of meaning in their research. These two aspects consisted of meaning as the ability to find a benefit in what had happened and meaning as a way of making sense of the loss. Attig (2001) further delineated the various conceptualizations of the search for meaning by distinguishing between meaning-making and meaning finding. *Meaning-making* refers to the conscious and active process of reinterpreting and bringing new meaning to one's experiences, actions, and suffering, and *meaning finding* refers to becoming aware of and accepting meaning that arises spontaneously out of grief and suffering. These two processes mix together as one rebuilds the assumptive world after a significant loss.

POSTTRAUMATIC GROWTH AND RESILIENCE

Research that has been published by Tedeschi and Calhoun (2004) suggests that there is potential for more than adjustment after exposure to "seismic" life events. The authors cite numerous instances in their research where individuals encountered tragic bereavement, catastrophic illness, violence, or political oppression, and their exposure to such events led to significant personal accounts of positive growth and development. The authors' use of the term *posttraumatic growth* describes the potential that individuals may have for transformation after exposure to trauma, highly stressful events, and crises. Growth in this sense is not a direct result of exposure to these types of events, but rather it results from the struggle that an individual engages in with the new reality in the aftermath of these events. Posttraumatic growth may also coincide with ongoing distress related to the negative event, as it can be viewed as both a process and an outcome but not necessarily an acceptance of the event.

Resilience and hardiness, which are two related concepts, speak to a potential for positive outcome after the experience of significant losses. Resilience tends to focus upon an ability to go on with life after hardship and adversity (instead of being paralyzed or destroyed by it). Resilience represents more of a "return to baseline" in regard to functioning and views about life. Hardiness is a concept that describes certain individuals' innate tendencies when confronted with challenge (Lang, Goulet, & Amsel, 2003). People who are "hardy" are those who tend to expect that life will bring challenges and that they can find personal development in meeting these challenges. Individuals who experience posttraumatic growth may or may not have these characteristics, although individuals who score high on hardiness would be very likely to experience posttraumatic growth after a significant loss.

Perhaps what is most salient to this discussion are the aspects of posttraumatic growth that reflect upon personal strengths that are developed when some individuals face an assault on their deeply held assumptions about the world. Personal strength may include descriptions of greater self-reliance, fortitude, and self-respect. Janoff-Bulman (2004) gave an account of a client who survived a debilitating accident who, after months of intense rehabilitation and therapy, stated, "I guess I really am strong . . . I never knew I had it in me" (p. 30). She also quotes a rape survivor who stated, "I feel stronger now . . . I came through with my integrity—I got through those months of hell and I know myself as a strong person now" (p. 31). In their descriptions, survivors of traumatic loss events often recognize that they have gone through agony and that they have grown as a result. In the backdrop of suffering, pain, and adversity, individuals may recognize the preciousness of life and be able to identify what is truly "most important" in their lives, which may not have been as easy before the experience.

DISENFRANCHISED GRIEF

We earlier discussed that it is important to view bereaved individuals and their experiences of grief in the social and political context in which they live and are identified. It is important to keep in mind that how an individual will interpret a loss experience and express grief will be moderated by how that individual has been socialized to view certain losses. What is important to keep in mind is that whether loss experiences are recognized or considered valid by an individual and whether an individual is identified as a legitimate griever relate to social norms and rules that are established in the social and political structures in which that individual is identified.

Grief that is not socially recognized or sanctioned, or a grief response that veers too far from what is seen as "normal" within a social framework is disenfranchised socially in some way. Doka (1989, 2002) described the term disenfranchised grief to apply to situations where the loss is not recognized as valid, the griever is not recognized as a valid person to mourn the loss, the grief response of the individual falls outside of social norms, or where the loss itself has a social stigma attached to it. The implications for disenfranchised grief usually involve inadequate or no social support to the bereaved individual, or social stigma or shunning becomes attached to the individuals identified with this loss. For example, the loss of a beloved pet is often a disenfranchised loss because pets are not typically seen as members of a family and not equivalent to human beings; however, many pet owners experience significant and profound grief after the loss of a beloved animal.

CONCLUSION

Through the work of bereavement researchers, clinicians, and academics, the present-day thinking of bereavement has been extrapolated. It is generally thought that the grief process has evolved as part of our survival instinct to enable us to integrate the experience of loss into our lives so that we can continue to function and maneuver in a world that is not in our control. We now realize that the grief response helps us to move forward in life, learning how to live again in a world that now does not feel as safe anymore, often without someone who was an integral part of our lives. Grief is seen as healthy and the process as an adaptive, albeit painful one. Grief counseling serves to facilitate the natural unfolding of the grief process as it is experienced by an individual. It is important for counselors to remember that the main goal of grief counseling is not to make someone feel better (which is usually not possible anyway), but to provide support and assistance and to journey alongside the bereaved so that they will not have to go through this painful process alone.

Glossary of Terms

Continuing bonds theory it states that bereaved individuals may be well-served to find ways to reconnect to their deceased loved ones in ways that are meaningful; often summed up in the statement that death ends a life, but not a relationship.

Disenfranchised grief   it refers to situations where the loss is not recognized as valid, the griever is not recognized as a valid person to mourn a loss, the grief response of the individual falls outside of social norms, or where the loss itself has a social stigma attached to it.

Dual process model   a model of grief that posits that bereaved individuals will "oscillate" regularly between restoration orientation (such as activities of daily living, distractions, and focusing on life) and loss orientation (such as remembering the deceased individual, reminiscing about life before the loss, and feeling the pangs of grief).

Grief   the normal and natural reaction to loss.

Hardiness   it refers to a trait in individuals who tend to expect that life will bring challenges and that they can find personal development in meeting these challenges.

Loss   the real or perceived deprivation of something that is deemed meaningful.

Master narrative   coherent overarching story and understanding of one's life and experiences, along with the meanings that are attached to these experiences.

Posttraumatic growth   the potential that individuals may have for transformation after exposure to trauma, highly stressful events, and crises.

Resilience   the ability to go on with life after hardship and adversity (instead of being paralyzed or destroyed by it). It represents more of a "return to baseline" in regard to functioning and views about life.

Two-track model of grief   it explores both the bereaved individuals' ability to function and navigate the world after a significant loss (track I) and the relational aspects of the grief that relate to maintaining a connection with the deceased individual over long periods, and even indefinitely (track II).

Questions for Reflection

1. Before you read this chapter, or before you had any exposure to the current thinking about bereavement, what were your thoughts about grief and the grieving process? Can you think of what may have shaped your thinking before you began reading about grief and bereavement?

2. A client comes to seek your assistance for grief counseling after the death of her abusive husband, who was an alcoholic and caused her a great deal of harm and terror. Since her husband's death, she has experienced a great deal of anxiety, and she finds herself ruminating about their relationship. Most of her friends and family tell her that she should be relieved, and she does feel a relief from the exposure to his unpredictability and her feelings of powerlessness to control her family life. She tells you that, mostly, she feels "lost" and paralyzed. Based upon the discussion in this

chapter regarding attachment and grief, and some of the other theoretical models, can you suggest what is happening to her?

3. Think of a significant loss experience that you have had or that someone you know has experienced. After reading this chapter and the various explanations of adjusting to loss, which of the theories of bereavement seems to best describe the process you went through after this loss occurred?

4. Think of examples of disenfranchised grief. What do you think makes some losses more socially acceptable than others? If you have experienced a disenfranchised loss, how was that experience different for you than if the loss was recognized and validated?

References

Albom, M. (1997). *Tuesdays with Morrie*. New York, NY: Doubleday.

Attig, T. A. (1996). *How we grieve: Relearning the world*. New York, NY: Oxford University Press.

Attig, T. A. (2001). Relearning the world: Making and finding meanings. In R. A. Neimeyer (Ed.), *Meaning reconstruction and the experience of loss* (pp. 33–53). Washington, DC: American Psychological Association.

Berman, W. H., & Sperling, M. B. (1994). The structure and function of adult attachment. In W. H. Berman & M. B. Sperling (Eds.), *Attachment in adults: Clinical and developmental perspectives* (pp. 3–28). New York, NY: Guilford.

Bowlby, J. (1969). *Attachment and loss: Attachment* (Vol. 1). London, UK: Hogarth.

Bowlby, J. (1973). *Attachment and loss: Separation* (Vol. 2). New York, NY: Basic Books.

Bowlby, J. (1982). *Loss: Sadness and depression (attachment and loss)*. New York, NY: Basic Books.

Bretherton, I. (1992). The origins of attachment theory: John Bowlby and Mary Ainsworth. *Developmental Psychology, 28,* 759–775.

Cassidy, J. (1999). The nature of the child's ties. In J. Cassidy & P. R. Shaver (Eds.), *Handbook of attachment: Theory, research, and clinical applications* (pp 3–20). New York, NY: Guilford.

Davis, C. G. (2001). The tormented and the transformed: Understanding responses to loss and trauma. In R. A. Neimeyer (Ed.), *Meaning reconstruction and the experience of loss* (pp. 137–155). Washington, DC: American Psychological Association.

Davis, C. G., Nolen-Hoeksema, S., & Larson, J. (1998). Making sense of loss and benefiting from the experience: Two construals of meaning. *Journal of Personality and Social Psychology, 75*(2), 561–574.

Davis, C. G., & Nolen-Hoeksema, S. (2001). Loss and meaning—how do people make sense of loss? *American Behavioral Scientist, 44,* 726–741.

Doka, K. J. (1989). *Disenfranchised grief: Recognizing hidden sorrow*. Lexington, MA: Lexington Books.

Doka, K. J. (2002). *Disenfranchised grief: New directions, challenges, and strategies for practice*. Champaign, IL: Research Press.

Field, N., & Wogrin, C. (2011). The changing bond in therapy for unresolved loss: An attachment theory perspective. In R. Neimeyer, D. Harris, H. Winokuer, & G. Thornton (Eds.), *Grief and bereavement in contemporary society: Bridging research and practice* (pp. 37–46). New York, NY: Routledge.

Frankl, V. E. (1963). *Man's search for meaning: An introduction to logotherapy.* New York, NY: Washington Square Press.

Harlow, H. F. (1961). The development of affectional patterns in infant monkeys. In B. M. Foss (Ed.), *Determinants of infant behavior* (pp. 75–97). New York, NY: Wiley.

Hazan, C., & Shaver, P. (1987). Romantic love conceptualized as an attachment process. *Journal of Personality and Social Psychology, 52,* 511–524.

Hinde, R. A. (1982). Attachment: Some conceptual and biological issues. In C. M. Parkes & J. Stevenson-Hinde (Eds.), *The place of attachment in human behavior* (pp. 60–76). New York, NY: Basic Books.

Hinde, R. A. (1992). Developmental psychology in the context of other behavioral sciences. *Developmental Psychology, 28*(6), 1018–1029.

Janoff-Bulman, R. (1992). *Shattered assumptions: Towards a new psychology of trauma.* New York, NY: Free Press.

Janoff-Bulman, R. (2004). Post-traumatic growth: Three explanatory models. *Psychological Inquiry, 15,* 30–24.

Klass, D., Silverman, P., & Nickman, S. (1996). *Continuing bonds: New understandings of grief.* Washington, DC: Taylor & Francis.

Kobak, R., & Hazan, C. (1991). Attachment in marriage: Effects of security and accuracy of working models. *Journal of Personality and Social Psychology, 60*(6), 861–869.

Kübler-Ross, E. (1969). *On death and dying.* New York, NY: MacMillan.

Lang, A., Goulet, C., & Amsel, R. (2003). Lang and Goulet hardiness scale: Development and testing on bereaved parents following the death of their fetus/infant. *Death Studies, 27,* 851–880.

Maciejewski, P., Zhang, B., Block, S., & Prigerson, H. (2007). An empirical examination of the stage theory of grief. *Journal of the American Medical Association, 297*(7), 716–723.

Miles, M. S., & Crandall, E. K. B. (1983). The search for meaning and its potential for affecting growth in bereaved parents. *Health Values: Achieving High Level Wellness, 7*(1), 19–23.

Neimeyer, R. A. (2001). The language of loss: Grief therapy as a process of meaning reconstruction. In R. A. Neimeyer (Ed.), *Meaning reconstruction & the experience of loss* (pp. 261–292). Washington, DC: American Psychological Association.

Neimeyer, R. A., Botella, L., Herrero, O., Pecheco, M., Figueras, S., & Werner-Wilder, L. A. (2002). The meaning of your absence. In J. Kauffman (Ed.), *Loss of the assumptive world: A theory of traumatic loss* (pp. 31–47). New York, NY: Routledge.

Parkes, C. M. (1971). Psycho-social transitions: A field for study. *Social Science & Medicine, 5,*101–115.

Parkes, C. M. (1996). *Bereavement: Stories of grief in adult life.* London, UK: Routledge.

Parkes, C. M., & Weiss, R. S. (1983). *Recovery from bereavement.* New York, NY: Basic Books.

Prigerson, H., Horowitz, M., Jacobs, S., Parkes, C., Aslan, M., Goodkin, K., . . . Maciejewski, P. K. (2009). Prolonged grief disorder: Psychometric validation of criteria proposed for *DSM-V* and *ICD-11. PLOS Medicine, 6*(8). Retrieved August 12,

2010, from http://www.ncbi.nlm.nih.gov/pmc/articles/PMC2711304/pdf/pmed .1000121.pdf/?tool=pmcentrez

Rando, T. (1993). *Treatment of complicated mourning*. Champaign, IL: Research Press.

Rubin, S., Malkinson, R., & Witzum, E. (2011). The two-track model of bereavement: The double helix of research and clinical practice. In R. Neimeyer, D. Harris, H. Winokuer, & G. Thornton (Eds.), *Grief and bereavement in contemporary society: Bridging research and practice* (pp. 47–56). New York, NY: Routledge.

Rubin, S. S. (1991–1992). Adult child loss and the two-track model of bereavement. *Omega, 24*(3), 183–202.

Rubin, S. S. (1999). The two-track model of bereavement: Overview, retrospect, and prospect. *Death Studies, 23*, 681–714.

Sanders, C. (1999). *Grief: The mourning after: Dealing with adult bereavement* (2nd ed.). New York, NY: Wiley.

Sarte, J. P. (1966). *Being and nothingness: A phenomenological study of ontology.* New York, NY: Washington Square Press.

Sroufe, L. A., Egeland, B., & Kreutzer, T. (1990). The fate of early experience following developmental change: Longitudinal approaches to individual adaptation in childhood. *Journal of Child Development, 61*, 1363–1373.

Stroebe, M. (2002). Paving the way: From early attachment theory to contemporary bereavement research. *Mortality, 7*(2), 127–138.

Stroebe, M., Schut, H., & Stroebe, W. (2005). Attachment in coping with bereavement: A theoretical integration. *Review of General Psychology, 9*(1), 48–66.

Tedeschi, R. G., & Calhoun, L. G. (2004). Posttraumatic growth: Conceptual foundations and empirical evidence. *Psychological Inquiry, 15*, 1–18.

Weiss, R. (1975). *Marital separation*. New York, NY: Basic Books.

Wheeler, I. (2001). Parental bereavement: The crisis of meaning. *Death Studies, 25*, 51–66.

Worden, J. W. (2009). *Grief counseling and grief therapy: A handbook for the mental health practitioner* (4th ed.). New York, NY: Springer Publishing Company.

Worden, J. W., & Winokuer, H. (2011). A task-based approach for counseling the bereaved. In R. Neimeyer, D. Harris, H. Winokuer, & G. Thornton (Eds.), *Grief and bereavement in contemporary society: Bridging research and practice* (pp. 57–68). New York, NY: Routledge.

CHAPTER 4

The Practice of Presence

When I (D.L.H.) was a nursing student, I was assigned to the care of an elderly patient named Ella who had metastatic colon cancer. Ella was a feisty and funny woman, and she would readily share her thoughts and opinions with me as I was assisting her with her personal care. We had a good rapport, and I was a primary caregiver to her for several weeks while on this particular rotation in my nursing program. One day, I arrived for my clinical rotation on Ella's floor and was told by the nurse in charge that Ella had taken a turn for the worse. I prepared myself emotionally before going into Ella's room, not sure of what I would find there and how I would feel when I saw the changes that were described to me by the charge nurse.

I walked into Ella's room and found her asleep on her side, facing away from the door. Her breakfast tray was untouched. When I went up to her and said her name, she smiled a little weakly and then nodded back off again. Not knowing what else to do, I completed Ella's bath and changed her sheets as usual. That took a very small amount of time because Ella kept her eyes closed and did not answer me when I spoke to her. When I finished with her personal care, I had a lot of time to spare, as in the past our conversation usually filled in the time that I was allotted to spend with her. Not knowing what else to do, I proceeded to water the plants at the window. I then straightened out and organized her personal items in the bathroom, which had not been used in a good while. I cleaned off her bedside table, and filled her water pitcher with fresh ice water, knowing very well that she would never drink it. I began monitoring the doorway, concerned that my clinical instructor would walk by and see that I was not busy and think that I was not doing what I was supposed to do. I added a blanket to Ella's bed, and I was in the midst of adding another pillow when

Ella reached out and grabbed my arm, opened her eyes, and said simply, "SIT." So I sat on the edge of a chair next to her while she rested, her hand gripping my arm . . . and I watched the doorway, concerned that I would be reprimanded for sitting down while "on the job." When I directed my focus to Ella, she seemed to be sleeping and unaware of my presence. However, whenever I tried to move away, her grip would tighten on my arm. Ella could not engage with me verbally, and she did not want me to be scurrying around her in a lot of busyness, but she obviously wanted my presence with her.

Many years later, when I entered my graduate training program in counseling psychology, I recalled this experience. It was my first lesson in the gift of presence. I now sometimes do a parody with my students about the lesson I learned from Ella that day: Do not just do something; sit there! In my readings about this topic, I came across the concept of presence. Being present is described as something that is multilayered—that in addition to offering our physical presence, there are deeper forms of "being with" someone. For example, being psychologically and emotionally present and attentive with someone involves good listening, empathy, being nonjudgmental, and fully accepting of that person and his or her experience. A further expansion of this concept, described as *therapeutic presence* by McDonough-Means, Kreitzer, and Bell (2004), described this kind of presence with another as a "spirit-to-spirit connection," requiring "that the caregiver have skills of centering, intentionality, intuitive knowing, at-one-ment, imagery, and connecting" (p. 25).

We live in a world that values individuals for their productivity and their efficiency. People tend to lead very busy lives, and if you are not busy, there is an implicit assumption that something must be wrong with you. When at a social gathering, one of the first things people will ask is "What do you do?" Our lives and mentality are built around doing, producing, and consuming. However, one of the most important skills required of a counselor is the ability to "be with" someone and not what to "do to" someone. Learning theory and acquiring skills for interventions with clients are both important to being a good counselor. However, interventions and book knowledge are not going to be enough when you have a client sitting in front of you who is experiencing intense emotional pain.

Most training for counselors focuses upon the content of the therapeutic encounter, emphasizing the development of communication skills and possible approaches and interventions to specific client issues (Hick & Bien, 2008). Very little training explores the counselor's quality of "being with" the client, and yet there is a good amount of research indicating that what fosters the most growth and change in therapy springs from the relationship that clients form with their counselor, and the awareness of their counselor's ability to journey alongside them, rather than the specific techniques that were utilized and the theoretical orientation of the counselor (Geller & Greenberg, 2002; Wampold, 2001; Yalom, 2002). In short, the relationship with the counselor and the sense of the counselor's attentive, engaged presence provides the foundation from which much of the work of the therapeutic encounter extends.

"BEING WITH"

When you are starting out in the work of grief counseling, you might find that you get "stuck" in the process because you might not know what to say to a client or you may not know what to "do" when a client shares something that is deeply painful. You may be afraid of saying the wrong thing and making the client feel worse or of not saying enough and thus falling short of the desire to assist your client. Often, what happens is that a great deal of time in the session is spent with the budding counselor nervously trying to decide what to say and how to respond to a client, and experiencing a great deal of anxiety about what should be said and done, when it might be much more productive and meaningful to learn how to simply be with a client before uttering a single word. We would like to take this chapter as an opportunity to address some of these concerns from the standpoint that sometimes, less is really not just more—but best.

Beginning counselors often find themselves unsure about what to say to clients, and they often feel pressured to say and/or do something that will make a difference to their client. However, if you really stop and think about it, there is nothing you can say that will make a bereaved individual feel better, as you cannot bring back the lost person and you cannot return someone's world back to the way it was before the loss occurred. The main issue, which is the significant loss of a loved one or of an aspect of the self that has been profoundly altered, is not something that can be fixed, changed, or reversed. There are no "ah hah" moments that will make a bereaved person all of a sudden look up and tell you that she or he is now "better." Nothing you can say or do will reduce the pain that a person is experiencing from the loss she or he has experienced.

In their everyday lives, most bereaved individuals are aware of a fair degree of social distancing by others who are afraid of saying the wrong thing or who do not want to make them feel worse by what they say—so the tendency is to avoid the person and the discomfort that is aroused by the uncertainty (Harris, 2009–2010). It is very important that grief counselors not perpetuate this scenario. A helpful stance in working with bereaved individuals might be an understanding that you may not be able to help the bereaved individual to feel better; however, you can still make a tremendous difference by remaining fully present to that person and his or her experience as it is shared. With the advent of modern medicine's focus upon cure and fixing what is broken as the goal of professional helping, the emphasis upon outcome and recovery has permeated our thinking about other aspects of life that may not fit very well into such a model. *Healing*, in this context, is more about care and process than about cure and outcome. Thinking "I cannot take this pain away from this person, but I can ensure that s/he will not have to go through this pain alone" may help to reframe some of the expectations around the role of the grief counselor (Kurtz, 1990).

As we discussed previously, grief is not a pathological state, but an adaptive process that allows us to adjust and accommodate to significant loss events in our lives. In light of this understanding, one of the main goals of grief counseling would be to allow the adaptive aspects of grief to unfold without hindrance so that the bereaved individual can integrate the loss experience into his or her life. Thus, as a grief counselor, it is important to learn to "sit with" grief, even though it can be a very difficult and intense process at times. This "sitting with" someone involves cultivating a sense of presence that is open, engaged, and compassionate. We will now attempt to describe what is meant by the term "therapeutic presence" and how to cultivate the practice of presence with oneself and with clients.

CULTIVATING PRESENCE

Perhaps the best way to establish a strong therapeutic relationship with a client is to begin with your relationship to yourself. It has been said by many wise individuals that we cannot offer to others what we are not offering to ourselves. Indeed, the concept of the "wounded healer" (Nouwen, 1972) implies that we allow the painful life experiences that we have endured to sensitize us to the pain of others when they are in similar dark places. Much has been written in the counseling literature about the counselor's use of self as a source of healing in the therapeutic relationship (Baldwin, 2000; Geller & Greenberg, 2002; Geller, Greenberg, & Watson, 2010; Wosket, 1999; Yalom, 2002). In this section, we will look at important ways of thinking and being that will be of benefit when supporting others who are experiencing difficult and painful losses.

Safety Inside/Safety Outside

This phrase does not have to do with locking windows and doors, but of taking stock of what it is like to feel emotionally comfortable and safe with ourselves and others. If you think about those who are closest to you and whom you trust, consider what allows you to trust them and to feel safe sharing some of your deepest thoughts and feelings with them. When you know that someone will be honest with you, but will also show respect and regard for you, there is a sense of feeling safe with that person. Rogers (1995) stated that human beings crave unconditional love and regard, and this is not a narcissistic tendency, but a real need to feel safe and deeply appreciated.

When we speak of "safety inside," we are referring to your inner world—your thoughts, feelings, and reactions to yourself. For example, an individual who is continually driven to perfectionism and strives constantly to achieve may have an inner world filled with negative thoughts about himself or herself about not "measuring up," or needing to prove his or her worth, or that he or she is lacking in some way. It is not unusual to hear someone say out loud, "I am so stupid!" These reactions can be comedic, and they are often not taken seriously—but it is important to listen deeply to the thoughts you tell yourself on a regular basis about how you perceive yourself and how you respond to life situations. Cultivating a feeling of being safe with yourself means that you are careful with yourself just as you would be careful with the words you share with someone whom you love—and you are no different from someone else who deserves your love and respect.

Shame, the sense that something is deeply wrong with us, is a very painful experience, and the debilitating effects of feeling shamed by someone else can have a profound effect upon that person. Shame differs from guilt in that when there is guilt, it is usually over something that we have done, which can hopefully be corrected or for which amends can be made. On the other hand, shame implies that there is something wrong with who we are, and we are paralyzed in our attempts to address it because there is no specific source or action—just a deep-seated sense of being inferior, feeling worthless, or like damaged goods (Harris, 2010). Shame in this sense leaves us unable to connect with others in a meaningful way because we cannot move beyond the need to avoid the pain of it, while we are inescapably drawn to try to alleviate the ineffable source of the shame at the same time (Harris, 2010).

Checking in with the dialog that occurs inside your mind is often referred to as listening to your "self-talk," and it can be a very important place to start when you want to be a counselor. If you are in the habit of respecting yourself and being kind with yourself, while you are also honest in your self-appraisals, you can "sit" with yourself in calm and patient awareness. If not, "sitting with" yourself or with someone else will be much harder because you really are not safe in the silence—as these times of quiet can become the moments when your mind can be permeated by negativity, self-loathing, and insecurity, and nobody would want to remain in that place very long.

Self-Awareness and Reflection

Presence begins with the therapist's self-reflective abilities and personal work as preparation for being with another person who is seeking the therapeutic encounter. Being able to understand yourself and what makes you "tick" may be very important when you are with clients whose experiences may be similar to yours or with individuals who may "trigger" some of your painful past experiences and associations. In our classes, we often give students an assignment that requires them to complete an inventory of the loss experiences of their lives, from birth to the present (*see the loss line exercise at the end of this chapter*). These loss experiences may or may not involve the death of someone close; rather, they are experiences where life took a turn that was unplanned and unexpected and required a period of adjustment and grief. Often, students will identify moving from one place to another, the loss of friends through changes in life situations, the ending of romantic relationships, and lost hopes and dreams alongside losses that have occurred after the death of someone significant. The purpose in assigning this exercise is to allow for an opportunity to reflect on how these losses have shaped their lives and to see places where there may be some lingering vulnerability, enabling an ability to separate feelings and experiences from those of a client who may share a similar experience and feelings.

In the development of greater self-awareness and open reflection upon one's life and experiences, there is an invitation to self-correct when necessary. The ability to *respond* to a situation by choice after reflection rather than to *react* quickly without much thought is certainly much more conducive to living in a way that is in line with your true intentions and values. This way of being will certainly give you a greater capacity to listen with openness to others who need to know that you will listen and reflect on what they share with you rather than jumping in with quick advice and conclusions.

Cultivation of Compassion

Compassion is defined as the ability to demonstrate kindness, understanding, and nonjudgmental awareness toward human responses, especially those which involve suffering, inadequacy, or perceived failure of some sort (Bennett-Goleman, 2001; Brach, 2003; Neff, Kirkpatrick, & Rude, 2007; Salzberg, 1997). These same authors state that compassion serves as a buffer against anxiety and leads to enhanced psychological well-being. Berlant (2004) saw compassion as a way of responding to others out of the recognition of shared human experience. She discusses the withholding of compassion as a form of cruelty that can be manifested in individual and social responses. Compassionate responses take into account the awareness that we all share common human experiences and traits. Nobody is perfect; nobody is immune from painful life experiences and nobody is spared from some kind of suffering at some point in time.

Individuals who gravitate toward the helping professions often have a great deal of compassion for others, but they often have difficulty feeling compassion toward themselves. To deny compassion for ourselves can be highly detrimental, as to separate ourselves out from the compassion we may extend to others may then require that we constantly need others in our lives to prove that we are valuable and worthy because we are unable to do this for ourselves. It can be dangerous to have this kind of mentality and to be working with vulnerable individuals, as without a strong sense of self-compassion, the helper will need clients to bolster his or her weak sense of self and in the process may inadvertently use clients for his or her own needs, thus violating the objective of the therapeutic relationship to place the client's needs as primary.

Stop and think for a minute about how you define compassion. If you were to describe someone who is compassionate, what would their attributes be? People who are identified as compassionate are often those who see the suffering of others and are moved to address this suffering in some way. Cultivating compassion involves a willingness to see the pain of others, to allow yourself to be exposed to others' suffering, and to choose to be an instrument of relief to that suffering in ways that are possible. Because we cannot remove many of the causes of suffering in human beings, such as death and significant losses, we resonate with those who suffer by bearing witness to their pain, journeying alongside those who are grieving, and being present and nonjudgmental to those who suffer. Far from being a passive process, demonstrating compassion requires us to actively and decisively "be with" another individual when others may leave quickly or get frustrated because they cannot "fix" what has happened. Being compassionate requires a great deal of inner strength and awareness, and it takes time and practice to learn how to "be with" others in such an engaged and open way.

In a qualitative study with expert therapists, Geller and Greenberg (2002) explored what is involved in the experience of presence in the therapeutic relationship. They concluded that being fully present to clients in the therapeutic encounter involves the following:

- *preparation for presence*, which entailed the therapist making a philosophical commitment to practicing presence in his or her personal life and developing an attitude of openness, acceptance, and nonjudgment prior to work with clients;
- *the process of presence*, which involved being authentic in the session with the client, being open and receptive during sessions, and listening with the "third ear;" and
- *experiencing the presence*, which allowed for deep absorption in the client's world without becoming attached to outcomes, and being fully aware, alert, and focused upon the client during that time.

These authors state that,

> Therapists' presence is understood as the ultimate state of moment-by moment receptivity and deep relational contact. It involves a being with the client rather than a doing to the client. It is a state of being open and receiving the client's experience in a gentle, nonjudgmental and compassionate way . . . being willing to be impacted and moved by the client's experience, while still being grounded and responsive to the client's needs and experience. (p. 85)

(For more specific information about presence and what is entailed in looking at the construct of presence in research, see Geller, Greenberg, & Watson, 2010.)

Presence is one of the most difficult concepts for individuals in Western society to grasp, just as the opening scenario of this chapter with Ella describes, as the main focus in helping professions is typically upon "doing something" rather than "being with" someone. Our ability to offer our full attention and empathetic presence to another human being is one of the greatest gifts that we have. Learning how to be fully present to others begins with learning how to be fully present to ourselves and our experiences.

A relatively new area of exploration is the intersection of Eastern philosophy with Western psychology, more specifically in the application of mindfulness to the therapeutic venue. Several authors describe the value of regular meditative practice or the development of mindfulness practice for the therapist as a means to learn how to be fully present on a daily basis in one's life and to apply this same practice of presence to being fully present to clients as they seek counseling (Epstein, 2007; Geller & Greenberg, 2002; Hick & Bien, 2008). Some therapeutic modalities draw directly or indirectly from these same practices to assist clients in developing ways of being and thinking in their lives that will facilitate deeper engagement with life while providing an opportunity to let go of their expectations and ways of thinking that interfere with living more fully (Kabat-Zinn, 2005; Kumar, 2009: Kurtz, 1990; Welwood, 2000). Although many of these authors emphasize the value of a formal meditative practice, the key aspect of this type of practice involves the development of a philosophy that allows for letting go of expectations and outcomes, learning to live from moment to moment in the present, and being able to cultivate greater awareness and presence with one's self and with others.

Many forms of therapeutic training require student counselors to be in counseling themselves as part of their training. There is certainly merit to this approach, as one of the best ways to develop empathy for clients in the therapeutic setting is by being a client yourself. Being a client is also an excellent way to see the process modeled through your encounter with a trained counselor and also a good start to developing skills for self-awareness and reflection. There is perhaps no better way to learn than by doing!

PRACTICE OF AWARENESS AND PRESENCE

The following exercises are suggestions to assist you in the process of self-awareness, self-reflection, and the cultivation of a sense of presence. We suggest that you spend time exploring each of these exercises and find someone who will honor your process and with whom you can share your experiences and responses.

Loss Line Exercise

A personal loss is any loss that results in a significant change to our lives. Personal losses include the death of a significant person, relationship loss, job loss, pet loss, loss of dreams, divorce, immigration, loss of health, or loss of self.

1. Create a list in chronological order of all of your personal losses. Include only the year and who or what was lost. For visual impact, it is helpful to diagram these losses on a timeline on a sheet of paper.
2. Look over this "loss line" that you have made. Think about each loss that you have indicated on the sheet of paper and its impact on your life. Make note of developmental or maturational differences at each stage of life that is highlighted in the loss history. How have your losses shaped you as a person now? What losses still feel "raw" or continue to overshadow your life at this point in time? How might the way you have handled your losses affect how you might work with a client who has encountered losses similar to yours?

Presence Exercise (You Will Need a Partner for This Exercise)[1]

Ideally, partners are not too familiar with one another, although this might be unavoidable. It might be helpful to have a third person read this exercise aloud for the two partners who are participating in it.

Part One

Please sit facing your partner, a comfortable distance apart but close enough that you could lean forward and whisper to one another.

Begin by closing your eyes and settling into your body. Try to recall a time when you opened your eyes on the world in innocence and wonder. If you cannot recall such a time, simply visualize that you now have those eyes which are about to open on the world, as if for the first time. Take a few moments to try to discover this inner sense of wonder and innocence.

Now, opening your eyes, you will keep your gaze lowered and try to maintain a soft, slightly unfocused seeing, as opposed to staring or glaring . . . And you will be looking in the area of your partner's knees or lap. Please open your eyes softly now.

You become aware of the presence of another. In your visual field, there is something that all of your senses tell you is not simply an inanimate object. Even just looking into this area of the person before you, your innate knowing tells you that this is a living being, just like you. Even at this stage you may sense the movement of breath in the other.

And now very slightly and gently raise your field of vision to include the lower abdomen of your partner—focusing on the area below the rib cage. Now you clearly become aware of the breathing of another. It may happen that the rhythms of your in-and-out breaths begin to harmonize. Do not strive to consciously make this happen—just gently observe if this synchronicity arises naturally. Calmly and silently stay with this awareness for a few moments.

This time, raise your vision very slightly, keeping this field soft and unfocused, from the shoulders down to the lap, so that you are gently taking in the whole upper torso of the person before you. You become aware, in looking at this other and feeling your own breath, that breathing involves the entire upper body—not just the nostrils, not just the lungs. Now you can more fully sense the presence of this person in front of you.

---

[1] This exercise is shared with permission from Brad Hunter.

Now, slowly, gently, and with compassion for both yourself and the other, please look into the face of your partner. You behold a face completely unique in the world and yet, fundamentally, not so different from yours. You can see in this face, as if looking in a mirror . . . this face that has known countless moments of loss and grief of all degrees . . . this face that has yearned for the same joys as you . . . this face that has been thrilled with love and acceptance . . . and torn by rejection and shame . . . this face that expresses the whole history of the heart . . . this person who longs for the same peace and happiness you do . . . this universal longing for the end of suffering . . .

Just gently allow yourself to look into the eyes and face before you for a few more moments. At this point, sometimes some giddiness or reluctance arises because doing this part of the exercise can be uncomfortable, and you may feel self-conscious. If this occurs, try to raise your sight one last time and simply look innocently and deeply into the face of your partner. When you follow this instruction *please do not avert your gaze*. If it feels too intense for an instant, just close your eyes and locate that innocent, nonjudgmental vision again.

Part Two

At this point, you will need to think of a true story of personal loss. How current and how profound the loss is completely up to you. But obviously, the more profoundly you share, the more powerful this experience will be. Just take a second to decide who is going to share first. The listener who is bearing witness to the story of loss *just listens*. It is vitally important for this that there be no cross-talking. Please hold back your impulse to reach out and touch or comfort the person for now. You do not have to sit poker faced— your body language and facial expressions are going to naturally respond to the story, but please do not speak.

Allow about 3 to 5 minutes for the telling of the story. When the first partner has completed telling his or her story, then signal that the second partner can then begin to share his or her story.

When the second partner has completed telling his or her story, allow a few moments to close your eyes and be with your partner. Then, share with each other what it was like to do this exercise. What was it like to listen without being able to "do" or say something? How did it feel to share in this context?

This exercise is often a poignant demonstration of how difficult it is to simply be fully present to someone else without "doing" something. It gives an idea of how to engage with someone by offering presence without interfering with the other person's flow or process.

Simple Presence Practice

This is a practice that you can do at any time, in many different situations. Do this for just a minute or two at a time. When you are in a situation where there is sharing of some sort, whether it be a social setting or a more clinical setting, begin to focus on one person near you. Notice that person's body language. Close your eyes and listen to the tone of that person's voice and the quality of his or her speech. Then, listen to the words that the person is using and how these words are conveying feelings, thoughts, and ideas. If the person is not talking or stops talking and is silent, allow your breathing patterns to match his or hers briefly. Reflect on what you learned about that person (or yourself) from your focused attention for this brief period.

Glossary of Terms

Compassion   the ability to demonstrate kindness, understanding, and non-judgmental awareness toward human responses, especially those which involve suffering, inadequacy, or perceived failure of some sort.

Presence   the act and intention of "being with" another individual, with full attention and engagement.

Therapeutic presence   it involves the counselor engaging the skills of centering, intentionality, intuitive knowing, at-one-ment, imagery, and connecting with the client.

Wounded healer   it implies that we allow the painful life experiences that we have endured to sensitize us to the pain of others when they are in similar dark places.

Questions for Reflection

1. In your own experience, what might hinder your ability to be fully present to another person as described in this chapter? How does presence in this chapter concur with or diverge from how you have viewed being a helper to those who are in painful circumstances?

2. Complete the two exercises described in the chapter with someone whom you trust. What was the experience like for you? How about for the person who completed the exercises with you?

3. We are often conditioned to think of healing to be the same as cure or being relieved of a painful situation. Based upon the concepts in this chapter, how can healing include times when it is not possible to change someone's circumstances or relieve their pain?

4. Think of times when you have been uncomfortable because you did not know what to say or do. Can you think of other ways to remain in these situations, using the concepts about presence that were presented in this chapter?

References

Baldwin, M. (2000). *The use of self in therapy* (2nd ed.). Binghamton, NY: Hayworth.

Bennett-Goleman, T. (2001). *Emotional alchemy: How the mind can heal the heart.* New York, NY: Three Rivers Press.

Berlant, L. (2004). *Compassion: The culture and politics of an emotion.* New York, NY: Routledge.

Brach, T. (2003). *Radical acceptance: Embracing your life with the heart of a Buddha.* New York, NY: Bantam.

Epstein, M. (2007). *Psychotherapy without the self.* New Haven, CT: Yale University Press.

Geller, S. M., & Greenberg, L. S. (2002). Therapeutic presence: Therapist's experience of presence in the psychotherapy encounter. *Person-centered and Experiential Psychotherapies, 1*(1–2), 71–86.

Geller, S. M., Greenberg, L. S., & Watson, J. C. (2010). Therapist and client perceptions of therapeutic presence: The development of a measure. *Psychotherapy Research, 20*(5), 599–610.

Harris, D. L. (2009–2010). Oppression of the bereaved: A critical analysis of grief in Western Society. *Omega, 60*(3), 241–253.

Harris, D. L. (2010). Healing the narcissistic injury of death in the context of Western society. In J. Kauffman (Ed.), *The shame of death, grief, and trauma* (Vol. 1, pp. 75–87). New York, NY: Routledge.

Hick, S. F., & Bien, T. (2008). *Mindfulness and the therapeutic relationship.* New York, NY: Guilford.

Kabat-Zinn, J. (2005). *Full catastrophe living.* New York, NY: Bantam.

Kumar, S. M. (2009). *The mindful path through worry and rumination.* Oakland, CA: New Harbinger.

Kurtz, R. (1990). *Body-centered psychotherapy: The Hakomi method.* Mendocino, CA: LifeRhythm.

McDonough-Means, S. I., Kreitzer, M. J., & Bell, I. R. (2004). Fostering a healing presence and investigating its mediators. *The Journal of Alternative and Complementary Medicine, 10*(Suppl. 1), 25–41.

Neff, K. D., Kirkpatrick, K. L., & Rude, S. S. (2007). Self-compassion and adaptive psychological functioning. *Journal of Research in Personality, 41,* 139–154.

Nouwen, H. J. (1972). *The wounded healer: Ministry in contemporary society.* New York, NY: Doubleday.

Rogers, C. (1995). *On becoming a person.* New York, NY: Houghton Mifflin.

Salzberg, S. (1997). *Loving kindness: The revolutionary art of happiness.* Boston, MA: Shambhala.

Wampold, B. E. (2001). *The great psychotherapy debate: Models, methods, and findings.* Mahwah, NJ: Lawrence Erlbaum.

Welwood, J. (2000). *Toward a psychology of awakening.* Boston, MA: Shambhala.

Wosket, V. (1999). *The therapeutic use of self: Counselling practice, research, and supervision.* New York, NY: Routledge.

Yalom, I. (2002). *The gift of therapy.* New York, NY: HarperCollins.

CHAPTER *5*

The Basics of Counseling Practice

*A*lthough we firmly believe that counseling practice is rooted in the counselor and the relationship that is formed between the counselor and the client, there are some therapeutic techniques and responses that you might find helpful to "give words" to your intentions with clients. Counselors who are newer to the field will often say that they are concerned that they will either say something that will make the bereaved person feel worse, say something that is inappropriate, or that they will not say anything and will feel foolish because they are tongue-tied. Hopefully, this chapter will provide some ideas for responding sensitively to bereaved individuals, and perhaps more. We will start with some basic skills to incorporate into your regular, everyday practice, and then discuss how to get started with a client. We then go to some "trickier" areas that you might want to consider as you begin working with clients.

SETTING UP THE GROUNDWORK

As we have discussed previously, establishing the therapeutic alliance is the most important step in beginning the counseling process. Learning how to be fully present to yourself and your client in a way that is open and receptive sets the stage for building up the work of the sessions. As we have discussed presence and the conditions of the therapeutic alliance already in great detail, let us move forward from how to "be" with clients to what to say and "do" with clients that will best express your intentions and journeying alongside with your clients. We will start with a description of basic attending skills and what these are. Next, we will explore the role of empathy in the therapeutic relationship. We will then discuss some practical ideas about how to help clients to tell their stories and what might provide the best support to them as they walk through their grief journey.

ATTENDING SKILLS

Attending skills are very basic things to which you need to "attend" both in yourself and in your client. When you are attending to your client, you are focused upon what your client is sharing, upon your client's body language, and upon your own inner responses and body language as well. It is important to keep in mind that much of our communication with others is nonverbal, even when someone is talking. So we listen to someone's words, but also perceive their body language to identify what may be "underneath" the words—and clients do the same with you as well. So, it is important that your body language and your focus be congruent with your intentions and the words, thoughts, and feelings that you share with the client. Here are some basic thoughts about attending:

1. *Eye contact*—involves looking at clients in a culturally appropriate way. This does not mean maintaining an unrelenting gaze, but, rather, looking into their eyes from time to time, especially when they are speaking, so that they are connected with you and they know you are focused upon them. It is very important to remember that not all cultures interpret eye contact as comfortable or appropriate. If you notice that your client seems uncomfortable with maintaining eye contact with you, you may want to modify your gaze to looking just to their side some or occasionally looking down from their eyes for brief periods. If the eye contact discomfort seems obvious, it is a good opportunity to check in with your client about comfort and expectations around this issue. Another reason that clients may feel uncomfortable with eye contact is that some people are unaccustomed to being the intense focus of another person's attention in the way that a counselor may focus on a client in a session. These feelings and issues provide a chance to deepen the trust and respect in the encounter if they are approached in a sensitive and respectful way.
2. *Vocal qualities*—we need to think about our rate of speech, the volume of our speech, and our tone when speaking with clients. We tend to speak very quickly because we are accustomed to quick responses and sharing a lot of information in short snippets of time either through technological means or in short encounters with

others. It is important in the counseling session to consciously slow things down, to take the time to focus not only on what is being said, but on *how* it is being said. We should think about how we speak so that we are easy to hear—not too high, too low, or monotonous. Ask a trusted friend for feedback on your verbal quality, or listen to yourself on a recorded device—the voice is an instrument that can be fine-tuned, if need be.

3. *Verbal tracking*—involves active listening on the counselor's part, where he or she follows the client's story, asking relevant questions that permit deeper understanding. We do not interject our own ideas, unless they would be helpful to the client, and we conduct the session so that the client does most of the talking. We cannot follow every detail of the client's narrative, and some clients are confused and scrambled in their account, but we search for the main threads and themes that make a complete whole. Another related aspect of verbal tracking is sometimes referred to as "intuitive tracking," which focuses not as much on the details as on the implicit feelings and meanings that a client shares with us. This may take some time to develop, and may be a skill that is easier for some than for others to practice.

4. *Attentive body language*—the positioning and physical presence of the counselor can send a powerful signal to clients that he or she is tuned in to them. The same can be said for when our body language might demonstrate disinterest, impatience, or distraction. Think about the bodily clues that indicate to you that someone is listening to you and engaged with you. We usually suggest that where you are sitting be about four feet from the client, and often not directly facing the client, but turned to the side a little. When listening, you may wish to lean slightly in the direction of your client, and to not be afraid to use hand gestures and facial expressions that help to convey your thoughts. When watching videotaped sessions of clients and counselors, it is common to see that the counselor begins to mimic the client's body language, facial expressions, and gestures. This synergy between the counselor and the client is common, and it often indicates that there is a comfort and sense that the counselor and client are "in tune" together.

　　Clients tend to feel uncomfortable if the counselor is too close, too intense in body language, or if the counselor's body language appears closed or distracted, such as looking at a watch, crossing the arms across your chest, or if you tend to be someone whose foot tends to move rapidly when you are talking. Remember, clients often feel that the process can be intimidating and there is vulnerability in sharing things that are so intimate about oneself, so it is important to consciously think about how your body language will be perceived by a client.

A related issue is whether to take notes during a session. We feel this is a personal decision that each counselor will need to decide. If you find that you need to take notes to keep track of details and to monitor the process during the session, then you might wish to share with your client at the beginning of the first session how you use your notes and why you are taking notes. Keep in mind that clients will be very aware of your writing during a session, and they may be influenced if you tend to write a lot when they share about one aspect of their experience or if you do not seem to note something that they think is important. Always ensure that taking notes does not prevent you from fully engaging your client and that the notepad is not "in the way" of your ability to maintain your presence and, focus upon the client at all times. Remember, the client is in front of you and *the story is the client*.

5. One of the easiest algorithms to remember about attending skills with clients is the SOLER model, described by Egan (2009) in his work entitled *The Skilled Helper*. In the SOLER model, we keep in mind the following:

   S—**squarely face** the client, or be at a 45-degree angle. Do not have a desk or table between you.

   O—**open posture**, avoid crossing arms; leg crossing is okay in our culture, but not with the ankle across the knee.

   L—**lean forward slightly**, bend slightly toward the client to invite conversation.

   E—**eye contact**, appropriately, means looking directly at the client at times, but also breaking contact to give the person a break.

   R—**relaxed posture and body language**, not holding tension or anxiety; natural and comfortable position.

OBSERVATION AND TRACKING SKILLS

Observation skills help us to ascertain information about the client through careful observation on the part of the counselor. Most of us already use our observational skills to "read" others' nonverbal cues, and sometimes you might remember the "gist" of a conversation, or how someone was feeling, but not be able to remember everything that was said to you in that conversation. As a counselor, learning how to focus simultaneously on both nonverbal and verbal cues that the client gives is an important skill to develop. Many clients do not have words to express their thoughts or feelings accurately, but you may be able to help them to do so by observing their expressions, body language, and behaviors during a session. In noticing these things with a client, you might be able to incorporate your observations into the material of the session to help a client articulate deeper thoughts and feelings. For example, you might say something like, "I noticed some hesitation when you said that everything is going well. Can you tell me a little bit more about that hesitation?" Another example may be to note nonverbal cues in the absence of words, such as, "I noticed a sad expression on your face just now. . . . can you tell me about that?" Many times, counselors will automatically mirror a client's posture or gestures without even thinking about it. This alignment with the client's body language can be called "movement synchrony," and you will usually see it occur when the client and counselor are deeply engaged in the session.

Verbal tracking is used by the counselor to more closely follow the client's story or how a client tends to share about an experience. In verbal tracking, the counselor tends to "pick out" things that point to a deeper level of a client's experience or awareness. Clients tend to illustrate their life themes by underlining words with significant meanings. When clients use words that indicate strong feeling states, or have an intense association or connotation, it is important for the counselor to take note and not miss these cues. Examples of these types of words might be *hopeless, helpless, at a dead end, overwhelmed, paralyzed,* or *lost.* These words often carry a great deal of significance for how the client perceives what has happened, or where the client's "crux" issue may reside. One important point to make when discussing this aspect of verbal tracking is to be aware that counselors may have their own selective attention—meaning that we might tend to focus on what we think is important and, in so doing, we could miss what the client feels is important. Awareness about our own biases and areas where we are more comfortable in a dialogue may help to prevent us from tracking clients in a way that is more suitable to our needs than to what a client may need.

Another form of tracking is to follow the use of language that the client uses. For example, some clients tend to be very concrete in their thinking, and literal in how they share their experiences. These clients may be uncomfortable if the counselor uses metaphors and abstract interpretations in their discussions together, and they may be more comfortable discussing things in a more concrete and behaviorally oriented way. Other clients may readily want to discuss patterns in their lives and seek to understand their underlying feelings and motivations. Matching a client's style may help the client be more comfortable, especially in the beginning of the counseling relationship. With time, clients may experience more growth and expand their awareness of themselves and others if they are challenged to think in ways that might, at first, seem a little "out of the box," but this type of challenge is usually not helpful until the therapeutic alliance is well established.

When clients make statements such as "I think . . .," "I feel . . .," or "I believe . . .," they are making "I" statements. These statements are important indicators of the inner world of the client, and need to be attended by the counselor. Many clients have a great deal of difficulty making these kinds of statements because they are not accustomed to being heard or valued; if this is the situation, the counselor might have to encourage the client to make these statements in the sessions in order to try out their use in conversation.

One final aspect of verbal tracking is paying attention to the client's verbal style. Most people demonstrate a clear preference in verbal styles, and if you listen carefully to the words that a client chooses in his or her descriptions, you can "match" your client's style more readily, and the client may feel more comfortable sharing. In addition, matching a client's verbal style invites rich descriptions and explorations of the client's world and feelings, which is often very helpful in the counseling process. When a counselor attends to this aspect of the client's sharing, the client often feels deeply understood and quite comfortable in the exchange. Examples of verbal styles might be as follows:

- Visual—the client uses words that speak about *seeing, imagining, visualizing,* and *providing details.*
- Auditory—the client uses words that focus on what is heard and may say things that incorporate words and phrases like *hearing, sounds like, harmony, noisy,* and *dissonant.*
- Kinesthetic—the client focuses on *movement, action, doing, feeling, touching, warmth,* and *sharpness.*

APPROPRIATE USE OF QUESTIONS

Questions are typically the way we elicit information from others. Certainly, in some of the humorous skits that are done of a counseling scenario, the counselor asks the client a question, and then writes something down on a notepad, sometimes with a scratch of the chin and a comment like, "hmmm . . . that's very interesting . . . " There are some important things to remember about asking questions of clients. First, asking a question puts the counselor in charge of the session, and if you recall from our earlier discussion, we want to empower the client to take the lead in the counseling session; by asking a question, you are requesting a response with a specific answer, and taking the session in a direction that may be different from where the client may have initially wanted to go. Asking too many questions in a row can cause a client to feel more like he or she is being interrogated rather than being heard. In addition, it is important to be careful not to use asking questions as a means to "fill" silence in a session because you are uncomfortable with it. Silence and pauses in the session may be important times for the client to be able to sort through some of his or her thoughts and feelings without interruption. Beginning counselors often report that they experience pauses, silence, and breaks in the conversation as awkward and uncomfortable. If there is a pause in the session, stop and take a breath before you speak. Allow yourself to wait for a minute or two—follow your client's lead—and see if this poignant time gives your client a chance to gather his or her thoughts a little and to go deeper with the material rather than being immediately sidetracked by having to answer a question that you have interjected.

There are basically two types of questions, and each can serve a good purpose. *Closed questions* are those that can be answered with a "yes" or "no" answer, or often with a single word. They often provide the facts such as address, age, length of time since an event, and so on, and often begin with where, is, are, and do. Closed questions are helpful in asking for specific information, such as demographics, and questions that are pertinent to counseling, but are not necessarily part of the process. Examples might be "Have you seen a counselor before?" or "Do you have a regular medical doctor?" Of course, many clients will often answer a closed question as if it were an open one because of their need to talk. Sometimes, an entire session will open with a simple question that is asked of the client, and the client chooses to elaborate on the answer because she or he feels it is something that is important.

Open questions begin with what, how, why, and could and allow clients to respond according to their needs. These types of questions invite clients to elaborate on their story and add the details as they wish. Open questions usually cannot be answered briefly, and they often require some thought or expression of feeling. Open questions are used for the following purposes at specific times:

- To begin the session, or to move the client forward in a story, indicating that you are listening and wanting more detail:

    "Can you share with me a little about what brought you to counseling?"

> "What are your thoughts about what is happening in your life right now?"
> "After the death, what were things like among the other family members?"

- Used to move the client more deeply into his or her world or experience:

  > "Could you tell me more about that?"
  > "What has this experience been like for you?"

- Used for specific information about what the client has shared:

  > "Can you give me an example of what you mean?"
  > "How have you managed to get through this time?"

- Used to make assessment of the client's situation:

  > "Who has been there to support you the most?"
  > "What is your typical day like right now?"

Questions that start with *who, what, how, when, why,* and *where* might be open or closed, but in beginning a sentence with one of these words, you are asking for an answer. The word you use to open a sentence determines the focus of the answer:

- Who—people
- What—facts
- How—feelings and reactions
- When—temporal aspects
- Why—reasons (use sparingly)
- Where—environment and setting
- Could—might be the most open and productive of all questions

Here are some guidelines to keep in mind in regard to the use of questions:

1. Use questions consciously and selectively when you need the information and can "go for it" when needed.
2. Think of how you can incorporate awareness-expanding questions into your sessions:

   > "Can you describe your ideal . . ."
   > "How might your life look like if this was changed?"
   > "What is the hardest part of your daily life right now?"

3. All questions and probes need to be grounded in empathy— understanding that there are valid reasons why a client has made

choices and an appreciation of what that person has gone through before getting here.

4. Build in an internal alarm that goes off if you ask two or more questions in a row and look at why. Pay attention to this and seek out why. Asking too many questions stops the flow, tends to keep the client in his or her head, and leads the client too much.

5. Base questions on the context of the session and what the client is bringing up.

6. You *must* ask questions if a person seems suicidal (we will discuss this more in detail later on).

7. Avoid using questions when you want to show empathy—use a statement instead. For example, you can say, "This is a very hard time right now," instead of asking, "How difficult is this for you right now?"

8. Avoid closed questions as much as possible when you are in the midst of a session.

9. Try to avoid using the word "why" when asking a question, as it may tend to appear judgmental or accusatory to a client.

EMPATHY

Empathy is perhaps one of the most essential components of counseling practice. The ability to join empathetically with a client involves your ability to essentially "get into the client's shoes" and see and experience things as if you were the client. Carl Rogers (1959), the founder of person-centered therapy, described empathy as the counselor's ability,

> To perceive the internal frame of reference of another with accuracy and with the emotional components and meanings which pertain thereto as if one were the person, but without ever losing the "as if" condition. Thus, it means to sense the hurt or the pleasure of another as he [or she] senses it and to perceive the causes thereof as he [or she] perceives them, but without ever losing the recognition that it is *as if* I were hurt or pleased and so forth. (p. 185)

Responding to a client with empathy means you intentionally move into your client's frame of reference—how things seem and feel to your client, trying to experience the world as your client does, while maintaining your awareness that this frame of reference and experience is not yours. All good counseling practices aim to increase our empathetic understanding of our clients with the intention that joining with clients in this way helps them to feel deeply understood and accepted. You have probably heard the phrase "walk a mile in my shoes." Empathetic joining is your attempt to do just that—to walk in your client's shoes, see through his or her eyes, and think about how the world is experienced by him or her. When we are empathetic in our stance with our clients, we share a valued sense of *resonance* with them, and this experience can be very powerful for our clients.

Sometimes, in the process of trying to experience the world as your client does in empathetic joining, you may get an intuition about something that the client may not have stated openly, but seems to be apparent once you begin to join more with that client. This occurrence is sometimes referred to as *advanced empathy*. It is important to note that you might actually be aware of something in the client's experiencing that may not necessarily be in the client's conscious awareness, but it is there—the client is generating it and you perceive it. When we listen empathetically with clients, we are often listening not just to their words and using the attending skills described above, but, rather, there can be a deeper form of listening that involves your intuition and your own responses to the client's material. Yalom (2009) spoke of using the "rabbit ears" of the therapist—picking up on often understated, but very significant aspects of the client's story and experiences. When we listen empathetically with clients, we are often listening not just to their words and using the attending skills described above, but, rather, there can be a deeper form of listening that involves your intuition and your own responses to the client's material. Paul Wong (2004), the President of the International Network on Personal Meaning, describes what is meant by advanced empathy,

> Advanced empathy requires the listener to go beyond verbal and non-verbal expressions, to develop an insightful awareness and understanding of another person's intentions, desires and unspoken concerns. It requires the skill to listen with the sixth sense, to feel the pulse of the innermost being, and to make explicit what is hidden beneath consciousness. It involves the insightful construing of meaning and significance from a variety of seemingly trivial clues. It tests hypothesis about the missing pieces of the puzzle and anticipates solutions. (para. 25)

Whenever you think you are "tuning in" to your client in this deeper way, and you believe that you have an insight for the client as a result, it is important to check your perceptions out with your client. You can let the client know that you have a "hunch" about something and want to know his or her thoughts about it. Using advanced empathy in this way is not an interpretation or even a "brilliant figuring out" of the client's material, but an opportunity to share in your client's world in a deeper way. When you are experiencing advanced empathy, you may sense a pattern emerging and you really "get it"—the connections begin with the client's story, experiences, feelings, and thoughts, and there is a certain clarity that you then reflect back to the client. Remember to offer your hunch as a possibility—invite the client to look at it, and if the client pulls away or does not agree, immediately move on to something else and do not dwell on it.

Empathy is more than a set of skills, and for many counselors, it is an innate quality that they just naturally possess. Learning what empathy is and how to enhance your ability to enter your client's world in this way is of paramount importance to the development of the therapeutic alliance, where clients feel safe to share their thoughts and feelings and engage with you in a meaningful way. For empathy to be effective, the therapist needs to develop the attitude or mindset of empathy. In other words, empathy works only when it comes from a person who really cares about people and who truly has a compassionate heart. Knowing that your counselor truly cares about you and values you is far more important in this process than intellectual understanding and knowledge of details. This type of caring about your clients will "cover" a lot of counselor errors in timing, misunderstandings, and inadvertent miscommunication. A counselor can come across to a client as patronizing, judging, or condescending in the absence of an empathetic connection.

ENCOURAGING, PARAPHRASING, AND SUMMARIZING

These skills involve verbal responses (not questions) that demonstrate to a client that you have listened to their story and understood their thoughts and feelings. These skills also provide clients with an opportunity to reflect upon their stories, clarify what they have shared, and go deeper into their thoughts and feelings.

- *Encouragers*—are head nods, hand gestures, and positive facial expressions that invite the client to continue talking. They include minimal verbal expressions, such as "uh huh," that go along with the nonverbal engagement and interest that are displayed by the counselor.
- *Paraphrasing*—feeds back to the client the essence of what he or she has said, using some of their words and also some of your own. Paraphrasing can be helpful when you want the client to know that you have "taken in" what they have shared, or if you want to try to focus on one aspect of the interaction or story. A good way to paraphrase what a client has shared with you is to start with a

sentence stem, based upon what you think the client's verbal style is, and then condense the material in your own words to check with the client for accuracy:

> Sight—"As I see things …"
> Sound—"As I hear you speak …":
> Movement: "You appear moved by this …"
>   For example, "Let me see if I have heard you correctly. What I think you are saying is that this is all just too much to absorb—it is too many losses and too many adjustments without a chance to catch your breath in between. Does that sound about right?"

- *Summarizing*—similar to paraphrasing, but a summary will cover a longer time frame and more information. Summarizing can be used to *begin the session*, for example, "Last time we were together, we talked about. . . . What has happened since?" In the *middle of the session*, summarization may help to wrap up one part of the session, before going on to something else: "Up until now we have talked about how it was at the funeral. You have mentioned what happened that day, some of the issues with your family that arose, and how you felt just before the funeral . . . so, I wonder now what took place in the weeks following his death?" A good summary is often very useful at the *end of the session* to review what has taken place during the session time. Use the sentence stem, a summary of important events and the feelings and key descriptors connected with them, and end with a check-out for accuracy.

> For example, "As I see the situation, you have been distraught over the death of your sister, partly because it was accidental and you had no time to prepare. You have had to be the strong one in the family and support your parents and siblings in their grief. It is possible that you have not taken the time to feel your own grief in the face of all that you have had to do, and now you are over-whelmed and seem ready to collapse. It sounds like there is a lot on your plate, and perhaps we can start with these issues at our next session."

IMMEDIACY

The client–counselor interaction often closely mirrors the way that clients interact with others. If you find the client to be difficult, nonemotional, scattered in thinking, or irritating in some way, most likely other individuals in the client's world experience the client in a similar way. Using immediacy involves looking at the here and now—at what is happening in the counseling sessions as grist for the mill in the client's process. We can move through past, future, and present tenses when clients share their stories, but staying in the present is probably what is most powerful (and helpful) for the client. In his guide book for therapists, Yalom (2009) discussed the use of immediacy and staying in the "here and now" with clients as vital in assisting them toward growth and healing.

It is important to remember that timing is crucial when you decide to draw attention to something that you experience with the client in the session. Immediacy is a bit of a "dance" between self-disclosure and feedback, as you choose to share something that you experience with the client in the here and now. Because this type of feedback is uncommon in most people's lives, clients may not know exactly how to handle your sharing of your experience of them during sessions so forthrightly, and some clients may feel that you are challenging them, or that you are criticizing them. Using immediacy requires skillful communication, and perception of both the self and the client by the counselor. We are taught socially not to address issues in this way, so it involves a relearning process. Using immediacy means we are naming what is going on and bringing it up into the conscious awareness in the room. You are noticing what you are seeing and talking about it openly. Yalom (2009) gave an example of how he might use immediacy with a client who casually makes a statement prior to repeating an oft-told story to him during a session:

> "I know you've heard this story before but …" (and the patient proceeded to tell a long story).
> "I'm struck by how often you say that I've heard the story before and then proceed to tell it. What's your hunch about how I feel listening to the same story over again?"
> "Must be tedious. You probably want the hour to end—you're probably checking the clock."
> "Is there a question in there for me?"
> "Well, do you?"
> "I am impatient hearing the same story again. I feel it gets interposed between the two of us, as though you're really not talking to me. You were right about my checking the clock. I did—but it was with the hope that when your story ended we would still have time to make contact before the end of the session." (pp. 24–25)

Keep in mind that clients may not be used to this type of interaction, and they may interpret it as judgment, shaming, or "calling them on the carpet" when that is not your intention. It is, therefore, very important that you ground any feedback like this in empathy and that you are careful and considerate when you first begin to incorporate its use in your work with a client. Some other examples of immediacy might be like these: "I noticed you sighed just now. I wonder what that's about …"

"Your face grimaced as you talked about that …"
"I am feeling this right now … how about you?"
"I find it difficult that you are smiling right now, but your story is very troubling. Can you tell me a little about that?"

SELF-DISCLOSURE

This skill involves the counselor sharing her or his own story and own person-hood at appropriate times in the process. Yalom (2009) described three kinds of counselor self-disclosure: (1) the mechanism of therapy, (2) feelings that are present in the here and now, and (3) sharing from the therapist's personal life and experiences. Probably the most difficult form of self-disclosure to gauge is that of your own personal experiences. There are some potential positive effects for clients when counselors disclose aspects of themselves to their clients. Some of these positive results with counselor self-disclosure may be that it:

- helps to normalize the client's experiences;
- helps to give realistic expectations;
- models self-disclosure for the client, especially if the client has difficulty disclosing information about self;
- communicates to clients that they are not alone; and
- can be helpful if you are sensing/feeling that you need to be more visible as a real person or that there is a need to try to equalize the power in the therapeutic relationship.

Self-disclosure has a lot to do with boundaries, and it is not a good idea to disclose material from your personal experiences if the boundaries of the client are shaky or not intact. Times when you should hold back from self-disclosure with a client might be in the following scenarios:

- Boundaries are not set or are problematic (i.e., the client may use the personal material you have disclosed in order to gain access to your personal life, or the client has difficulty with maintaining close relationships because of dependency needs or inappropriate behaviors).
- You are triggered and want to share something for your own release during the session.

- You sense that disclosing something personal with a client might change the relationship dynamic in an unhealthy or unproductive way.
- Your self-disclosure leads the client to try to focus on you instead of them; the client may want to talk about you and your experience more as a defense or the client has a habit of wanting to take care of others incessantly or to "rescue" others repeatedly.
- The client does not tolerate intimacy well. Your sharing something personal could backfire with a client who has difficulty being close to others, as he or she may not be able to handle having personal knowledge of you or feel overwhelmed by the information.

If you have established a good working therapeutic alliance with a client, and you feel that sharing something from your personal world may afford some benefit to your client, there are a few suggestions to consider beforehand. These might be as follows:

- Be conscious—know why you are doing it.
- Be brief—one or two sentences maximum; keep the focus of the session upon the client and not upon you.
- Check out whose need it is serving; if you are feeling a lot of emotional energy around sharing something with a client, stop and reflect upon your purpose in sharing this information.
- Limit the frequency—if you are doing a lot, explore why. Are you being set up as an avoidance? Are you frustrated because the client is not sharing deeply in the sessions?
- Use your intuition whether or not this is right for this client. If you have any uneasiness about it, wait to disclose until you can give it more time and thought.
- Use your common sense.
- Be aware of timing; in the beginning of counseling, the focus should be more upon hearing the client and "getting" the story. As you go on in time, and the focus of the sessions begins to move toward growth and the future, self-disclosure may be a very valuable tool.
- Clients vary enormously with the appropriateness of this technique, so be aware and follow the client's response as a guide. There is no one "right" way to approach this issue with all of your clients, so you would need to gauge your disclosure on a case-by-case basis.

- If you have any hesitation about whether to self-disclose or not, err on the side of not disclosing. Remember, once you have disclosed something to a client, you cannot take it back!
- Keep in mind that clients are not bound by the same adherence to confidentiality as a counselor is. Whatever you may share with a client can potentially be shared with many other individuals in the client's interactions with others outside of the session.

Self-disclosure certainly has its place in the therapeutic alliance. Counselors tend to vary widely in how they choose to disclose or not to disclose details of their personal lives with clients. Many counselors feel that the benefits of disclosure in regard to their transparency and shared humanity with clients are profound. What is most important to this discussion is that you be able to think about this topic and your comfort with self-disclosure so that you feel reconciled with whatever choices you make about this issue.

HONORING RESISTANCE

Even though a client freely chooses to begin counseling sessions, there may be times when you get the feeling that the client is holding back in the sessions with you, or that the client demonstrates behaviors that indicate to you that something may be awry in the therapeutic alliance. If you have this experience, you may be facing resistance from the client, and it is important to reflect upon what is happening. Keep in mind that for many individuals, the counseling process may be associated with stigma or with identification by others of being "weak." Counseling can also be expensive for clients, especially if they have very little or no insurance coverage to assist with the costs of sessions. In addition, the venue itself might seem pretty daunting—unsure of what to expect, clients are asked to enter into a relationship with a virtual stranger and share about personal experiences and feelings that they might not have shared previously with even their closest friends and family. For other clients, the choice to seek counseling help might not have been their own. They may have been coerced into counseling by a well-meaning family member, friend, minister, or health care professional, and as a result, they are not willing to fully commit themselves to the process. Given the unique dimensions of the counseling process, it is only natural that some clients will feel a sense of resistance toward the counseling process.

It is important for a counselor to know how to recognize resistance and how to best respond to its presence within a client. Keep in mind that when someone is feeling resistant, he or she is often feeling highly vulnerable and wanting to protect that vulnerability by putting up a barrier. Often, resistance stems from the client feeling coerced, outmaneuvered, or intimidated, even though these are the last things that a counselor would want to convey. In fact, the resistance may not have anything to do with the counselor at all, but be more of a reflection upon the client's anxiety, difficulty trusting, feeling shame, finding the interactions too intense, or the need to stay in the familiar and to be identified with what is known. Resistance is a normal response and needs to be honored as such.

It is imperative that you give the client space when this is happening and not push. In being resistant, the client is able to say "no," which can be a good thing. It is a natural response to get frustrated with a resistant client—however, it is a normal process, and it is important to see it as an opportunity to learn more about the client's feelings and world view.

Resistance may be manifested in many different ways. Clients may talk "around" an issue and change the subject when things are getting too close for their comfort. Some clients may attempt to use humor, try to focus the session on extraneous things like the weather or details that are not really important, or onto the therapist. When you sense there is resistance, back up and think about what is happening. If your goal is to honor the client's process, you will most likely pick up on the resistance and handle it with compassion, which is probably what the client needs at this time. Here are common reasons for why resistance may occur:

- The counselor is leading too much.
- The client does not feel that the counselor understands him or her.
- The session or process may be too intense.
- The counselor is not listening well enough or is not engaged enough with the client.
- The counselor is too challenging for the client.
- The counselor's body language may be misinterpreted by the client.
- The client feels the counselor is judgmental or advice-giving.
- There is transference on the part of the client that is interfering with his or her relationship with the therapist (i.e., the therapist reminds the client of someone who has been abusive, negative, or highly critical to him or her in the past).

Once you are aware that there is some resistance being manifested by your client, how is the best way to handle it? Here are some ideas:

- Remember that it is normal and normalize it—"It's okay."
- Accept where the client is and be respectful; remember that resistance has a purpose.

- Understand that resistance and reluctance are fear-based and are often related to feeling a loss of control, fear of the unknown, fear of change, and so on.
- Examine your own fear/resistance—what is your part? (as a counselor, are you afraid of failing, afraid of not working well with the client, or the client not doing well after seeing you?)
- Examine your interventions—especially any hidden agendas or current "hot issues" for you—are you pushing too hard? Could the client be feeling any subtle coercion or expectations?
- Go with the resistance and allow it to produce change. You can befriend the resistance—"I can sense you do not want to talk about that and it is okay."
- Be realistic, fair, and flexible. Do not be afraid to stretch. Maybe you are expecting too much. Allow the client to have control.
- Resistance is often felt as a challenge to *you*, but it may not be about you. Be willing to be open, honest, and look for solutions, and to be as honest with yourself as you can be in your work with clients.

GETTING STARTED—THE FIRST SESSION

As we have stated earlier, many people come to counseling without having a clear idea of what it is really about. Clients come to counseling for various reasons, but most initiate counseling in order to feel better, to learn how to cope more effectively with the experiences they have had, or to feel that they are not alone in their situation. So, with these thoughts in mind, let us think about our objectives for the first session that we see a client:

1. *Begin to build a trusting relationship.* We have discussed much of the groundwork involved in setting up the therapeutic alliance in previous chapters and in this one as well. This is now the time when you begin to orient the client to your way of being with him or her, and the client begins to have a good idea of your values and way of working therapeutically. Safety in the therapeutic relationship is built upon trust, and you need to be able to share with the client how you will keep his or her disclosures safe and private, and how you will begin the work. So, in addition to the intentional offering of your full presence, you will use the skills that we described in this chapter to lay the foundation for your future interactions. In addition, you will need to share with your client about the confidential nature of counseling, and any limits on that confidentiality that may be present.

2. *Teach the client about the gradual, unfolding nature of the counseling process.* Ask the client for his or her expectations and to share ideas about how the counseling process works from his or her perspective. You can also share a little bit about your philosophy of counseling and how you like to work with clients. However, it is also a very good idea to ask your client to identify what he or she might find most helpful as a starting point for this work together. You want to use this first session as a time to let the client know that you wish to follow his or her lead—not the other way around.

3. *Ask the client about his or her concerns and desired outcome from counseling.* Do not be afraid to ask the client to indicate to you what he or she hopes will happen as a result of coming to a counselor. It is also important at this time to engage in a dialogue about what the counseling process is and is not. For example, some clients will indicate that they want you to tell them what to do. You may then have to explain that you do not tell people what to do, but, rather, you try to help them to figure out what they feel is best to do after exploring all of the possibilities that are available.

4. *Discuss the collaborative nature of counseling.* Ask the client about how you can best support him or her in this journey. Do not be afraid to ask if he or she has seen a counselor in the past and to describe what that experience was like—and if you need to adjust your way of working with the client to better accommodate his or her needs and expectations. Remind clients that you will frequently "check in" with them during the sessions for their feedback and that you will also provide honest feedback to them, if they wish.

Some counselors may choose to have a written contract in place with their clients, delineating out the roles and expectations of each party in the counseling process. This contract may strengthen the therapeutic alliance by providing a clear understanding regarding what each party is expected to do when entering the contract.

CONCLUSION

Being a counselor can be a very challenging vocation. Being a skilled counselor requires a great deal of discipline, focus, commitment to self-awareness and understanding, and compassionate engagement with clients. Reading about these skills and the counseling process is interesting, but actually having the opportunity to "practice the process" and to spend time immersed in therapeutic encounters will help to refine the counselor's abilities and skills considerably.

Glossary of Terms

Advanced empathy   moments when the counselor is deeply attuned to the client and has an intuitive knowing about something that the client may not have stated openly, but seems to be apparent in the session.

Attending skills   include things to which the counselor needs to "attend," both in himself/herself and in the client. Include body language, eye contact, tone and volume of voice, use of language, and nonverbal cues.

Closed questions   questions that can be answered with a "yes" or "no" answer, or often with a single word. Closed questions often provide the facts, such as address, age, length of time since an event, and so on. Often begin with where, is, are, and do.

Empathy   involves the counselor intentionally moving into the client's frame of reference—attempting to experience how things see and feel to the client, trying to experience the world as the client does, while at the same time maintaining the awareness that this frame of reference and experience is the client's and not the counselor's.

Immediacy   the ability of the counselor to use the immediate situation within the session to invite the client to look at what is going on between them in the relationship.

Observation skills   the ability to ascertain information about the client through careful observation on the part of the counselor. Observational skills assist in reading nonverbal cues and filling in details about the client's story and situation.

Open questions   they cannot be answered briefly and often require some thought or expression of feeling. Open questions often begin with what, how, why, and could, and allow clients to respond according to their needs. These types of questions invite clients to elaborate on their story and add the details as they wish.

Resistance   the situation where a client withholds disclosure or engagement in the therapeutic relationship or session, often because of the client feeling threatened or uncomfortable for some reason. Resistance may or may not be conscious on the part of the client.

Self-disclosure   involves the counselor sharing her/his own story and own personhood at appropriate times in the process. Three kinds of counselor self-disclosure are (1) the mechanism of therapy, (2) feelings that are present in the here and now, and (3) sharing from the therapist's personal life and experiences.

Verbal tracking   used by the counselor to more closely follow the client's story or how a client tends to share about an experience. In verbal tracking, the counselor tends to "pick out" things that point to a deeper level of a client's experience or awareness.

Questions for Reflection

1. Practice your own skills of empathy and listening to others in social settings. For instance, when you are listening to someone describe an experience or their feelings about something, try to "tune in" by listening to what they are saying, and their feelings about the experience, without asking questions and without interjecting your opinions. What happens when you do this?

2. Ask someone you know to describe an event or an experience they have had. As they are speaking, you can engage with them, as long as you do not ask any questions. You may use statements, but not questions. What is it like to do this exercise? What can this exercise tell you about how you would interact with different kinds of clients?

3. Think of a "script" that you might use for your initial sessions with clients. Write out what you would say in the beginning of the first session to set the tone for the counseling and how you would describe your way of working with clients to a new client. You can practice your "script" with a friend or colleague to fine tune it before you use it with clients.

4. What are some reasons why a bereaved client might feel some resistance to sharing something with a counselor? How might you address resistance with bereaved individuals in the counseling process?

5. Practice listening to people as they share their stories and experiences with you. Do you find that you tend to remember details of the story more easily or that you tend to "tune in" to the tone of the person who is speaking, noticing their feelings and reactions more than the details of their story? What might this tell you about the way that you will work with clients?

References

Egan, G. (2009). *The skilled helper: A problem management and opportunity development approach to helping* (9th ed.). Belmont, CA: Brooks/Cole.

Rogers, C. R. (1959). A theory of therapy, personality and interpersonal relationships, as developed in the client-centered framework. In S. Koch (Ed.), *Psychology: A study of science* (Vol. 3, pp. 184–256). New York, NY: McGraw-Hill.

Wong, P. (2004). *Creating a kinder and gentler world: The positive psychology of empathy.* Retrieved January 5, 2011, from http://www.meaning.ca/archives/presidents_columns/pres_col_mar_2004_empathy.htm

Yalom, I. R. (2009). *The gift of therapy.* New York, NY: HarperCollins.

CHAPTER 6

Working With Bereaved Individuals

Many people are afraid to approach newly bereaved individuals, feeling concern that they may say the wrong thing or that they may actually make the bereaved person feel worse by saying something that is inadvertently insensitive or that provokes pain. In this chapter, we will give you some practical ideas for how to sensitively approach someone who is bereaved and to offer the best form of support that might be possible to that person.

We have already mentioned in a previous chapter that most bereaved individuals do not require professional support or therapy to cope with their losses and their grief. In this chapter, we are not going to focus so much on what professionals do or do not do, but upon what might be helpful to a bereaved person, whether you are a friend, colleague, or a counselor. Some people seek grief counseling not because their grief is complicated or because deeper unresolved issues in their lives have been triggered by the loss, but because they need a safe place to explore their grief in a healthy way with someone who can offer them unconditional support. In this chapter, we will first explore some of the common expressions of the grief experience, and then we will discuss some practical suggestions for how to be most helpful to a bereaved individual.

WHAT IS NORMAL?

This question is perhaps one of the most common queries we receive from clients and students alike. As there is so much variation in grief from one person to another, how would you know what is normal? One of our clients answered this question very well when she said simply, "Normal is a cycle on the washing machine. If you want normal right now, go to your laundry room and look for it to be written on the dial. That's where you will find normal when you are grieving." We laughed at the time when she said this statement, but we have shared it with many other clients, who will nod in agreement. When we encounter a significant loss—the "seismic life event" that we mentioned earlier, our entire world gets turned upside down. There is often a sense of being off-balance and unable to be the way we have known ourselves to be in the past, and sometimes there is an accompanying sense of paralysis or a dizzying need to remain very busy that is not normally part of who we are. So, let us start with how grief can be experienced by many individuals and then take a look at some of the more unique aspects of the grieving process as a way of exploring what "normal" grief may look or feel like.

How Is Grief Experienced?

Although grief is often considered primarily an emotional response, it can be manifested in many different ways with a great deal of variation between individuals. It is important to note that bereaved individuals will most likely experience grief in a way that is congruent with their personality and previous ways of coping with stressful situations. For example, a person who is not typically emotionally demonstrative with others will most likely not all of a sudden become highly emotional or seek out places to share his or her feelings after experiencing a significant loss. Grief can be manifested in many ways:

- *Emotionally*—although we expect to see sadness, that is not always the primary emotion bereaved individuals may feel. It is very common to feel angry because of what has happened, to feel robbed of the presence of someone we loved who is now gone, or to feel like we have lost a part of ourselves that we valued. Sometimes, the anger is expressed toward medical care providers, clergy, family members, or oneself. The anger can also be more covert, being expressed through sarcastic remarks or cynicism about life and people. Many bereaved individuals report feeling numb—a sense that they are unable to access their feelings or that they are flooded—that their feelings are very intense and overwhelming. Guilt and remorse are commonly expressed, either for lost opportunities, things said or done that they now wish they had not or that they will never have the opportunity to clear up, and these feelings are often expressed as "if onlys." It is important to remember that emotions do serve a valuable purpose when they are present, and the listener's role is not to talk the bereaved person out of these emotions, or to try to make him or her to feel better, but to listen and support the sharing of these emotions so that the bereaved individual can benefit from the purpose they are serving. We will talk more about working with strong emotions in a later chapter.

- *Cognitively*—it is common for bereaved individuals to complain that they just cannot focus well or that their minds seem to wander a lot. Many people describe difficulties remembering, organizing, and keeping track of things. Time may seem to warp as well; a day may seem like forever, or it may seem like a brief period. Days and nights can get switched around as well. Many of our bereaved clients describe their minds as "constantly busy," but not productively so. One client reported that she accidentally forgot to pick up her 2-year-old son from the day care. She stated that she had a nagging feeling that something was amiss, and when she got home, she realized that she had not picked up her son at the usual time of 4 p.m. (and it was now almost 6 p.m.)! This aspect of grief may be very hard if you work, as most people have limited time off work after the death of a loved one, and when they return to work, concentration and focus can be very difficult.

- *Physically*—our bodies often "carry" the weight of our grief through physical symptoms. Many bereaved individuals will share that they often have symptoms that mimic those of their loved one before she or he died. One client shared that she had gone to the emergency room three times with chest pain and shortness of breath that had never been present before her husband died suddenly of a heart attack. One very common description from clients is something that we term "restless exhaustion," where bereaved individuals may feel continually busy or agitated in their minds, but exhausted physically. When they try to lie down or rest, their minds become even busier; however, when they try to get something done or try to complete a task, they are overwhelmed by feelings of exhaustion and lethargy. Headaches, bodily aches and pains, difficulty sleeping, weight loss and weight gain, digestive problems, and accidents like falling, tripping, and knocking things over are commonly described as well (Hensley & Clayton, 2008; Luekin, 2008; Stroebe, Schut, & Stroebe, 2007). It is interesting to note that there is research linking certain types of bereavement to lowered immune function and to higher rates of morbidity and mortality in survivors (Buckley, McKinley, Tofler, & Bartrop, 2010; Goodkin et al., 2001; Hall & Irwin, 2001; Jones, Bartrop, Forcier, & Penny, 2010; Schleifer, Keller, Camerino, Thornton, & Stein, 1983).

- *Spiritually*—we have already discussed how a significant loss event can shake up an individual's assumptive world and the spiritual effects of a major loss often leave people questioning their beliefs about God or wondering if there is indeed any higher order or purpose in life. Over time, many bereaved individuals will often say that their loss experience deepened their faith or caused them to reexamine beliefs that they had taken for granted before. On a more practical level, clients will often share how their faith communities are sources of support and also, at times, sources of discomfort or disappointment. Although there are studies that examine the effects of spiritual beliefs upon bereavement outcome, most do not conclusively demonstrate either that religion or systems of faith have a direct impact upon the course of bereavement (Wortmann & Park, 2008). However, it is often thought that many individuals benefit from the sense of structure and ritual that a faith tradition may provide for them after a significant loss, such as the funeral liturgy, mourning rituals, and a sense of belonging to a community at a time when they may otherwise be isolated (Park & Halifax, 2011).

Balk (1999) stated that three things must be present for a life crisis to initiate spiritual change in a person: (1) the situation must create a feeling of destabilization that resists restabilization readily, (2) there must be time to reflect upon what has occurred, and (3) the crisis must be something that will be indelibly etched into the life story of the person who experiences it. Balk goes further to state,

> Bereavement contains all the necessary ingredients needed to trigger spiritual change. It is a dangerous opportunity, producing extreme psychological imbalance, and possessing sufficient intensity and duration to allow for serious reflection. Its effects color a person's life forever. (p. 488)

Fowler (1981) mentioned that the times in our lives when we end up questioning our beliefs and searching for meaning can produce what he calls a *transformed faith consciousness*, which allows for greater meaning and understanding in our lives. Thus, a significant loss event carries the possibility of spiritual destabilization and the potential for increased depth and personal meaning in life.

- *Socially*—there are many effects that grief has upon how bereaved individuals interact with others socially. If the bereaved individual has been a long-term caregiver, there is a good likelihood that the social network that was in place before so much time was spent taking care of a dying loved one is no longer in place. Others' lives have continued in a very different way from the life of the person who became a long-term caregiver and with increasing demands because of the illness of their loved one, there was likely little time left to socialize and stay in touch with their usual support network (Burton et al., 2008). Our bereaved clients often describe feeling socially isolated and aware that they do not "fit" into any identifiable social group, often feeling acutely aware that they are different in the way they react to things and to their needs in their close relationships than before they were bereaved.

Many bereaved individuals isolate themselves because they have a great deal of difficulty handling social situations where they may be triggered into their grief or where the effort to engage in small talk seems like a great deal of work because their lives have been filled with such deep grief and profound questioning of life and themselves. Many of these individuals have a difficult time fitting neatly in a social context—they may no longer be able to identify with the role that was associated with the deceased person—for example, a widow is no longer a wife; a parent to a deceased child is still a parent, but the child is missing. In addition, many bereaved individuals sense the discomfort of others around them, as people struggle finding the "right" words to speak or avoid them to prevent the discomfort of an awkward social exchange.

- *Economically*—we often do not ask our clients about this particular issue in bereavement, but it is an area that can be of immense concern to bereaved individuals. Two of the younger widows whom I (D.L.H.) saw in my practice had to declare bankruptcy after their husbands died because there was not enough life insurance to cover the debts in their husbands' businesses, and they could not deal with bill collectors and harassing phone calls and letters on top of their paralyzing grief.

If the bereaved individual takes time off work to be the caregiver to a terminally ill loved one, he or she may not only face lost income, but his or her jobs may have been given to someone else in his or her absence. In addition, those individuals who take a leave from their work after the death of a loved one may do so out of necessity to take care of the estate issues and to take care of themselves emotionally and physically, but this time may be unpaid leave from work, with the result being increased financial strain in addition to the grief. If the bereaved individual is the executor of the deceased person's estate, there are often time-consuming responsibilities associated with this role and there may be conflict with surviving relatives about the distribution of the estate, all of which will land in the lap of the grief-laden executor. Some clients have difficulties accepting insurance monies and proceeds from an estate, citing feelings of guilt that the death of the person they loved has now somehow benefitted them financially.

- *Behaviorally*— some of the behaviors in which bereaved individuals may engage can be quite subtle, but they may be very common. For instance, many bereaved individuals will describe feeling like they are *searching* for their lost loved one in a crowd, or they will automatically scan situations for familiar things that are associated with their loved one—a car that is similar to the one that your son drove before he died, and you realize that you are staring at the driver, looking for your son in the seat. Or, you find yourself going to places that your loved one would go, even if it is not a place where you went together beforehand. Some individuals find engaging in an activity that their loved one used to enjoy to be comforting— gardening, playing certain music that their loved one would listen to, feeding birds, collecting stamps, shopping, watching certain sports events and teams, eating at certain restaurants or certain types of food that your loved one enjoyed—all are commonly described by bereaved individuals, and the common thread is often an identification with the deceased person and an attempt to reconnect with that person in these activities. Clayton (1990) described attempts to cope by the increased use of alcohol, tranquilizers, hypnotics, and cigarettes often reported in bereaved individuals. Many bereaved individuals describe a sense of "going through the motions," or of being on "autopilot" for a long period after they experience a significant loss. One client described this experience as "showing up for work, but leaving my brain at home asleep."

Extraordinary Experiences

Bereaved individuals commonly describe feeling that their loved one has connected with them through a sign, a dream, a vision, or a hallucination. We have had clients give descriptions of radios tuned in to the favorite station of their loved one without them recalling changing the tuner themselves, a bird landing on windowsills that they believe represents a visit from the deceased person, a "sense" of something brushing against their skin, finding a book open to a page where there is a message for them, flickering lights, butterflies appearing from nowhere, or hearing the voice of their loved one speaking to them either silently or audibly. The "visitation dreams" that clients describe are often very vivid and totally engaging, often with the deceased person telling them that they are okay, and sometimes the feeling that there was physical contact with the deceased in the dream.

Many clients share that they have regular "conversations" with their deceased loved ones, most commonly described as silent discussions that occur in their thoughts, but sometimes in audible dialog as well. These conversations most often happen at the graveside or in a place that was most frequented by the deceased person, such as his or her office, a favorite recreation spot, or a special place that they shared together. Most bereaved individuals describe these experiences as comforting and helpful, which is also supported by Parker's (2005) research on the topic. What is important to note about these experiences is that they are common among bereaved individuals and they also tend to have a functional role in the grieving process rather than a pathological or unhealthy influence. These experiences are not breaks in reality that would occur in someone with a psychotic or delusional disorder, as the bereaved are aware that the experience is extraordinary when it occurs, and their interpretation of the event is often kept very private to avoid social stigma surrounding the experience or their mental state.

Resurgences

It is now known that grief may never be fully "resolved." It is more common (and more accurate) to use words such as "integration," "accommodation," and "adaptation" to loss rather than to refer to "recovery from grief," "resolution of a loss," or "acceptance." In fact, it is now recognized that grief may never really end. Although the intensity of the grieving experience usually diminishes over time, grief itself may be present in various ways throughout a person's lifetime. For example, a girl whose father dies when she is 8 years old may experience a resurgence of grief later in her life as she experiences significant life passages and realizes that her father is not there to participate in these times with her. There are times when grief that has abated in its intensity over time can be reactivated in a very real and intense way. Most commonly, these resurgences occur at significant times, such as anniversary dates, the date the loved one died, or at special family times or rites of passage, such as graduations, weddings, the birth of a baby, or some time or event that carries a reminder of a shared time with the deceased (Sofka, 2004). Some people call these "grief triggers" or "grief surges." Parkes (1975) used the term grief "pangs" to describe these resurgences of grief. Rosenblatt (1996) addressed the issue of the ongoing nature of grief, stating that grief may never really go away completely, and noting that it is probably unrealistic to think that a bereaved individual will just stop grieving at some point. Rather, he stated that grief resulting from major losses will probably recur at many points over a person's lifetime. Grief can essentially "sneak up" on someone when there is a new pang of grief that surfaces in response to a triggering situation or reminder. Rando (1993) described *STUG reactions* that are subsequent temporary upsurges of grief that occur in situations where the realization of the loss and its magnitude are brought into the active awareness of the bereaved individual, sometimes many years later. It is very important to recognize that there is no specific timeline for grief to end, and the resurgence of grief at various points in time after a significant loss is very common and normal.

Grieving Styles

Doka and Martin (2010) extrapolated on different patterns of the expression of grief in their descriptions of adaptive grieving styles. These authors described three main grieving styles on a continuum, with intuitive grievers at one end, instrumental grievers at the other, and a more blended grieving style between them. *Intuitive grievers* tend to express feelings and wish to talk about their experience with others. *Instrumental grievers* tend to grieve more cognitively and behaviorally and tend to express their grief in terms of thoughts, analysis, and actions. Individuals who have a blended grieving style may combine elements of both intuitive and instrumental grieving styles, but they usually have a predominate tendency toward one of the other style. This exploration of grief emphasizes that there is no "right" way to grieve; however, bereaved individuals are often expected to grieve in certain ways based upon gender socialization, and if they do not express grief in a way that is expected by others, their experience may be labeled as problematic or even pathological.

There have been times when a client or a family member of a bereaved individual will assume that a person has not "grieved well" unless he or she has expressed emotions about the loss. As we stated earlier, not all bereaved individuals will grieve through their emotions or will need to share their feelings and talk about their loss. Expressions of grief typically are congruent with an individual's existing personality, temperament, and preferences. For example, one of our colleagues recently lost his wife. They were extremely close, and her illness and subsequent death occurred over a few short months. He was back to work within a few weeks after the funeral. Many individuals in our work place assumed that he was avoiding his grief and attempting to bury himself in his work, and they expressed concern that he was "hiding" from his grief. However, when in speaking briefly with him, it was very apparent that he needed the structure of work to help him through his daily life, and he is by nature a more cognitively oriented individual who tends to process his experiences through his intellect and analytical thinking. His grief was very real to him, as is his profound loss, and his choice in returning back to work and focusing on everyday tasks was very congruent with his personality and previous ways of coping during times of stress.

For a long time, the goal of grief counseling seemed to be to get the client to emote and to "clear" the grief by having emotional catharsis. However, it seems much more appropriate (and humane) to think of grief counseling not with this type of goal in mind, but to support the bereaved individual in working out the process of grief in ways that are aligned with that person's values, view of himself or herself, personality, and temperament.

Although emotional expression is now not seen as an imperative in the way it once was, social support to bereaved individuals can be very important in assisting the bereaved individual. What is very important to remember about social support is that individuals will vary widely in what is seen as supportive and what is not. For instance, if we go back to the example of my widowed colleague, I doubt he would find it helpful if one of us showed up to his office, sat down, and asked him to talk about his feelings. Support to him has come in the form of snippets, which allow him to know that his colleagues are thinking of him and care about him, but not placing an expectation upon him to talk about his feelings at length. He also seems to greatly appreciate the ability to talk about his teenage children as they cope with the loss of their mother, and he has often requested information about specific aspects of teen grief and the loss of a parent.

Mediators of Mourning

The most important aspect of grief counseling is attending to the story and needs of the bereaved individual as he or she describes them. In this form of active listening, you might also "tune in" to the aspects of the grief experience that are unique to that person and his or her experience, and how these unique modifiers shape the landscape of grief for this person. Worden (2009) referred to these unique factors as the *mediators of mourning*, which include (a) identifying the relationship of the deceased person to the bereaved individual, (b) the nature of the attachment to the deceased person, (c) how the person died, (d) the bereaved individual's history of previous losses and stresses, (e) personality style and how the person has coped in the past with stressful situations, (f) perceived social support that is available, and (g) the presence of concurrent changes and crises that may be occurring at the same time. Worden cautioned that in identifying these variables, the focus is upon the multidimensional aspects of grief and the many variables that may have an impact upon the bereaved individual, and not an attempt to oversimplify grief and its antecedents.

WHAT MAY HELP—PRACTICAL SUGGESTIONS

Do Less, Be More

Many bereaved individuals have experienced others trying to "rescue" them because it is so difficult for others to see them struggling or because their own grief issues become triggered in the bereaved person's presence. We can certainly say that we agree with the dictum of the Hippocratic Oath that states "above all, do no harm" (Vaughn & Gentry, 2006, p. 165). The first rule of thumb is that you cannot "fix it" or even make it better. There is no "ah hah" phrase or intervention that "works." You cannot bring back the deceased person. You cannot replace what is irreplaceable. A person cannot go back in time and "unknow" what is now known through a significant loss experience. Grief counseling at its heart is very person-centered in its approach, and sensitive counselors know how to "lead from two steps behind their client" (Robert Neimeyer, personal communication, April 16, 2010). So, the real goal of helping in this context is to journey alongside the individual so that she or he will not have to go through it all alone. In our "being with" bereaved clients, we bear witness to their experiences, pain, and process. If you are not comfortable with strong emotions (yours or others) or with silence, you will have difficulty working effectively with grieving clients. As we discussed in the section on therapeutic presence, we are fully present and attentive to our clients, following their stories, listening with our ears and our intuition, and in so doing, we value and validate their experiences. You cannot take away the pain. You can, however, make a difference in how your clients journey through this painful experience.

Know Yourself

If you have any unresolved or "raw" grief issues, be aware that you are very likely to be triggered by working with grieving clients. If you have not worked through some of your own loss experiences, chances are you will inadvertently shut your client down emotionally to protect yourself or you will "need" your client in order to complete your own grief work. Self-awareness is one of the most important responsibilities of being a grief counselor. Loss issues, as we all know, do not always pertain just to death. We will address counselor issues in more depth later on, but suffice it to say that grief is a universal experience, and we all experience losses throughout our lives. It is important that counselors be aware of how their loss experiences have shaped and influenced their lives, and often their responses to clients. If we remain open to our own experiences, and address them with compassionate awareness, we can more readily maintain our focus on our clients' processes and needs.

Remembering

Although not everyone needs to talk and to share feelings about their loss, those who seek grief counseling are more likely to self-select toward this desire. Much of grief counseling involves "bearing witness" to your client's story of loss—who he or she was before the loss, the relationship to the person who died if the loss was a death, or the nature of the loss and its meaning, and what life has been since the loss occurred. If the loss is the death of a loved one, we often suggest that clients bring pictures of the person at different times in his or her life, with or without the client in these pictures. You can ask clients to "introduce" you to the deceased person, and in that process, you will learn much about the story of the deceased person, and also about the relationship between the client and the deceased person. We also invite clients to bring in "linking objects" to the sessions. These may be special items that serve as reminders of the loved one—pieces of clothing, jewelry, books, samples of the person's handwriting, cookbooks and recipe cards, and many other things, which invite memories and rich descriptions of the deceased person and the relationship that they shared together. We call this process "remembering," as you are putting the shattered parts (members) back together as the story of the person and the relationship come together through the sharing.

Many clients welcome the opportunity to speak freely and to share openly about their loss, their feelings, and their process since the loss. This type of sharing may also serve to remind the client of the times that were good or happy, especially if there has been a period of lengthy caregiving, difficulties, or pain prior to the loss. It is often helpful to use the name of the deceased person in the conversation and to try to use language that is similar in tone, words, and style to the client in responding to the sharing of the story. Bearing witness to a client's grief occurs when you listen intently and when you are fully present to the client as the story unfolds. In your listening and responding, you are also acknowledging the significance of the relationship as well as the painful loss and deprivation that are now part of the client's daily existence, and you are journeying alongside your client as he or she experiences the aftereffects of this loss.

Tuning In—and Then Changing the Channel

As described in the chapter on bereavement theories, recent thinking in bereavement research is that individuals who are grieving need to oscillate between their grief process and their everyday functioning (Stroebe, 2002). Distraction and "changing the channel" may be helpful at times and are not necessarily indicative of unhealthy denial or avoidance. If clients find that they have been mired down in their grieving process very heavily for a prolonged period of time and they are not "clearing" the grief, it might be helpful to suggest a way to "change the channel" for a while because the process is repeating itself and may be causing more harm by the repetition of the intense feelings without any movement or relief. This is especially important if traumatic material keeps coming up. Teaching containment in these instances might be very helpful. We will discuss the interaction of grief and trauma in more depth later on. However, it is important to keep in mind that sometimes being able to "zone out" with a funny movie, a good piece of music, or at times, becoming immersed in life's everyday details may be more therapeutic to a bereaved individual than hashing out the blow-by-blow details of a loss event with a counselor over and over. For this purpose, I (D.L.H.) have several guided relaxation and visualization CDs that I loan out to clients who need a way to disengage from distressing and repetitive thoughts that may interfere with their ability to sleep or function at times when they are feeling depleted and exhausted.

Rituals and Legacies

As we discussed earlier, much of the "work" of grief is the need to find meaning after a significant loss event. The initiation of rituals associated with the loss or of establishing legacies to commemorate a loss may be helpful in attaching meaning to what has occurred and to the life of the bereaved individual in the wake of a significant loss event. Although there are very few prescribed mourning rituals in current Western society, clients may find their own personal rituals that give meaning to their experience. Some people may wear the deceased's clothing in efforts to remain close in some tangible way. Some may write in a journal to their loved ones or to themselves, light a candle, play a specific piece or a certain type of music, and others may, like Queen Victoria upon the death of her beloved husband Albert, have the deceased's clothing laid-out every day for ensuing years (Lewis & Hoy, 2011). We will explore this aspect of working with bereaved individuals in more detail later on. Suffice it here to say that there is no limit to the creativity and ingenuity of ritualized acts as a response to human need born from loss and grief.

When to Refer for Additional Help and Assessment

Although normal grief usually abates in intensity over time, and most bereaved individuals do not require professional help in order to adapt to their loss, there are some instances where additional help from individuals with specialized training is indicated. We will explore this type of difficult, complicated grief in greater detail in Chapter 9.

CONCLUSION

Although grief is a healthy and adaptive process, bereaved individuals may wish to share their process with someone who can be fully present and "bear witness" to their experience. Understanding how grief often unfolds and learning about ways to offer support that are congruent with the bereaved individual's preferences and needs will help grief counselors to work with these clients in ways that can be meaningful and that might help to promote healing and growth.

Glossary of Terms

Extraordinary experiences   events in which a person believes he or she has been spontaneously contacted by a deceased loved one.

Instrumental grievers   individuals who tend to grieve more cognitively and behaviorally and who generally express their grief in terms of thoughts, analysis, and actions.

Intuitive grievers   individuals who tend to express feelings and wish to talk about their experience with others.

Linking objects   special items that serve as reminders of a deceased loved ones. These items often invite memories and rich descriptions of the deceased person and the relationship that they shared together.

Mediators of mourning   unique modifiers that help to shape the grieving process for a given individual.

STUG reactions   subsequent temporary upsurges of grief; occur in situations where the realization of the loss and its magnitude are brought into the active awareness of the bereaved individual, sometimes many years later.

Transformed faith consciousness   difficult times in people's lives that lead to greater questioning our beliefs and searching for meaning, with the result being a deeper appreciation of life and one's beliefs.

Questions for Reflection

1. Much of the experience of grief involves feeling out of control. Bereaved individuals have no control over the loss of their loved one or over the changes in their lives that have occurred as a result of a major loss. One exercise to explore loss of control involves having a blindfold placed over your eyes. Have a partner choose different foods—tastes, textures, spices, and temperatures—and your partner chooses which foods to feed to you without your knowing what they have chosen or what you will be fed. After you complete this exercise, talk with your partner about what it was like to not be able to make your own choices about what you were going to eat, or to know what was going to be fed to you. (Be sure to disclose any food allergies or major food aversions in advance!)

2. Think of a significant loss that either you or someone close to you has experienced. Look at the mediators of mourning written by Worden (2009), as discussed in this chapter, and describe how each mediator played a role in how you or the other person dealt with the loss experience.

3. In this chapter, we briefly discuss the possibility of assisting a bereaved individual to "change the channel" at times as a way to assist in the grieving process. What do you think makes this suggestion different from unhealthy avoidance of grief?

4. Think of some of the popular movies that you have seen where grief and loss have played a major role in the plot. How has the grief in these movies been portrayed? What were some of the responses from other members of the cast to the person in the movie who is bereaved? What messages do these movies convey about grief to the public?

References

Balk, D. (1999). Bereavement and spiritual change. *Death Studies, 23*, 485–493.

Buckley, T., McKinley, S., Tofler, G., & Bartrop, R. (2010). Cardiovascular risk in early bereavement: A literature review and proposed mechanisms. *International Journal of Nursing Studies, 47*(2), 229–238.

Burton, A. M., Haley, W. E., Small, B. J., Finley, M. R., Dillinger-Vasille, M., & Schonwetter, R. (2008). Predictors of well-being in bereaved former hospice caregivers: The role of caregiving stressors, appraisals, and social resources. *Palliative and Supportive Care, 6*, 149–158.

Clayton, P. J. (1990). Bereavement and depression. *Journal of Clinical Psychology, 51*(7), 34–38.

Doka, K. J., & Martin, T. L. (2010). *Grieving beyond gender: Understanding the ways men and women mourn.* New York, NY: Routledge.

Fowler, J. W. (1981). *Stages of faith: The psychology of human development and the quest for meaning.* San Francisco, CA: Harper & Row.

Goodkin, K., Baldewicz, T., Blaney, N., Asthana, D., Kumar, M., Shapshak, P., . . . Zheng, W. (2001). Physiological effects of bereavement and bereavement support group interventions. In M. Stroebe, R. Hansson, H. Schut, & W. Stroebe (Eds.), *Handbook of bereavement research: Consequences, coping, and care* (pp. 671–704). Washington, DC: American Psychological Association.

Hall, M., & Irwin, M. (2001). Physiological indices of functioning in bereavement. In M. Stroebe, R. Hansson, H. Schut, & W. Stroebe (Eds.), *Handbook of bereavement research: Consequences, coping, and care* (pp. 473–492). Washington, DC: American Psychological Association.

Hensley, P. L., & Clayton, P. J. (2008). Bereavement: Signs, symptoms, and course. *Psychiatric Annals, 38*(10), 649–654.

Jones, M. P., Bartrop, R. W., Forcier, L., & Penny, R. (2010). The long-term impact of bereavement upon spousal health: A 10-year follow up. *Acta Neuropsychiatrica, 22*(5), 212–217.

Lewis, L., & Hoy, W. (2011). Bereavement rituals and the creation of legacy. In R. Neimeyer, D. Harris, H. Winokuer, & G. Thornton (Eds.), *Grief and bereavement in contemporary society: Bridging research and practice* (pp. 315–324). New York, NY: Routledge.

Luekin, L. J. (2008). Long-term consequences of parental death in childhood: Psychological and physiological manifestations. In. M. Stroebe, R. Hansson, H. Schut, & W. Stroebe (Eds.), *Handbook of bereavement research and practice: Advances in theory and intervention* (pp. 397–416). Washington, DC: American Psychological Association.

Park, C. L., & Halifax, J. (2011). Religion and spirituality in adjusting to bereavement: Grief as burden, grief as gift. In R. Neimeyer, D. Harris, H. Winokuer, & G. Thornton (Eds.), *Grief and bereavement in contemporary society: Bridging research and practice* (pp. 355–363). New York, NY: Routledge.

Parker, J. S. (2005). Extraordinary experiences of the bereaved and adaptive outcomes of grief. *Omega, 51*(4), 257–283.

Parkes, C. M. (1975). *Bereavement: Studies of grief in adult life.* New York, NY: Penguin.

Rando, T. A. (1993). *Treatment of complicated mourning.* Champaign, IL: Research Press.

Rosenblatt, P. C. (1996). Grief that does not end. In D. Klass, P. Silverman, & S. Nickman (Eds.), *Continuing bonds: New understandings of grief* (pp. 45–58). New York, NY: Routledge.

Schleifer, S. J., Keller, S. E., Camerino, M., Thornton, J. C., & Stein, M. (1983). Suppression of lymphocyte stimulation following bereavement. *Journal of the American Medical Association, 250*(3), 374–377.

Sofka, C. S. (2004). Assessing loss reactions among older adults: Strategies to evaluate the impact of September 11, 2001. *Journal of Mental Health Counseling, 26*(3), 260–281.

Stroebe, M. (2002). Paving the way: From early attachment theory to contemporary bereavement research. *Mortality, 7*(2), 127–138.

Stroebe, M., Schut, H., & Stroebe, W. (2007). Health outcomes of bereavement. *Lancet, 370*(9603), 1960–1973.

Vaughn, K. S., & Gentry, G. K. (2006). Do no harm. In T. J. Vaughn (Ed.), *Psychology licensure and certification: What students need to know* (pp. 165–174). Washington, DC: American Psychological Association.

Worden, J. W. (2009). *Grief counseling & grief therapy* (4th ed.). New York, NY: Springer Publishing Company.

Wortmann, J. H., & Park, C. L. (2008). Religion and spirituality in adjustment following bereavement: An integrative review. *Death Studies, 32,* 703–736.

CHAPTER 7

Living Losses: Nonfinite Loss, Ambiguous Loss, and Chronic Sorrow

*I*n the process of living our lives, we encounter losses on a regular basis, but we often do not recognize their significance because we tend to think of loss in finite terms, mainly associated with death and dying, and not more generally in terms of adaptation to life-altering events and changes. We know that grief is the normal, unique response to loss. However, the assumption is often made that grief is only associated with losses that occur after the death of a loved one. We think that this view of grief is quite narrow. Of course, grief will normally follow the death of someone whom we cared about deeply. But does a person have to die for grief to occur? We think that grief is a process that enables us to rebuild our assumptive world after it has been broken, even shattered, by a significant loss event, and losses that are both death and nondeath related can assault our assumptions about how the world should work. In this chapter, we explore different types of losses that are not death related and their unique features and impact upon us.

Most of the current bereavement literature focuses on death-related losses, and many of the measures used in bereavement research are rooted in the identification of "separation distress" from another individual as the primary feature distinguishing grief from other responses and states, such as post-traumatic stress, depression, and anxiety (Prigerson et al., 1999). Separation distress is characterized by yearning, longing, preoccupation, and searching for the deceased individual (Jacobs, Mazure, & Prigerson, 2000). However, the emphasis on grief in terminology that relates only to the death of a person does not consider the possibility that the same grieving process also allows individuals to integrate significant losses that are perhaps not as tangible or overt. In reflecting upon this aspect of bereavement theory and research, we need to consider the possibility that the emphasis upon separation distress after the death of a loved one may be limited in scope. Grief can be more broadly defined as the distress that occurs when an individual's existing assumptive world is lost because of a significant life-changing event, or what Tedeschi and Calhoun (2004) would refer to as a "seismic" life event. Indeed, Bowlby's (1988) descriptions of yearning, pining, longing, and searching (which are all considered hallmarks of separation distress over the loss of a significant attachment figure) can be identified in various ways in the experiences of nondeath losses as well.

THE ASSUMPTIVE WORLD AND LOSS

Significant life-changing events can cause us to feel deeply vulnerable and unsafe as the world that we once knew, the people whom we relied upon, and the images and perceptions of ourselves may prove to be no longer relevant in light of our experiences. Grief is both adaptive and necessary in order to rebuild the assumptive world after its destruction. It would certainly follow that the process of making meaning, which is a part of the grief response, is applicable to both death-related and nondeath-related losses. We hope to see research in the future that addresses the process of grief after the experience of nondeath losses, as there are very few studies that explore grief after such events, and very few measures that would be appropriate to nondeath loss events.

As we have already discussed, attachment is often identified as a key element in grief, and the attachment model provides an ethological[1] element to the grieving process. Bowlby's (1988) research demonstrated that the searching and pining behaviors seen in young children who were separated from their mothers resemble the behaviors seen in young primates that were subjected to similar conditions. Parkes (1996) expanded this work into the area of adult bereavement and suggested that the attachment system, and the resulting grief when that system is threatened by separation, is an extension of a process that has evolved over time to optimize feelings of safety and to enhance the chances for survival of the individual. From the perspective of evolutionary biology, attachment and the resulting grief that comes with separation appear to confer a survival advantage on the individual.

---

[1] Ethology is concerned with the adaptive or survival value of behavior and its evolutionary history. It emphasizes the genetic and biological roots of development and behaviors that are instinctually programmed into an animal's normal repertoire of responses to given events.

If grief and attachment are thus interrelated, then to what are we attached when we grieve a nondeath loss, such as loss of a sense of safety, loss of our homeland, or loss of employment? It could be that these defining, overarching losses involve the loss of either an aspect of ourselves to which we are attached or our place in the world, which makes us feel safe and secure. For example, it is common for immigrants to yearn for their family and friends who are still present in their homeland, to search for what is familiar in their new environment, and to look for commonalities with their known culture in the new country of their arrival. The well-known term "comfort food" implies that identification with foods that are associated with our family and cultural roots provides a sense of comfort when we are stressed or in unfamiliar territory. Individuals who have lost their jobs may pine for their old lives or selves to return to them, reminiscing about what they used to do or who they used to be. The natural process of aging often catches us by surprise and we wonder, "Where did that woman in the mirror come from, and where did *I* go?"

The disequilibrium that results from these types of losses can activate the attachment system, motivating us to draw closer to what is familiar and safe, and the grieving process enables us to adapt to some part of ourselves or our life that is markedly different from what it was before. As discussed earlier, Janoff-Bulman (1992) drew a connection between one's assumptive world and one's attachment system, stating that how one relates to and views the world, others, and oneself is an extension of the attachment system that is formed at a very young age. Thus, it would make sense that threats to the assumptive world resonate back to the attachment system upon which that world was built.

NONFINITE LOSS AND CHRONIC SORROW

Patricia met James the week after her mother died from a prolonged fight with cancer. James was sitting at a table in a coffee shop, and the only empty chair in the entire place was next to him at the same table. He looked like he was content to read his paper while sipping his drink, and Patricia needed a place to set her laptop down to work while she drank her morning coffee. James was more than happy to offer the chair and table top to Patricia, and once they started talking, they hit it off very well. Patricia was 40 years old at the time, and James was 53. Over the next year, they dated, traveled together, and met each other's extended families and close friends. They were such a good fit—even their dogs liked each other! They were married the next year, and they settled into a comfortable routine of sharing meals, walking the dogs, traveling, and reading snippets of the paper to each other on Sunday mornings. They also began trying to have children, and they had discussed the possibility of either adoption or fostering a child to share their loving home with them.

One Sunday morning, James woke up and did not feel well. He was dizzy and felt weak. He called out to Patricia as he was getting out of the shower and then collapsed in a heap on the floor. Patricia called 911 and an ambulance came and took James to the emergency department of the nearest hospital. Patricia was told that James had suffered a stroke and that he would survive, but it was unlikely that he would be able to speak and he would not be able to use one side of his body. He would have a great deal of difficulty walking because of this weakness, and it was recommended that he spend a few months in a rehabilitation center to help him to gain as much function back as possible.

Patricia was now 44 years old. They did not have children. Both sets of their parents were older and had significant health problems. James was able to come home after Patricia made modifications to the house to accommodate a wheelchair and the special needs he had for personal care. She resigned from her position at work so that she could care for James, taking early retirement, which paid her less than half of her usual income. As time went on, fewer and fewer friends came over to visit; most of the time when the doorbell rang, it was someone from the home health agency arriving to provide care of some sort or to bring medical supplies that were needed. James could understand what Patricia said to him, but he would become very frustrated when she could not understand what he wanted or needed. After several months of care giving, Patricia slumped herself down in a chair in the corner of the bedroom while James slept. Tears flooded as she assessed her life—or what was left of it—in this room. She would never have children. She could not just run to the store to pick something up without making arrangements for someone to be with James. James could stay like this for years, or he could get worse, and she often worried that she would somehow neglect something important and cause a complication to occur. She was completely exhausted and alone.

The above scenario has many losses in it. However, none of the losses are because someone died; rather, the losses are ongoing, and they exist and mingle with the everyday life of Patricia and James as time goes on. We would call these losses living losses, and most of them would fit into the category of nonfinite loss. *Nonfinite losses* are those loss experiences that are enduring in nature, usually precipitated by a negative life event or episode that retains a physical and/or psychological presence in an ongoing manner (Bruce & Schultz, 2002). Some forms of nonfinite loss may be less clearly defined in onset, but they tend to be identified by a sense of ongoing uncertainty and repeated adjustment or accommodation. There are three main factors that separate this experience from the experience of a loss because of a death event. These factors are as follows:

- The loss (and grief) is continuous and ongoing, although it may follow a specific event such as an accident or diagnosis.
- The loss prevents normal developmental expectations from being met in some aspect of life, and the inability to meet these expectations may be because of physical, cognitive, social, emotional, or spiritual losses.
- The inclusion of intangible losses, such as the loss of one's hopes or ideals related to what a person believes should have been, could have been, or might have been (Bruce & Schultz, 2001).

In their writings, Bruce and Schultz (2001) go on to describe several cardinal features of the experience of nonfinite losses:

- There is ongoing uncertainty regarding what will happen next.
- There is often a sense of disconnection from the mainstream and what is generally viewed as "normal" in human experience.
- The magnitude of the loss is frequently unrecognized or not acknowledged by others.
- There is an ongoing sense of helplessness and powerlessness associated with the loss.

Jones and Beck (2007) further added to this list a sense of chronic despair and a sense of ongoing dread as individuals try to reconcile themselves between the world that is now known through this experience and the world in the future that is now anticipated.

In short, the person who experiences nonfinite loss is repeatedly asked to adjust and accommodate to the loss. At the same time, because nonfinite loss is often not well understood, the experience may go unrecognized or unacknowledged by others. Support systems may tire of attempting to provide a shoulder to lean on.

A related concept to nonfinite loss is that of *chronic sorrow*, a term that was first proposed by Olshansky (1962) after his observations of parents whose children were born with disabilities. He noticed that these parents experienced a unique form of grieving that never ended as their children continued to live and the hopes that they had for these children were repeatedly dashed as time went on. Shortly after the introduction of the concept by Olshansky, there were a few articles written about the adjustment and coping in parents of children with various developmental disabilities. Since then, most of the research associated with the concept of chronic sorrow has been reported in the nursing literature. The concept of chronic sorrow has been described in multiple sclerosis, parenting a child with a mental health problem, Alzheimer disease, autism, infertility and involuntary childlessness, mental illness, and caring for a child with disabilities. Chronic sorrow has also been linked to Parkinson disease, mental retardation, neural tube defects, spinal cord injury, schizophrenia, and chronic major depression (Roos, 2002). It is often found in situations involving long-term care giving.

Chronic sorrow is defined by Roos (2002) as,

> a set of pervasive, profound, continuing, and recurring grief responses resulting from a significant loss or absence of crucial aspects of oneself (self-loss) or another living person (other-loss) to whom there is a deep attachment. The way in which the loss is perceived determines the existence of chronic sorrow. The essence of chronic sorrow is a painful discrepancy between what is perceived as reality and what continues to be dreamed of. The loss is ongoing since the source of the loss continues to be present. The loss is experienced as a *living loss.* (p. 26)

Chronic sorrow remains largely disenfranchised and often escalates in intensity or is progressive in nature (Roos & Niemeyer, 2007). Although chronic sorrow is often linked to a defining moment, a critical event, or a seismic occurrence, it can just as easily be the hallmark of the slow, insidious realization of what a diagnosis means over time and how it has caused change for the lives in its wake. In our discussions, the term nonfinite loss will refer to the loss or event itself, and chronic sorrow will refer to the response to ongoing, nonfinite losses.

Burke, Eakes, and Hainsworth (1999) described chronic sorrow as akin to grief-related feelings that emerge in response to an *ongoing disparity* resulting from the loss of the anticipated and expected normal lifestyle of an individual. Teel (1991) stated that in addition to the disparity that exists between what is expected or hoped for and what actually is in reality, the chronicity of the feelings and the ongoing nature of the loss set chronic sorrow apart from other forms of grief. According to this author, chronic sorrow can be precipitated by the permanent loss of a significant relationship, functionality, or self-identity.

Lindgren, Burke, Hainsworth, and Eakes (1992) defined the characteristics of chronic sorrow to include (a) a perception of sadness or sorrow over time in a situation with no predictable end, (b) sadness or sorrow that is cyclic or recurrent, (c) sadness or sorrow that is triggered internally or externally, and (d) sadness or sorrow that is progressive and can intensify. Chronic sorrow is differentiated from the grief response after a death in that *the loss itself is ongoing, and thus the grief is also ongoing and does not end.* These authors stress the peaks and valleys, resurgence of feelings, or periods of high and low intensity that distinguish chronic sorrow from other types of grief responses. An individual's emotions might swing between the flooding of emotion and paralyzing numbness at the two extremes of an emotional pendulum. Most people who experience chronic sorrow generally reside somewhere between these two end points, but fluctuations are common.

Roos (2002) also stated that the loss involved in chronic sorrow is a lifetime loss and remains largely unrecognized for its significance. One's assumptive world is shattered, and there is no foreseeable end, with constant reminders of the loss. She stated that there is also an undercurrent of anxiety and trauma that separates this type of response from grief that is experienced after the death of a loved one, and the fact that the person usually continues to function separates it from primary clinical depression. Chronic sorrow differs from posttraumatic stress disorder because of the ongoing nature of the loss and the fact that it is not a reaction to an event that has occurred, even though there may be an event that defines when the loss began. The traumatic material in nonfinite loss is related to the degree of helplessness and powerlessness that is felt in light of a situation that has profound, ongoing, and life-altering implications for the individual.

Roos (2002) made the point that chronic sorrow may apply more to those who are caregivers, as the affected individual may not be able to internalize the world in such a way as to be able to have dreams or life goals, and the intensity of the experience of chronic sorrow is related to the potency and magnitude of the disparity between the reality of the situation and the dream to which a person may cling. The outcome is really unknown, or the progression of what will unfold is unknown, so unpredictability complicates the process. The ongoing presence of the person or the loss inhibits reinvestment into other aspects of life and there are "surges" of loss that are often triggered by various events, as might occur in individuals whose loss was related to the death of another individual (Teel, 1991).

AMBIGUOUS LOSS

Janice pulls her car into the garage and begins to unload the groceries into the kitchen. She knows that her husband, Richard, is at home because his car is in the garage, but she does not expect a greeting from him when she gets in the door, and she also does not seek him out to say hello when she gets home. Their two teenage children, Cynthia and Rachel, come in the door from school and immediately go upstairs to their rooms and close the doors. Janice finishes unloading the groceries and prepares dinner. She calls to them all when dinner is ready, and they sit at the table to eat together. However, Richard turns the TV on as they are about to sit down at the table, and he watches the news while eating, not saying much to Janice or the girls. Cynthia has begun hanging out with friends from the volleyball team, and she spends a good portion of the dinner time texting back and forth to them on her cell phone. Rachel has her iPod headphones on when she comes to the table, not bothering to remove them when she begins to eat dinner. Janice looks around at the table. She tries to make conversation and ask each one of them about their day. Richard mutters something quick, like "just fine . . . busy," whereas Cynthia tries to talk and text at the same time without success, and Rachel acts perturbed at having to remove her headphones to answer her mother's query. Finally, Janice eats in silence and watches the TV too. Later that night, Janice feels overwhelmed with sadness, but she does not know why. She goes downstairs to get a glass of milk, sits at the kitchen table, and begins to cry.

Many of the nondeath losses that are experienced by individuals are very difficult to name, describe, or validate. As stated previously, many losses are not clearly defined because there is no identifiable "death." For many individuals, it may be unclear exactly what has been lost. The loss may or may not involve a person and there may not be a defining experience to denote where the loss actually originates. In her development and exploration of loss experiences where there was significant ambiguity, Boss (1999) first used the term *ambiguous loss*. She described two situations where ambiguous loss occurs. In the first scenario, the *person is perceived as physically absent but psychologically present*. Examples may be when a person is missing, such as in divorced families when the noncustodial parent is absent but very much present in the minds of the children. Prisoners, kidnapping victims, relatives serving their country overseas, adoptive families, and situations when a person is absent or missing but very much present in the minds or awareness of their loved ones may also fit this description. Another frequent example would be grandparents who lose contact with their grandchildren after the parents of these children divorce, as they may frequently think of their grandchildren and miss them, so they are physically not able to spend time with them, yet thoughts of these children frequently occupy their minds and cause a feeling of grief.

In the second scenario described by Boss, ambiguous loss may be identified when *the person is physically present, but perceived as psychologically absent.* Examples of this type of loss may be when a family member has Alzheimer disease, acquired brain injury, autism, a chronic mental illness, or if there is a family member who is psychologically unavailable because of addictions or some type of ongoing distraction or obsession, as is the case for Janice with her family. Each of these scenarios leaves individuals feeling as if they are "in limbo" (Boss & Couden, 2002) as they struggle to learn to live with ambiguity (Boss, 1999, 2006, 2007; Tubbs & Boss, 2000).

Boss' first observations of this phenomenon occurred when she engaged with families in a therapeutic setting, where the family system was outwardly intact, but one of the members was absent psychologically from the family through obsessive workaholism or addiction.

Key aspects of ambiguous loss include (Boss, 2007) the following:

- The loss is confusing and it is very difficult to make sense of the loss experience (as when a person is physically present, but emotionally unavailable).
- Because the situation is indeterminate, the experience may feel like a loss, but not be readily identified as one. Hope can be raised and destroyed many times over—so many times that individuals may become psychically numb and unable to react.
- Because of ongoing confusion about the loss, there are frequent conflicting thoughts and emotions, such as dread and then relief, hope and hopelessness, wanting to take action and then profound paralysis. People are often "frozen" in place in their reactions and unable to move forward in their lives.
- Difficulty with problem solving because the loss may be temporary (as in a missing person) or it may be permanent (as in an acquired head injury).
- There are no associated rituals and very little validation of the loss (as opposed to a death where there is official certification of the death and prescribed rituals for funeral and disposal of a body).
- There is still hope that things may return to the way they used to be, but there is no indication of how long that may take or whether it will ever happen (e.g., if a family member enters treatment for an addiction or if a couple enters marital therapy).

- Because of the ambiguity, people tend to withdraw instead of offer support because they do not know how to respond, or there is some social stigma attached to the experience.
- Because the loss is ongoing in nature, the relentless uncertainty causes exhaustion in the family members and burnout of supports.

Boss (1999) and Weiner (1999) described the experience of ambiguous loss like a "never-ending roller coaster" that affects family members physically, cognitively, behaviorally, and emotionally. Physical symptoms may include fatigue, sleep disturbances, and somatic complaints that may affect various body systems. Cognitive symptoms may include preoccupation, rumination, forgetfulness, and difficulties concentrating. Behavioral manifestations may be expressed through agitation, withdrawal, avoidance, dependence, or a pressing need to talk at times. Emotionally, individuals may feel anxious, depressed, irritable, numb, and/or angry. It is not uncommon to be misdiagnosed with an anxiety disorder or a major depressive disorder (Weiner, 1999).

LIVING LOSSES

There is a great deal of overlap between losses that are nonfinite and losses that are ambiguous (see Figure 7.1). Perhaps much of the distinctions have to do with their origin in different fields of study, and thus the lens that is used to describe these experiences reflects different ways of viewing loss experiences that may have many similar features. In the literature, nonfinite loss is described more from an intrapersonal perspective, with the loss experience focusing on the individual's perception and coping (i.e., what did I have that I am now losing?), whereas ambiguous loss is a concept that was formulated within a family stress model, and the loss is described in terms of how the family members perceive and define the loss according to the boundaries of the family system (i.e., who is absent from the family system that should be present?). In the descriptions of nonfinite loss and ambiguous loss, the common features include (a) dealing with ongoing uncertainty that causes emotional exhaustion, (b) shattering of assumptions about how the world should be, and (c) a lack of rituals and validation of the significance of these losses. Nonfinite loss, ambiguous loss, and chronic sorrow may be linked not only to real losses but also to perceived, symbolic, or secondary losses. They may all be accompanied by shame and self-loathing that further complicates individual authenticity and truthfulness in other relationships, thereby adding

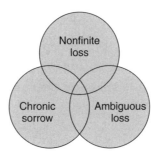

FIGURE 7.1
Overlap of Nonfinite Loss, Ambiguous Loss, and Chronic Sorrow.

to the struggle with coping. For example, Janice may blame herself by thinking that she has been a poor partner to Richard or an inadequate mother to
Rachel and Cynthia for her family to be so disconnected; this self-perception
could undermine her sense of self as worthy or valuable to others, which is a
core aspect of the assumptive world.

Although ambiguous losses, nonfinite losses, and chronic sorrow
are often disenfranchised (Boss, 1999; Casale, 2009; Doka, 1989; Roos, 2002),
the ongoing grief is normal and understandable. Recognition that life as
it has been or was expected to be is lost and has been replaced by an initially unknown, unwanted, and often terrifying and inevitable new reality
is extremely difficult, forcing a new appraisal of one's assumptive world.
Believing that life is predictable and fair and the notion of justice and compensation cannot survive in the new reality. The self and the world must be
relearned. This process is often a disturbing and ongoing focus of concern.
There exists a significant body of research on ambiguous loss that indicates a
relationship to depressive symptoms and family conflict (Boss, 2007; Carroll,
Olson, & Buckmiller, 2007).

IMPLICATIONS FOR COUNSELING

The practice considerations related to both ambiguous loss and chronic
sorrow underscore the importance of normalizing the ongoing grief that is
present. Because these losses may have no real resolution, and they may unfold as *living losses*, the grief persists for a prolonged or undetermined time.
It is important to recognize that in these scenarios, the ongoing grief is a normal reaction, whether the loss is related to a person or thing that is greatly

valued, or something less tangible, such as a hope or expectation. Flexibility in providing counseling to an individual, couple, family, and group in various constellations at different times can assist in supporting those who are taking on most of the responsibilities. Finding ways to adjust and redefine roles in the family can help to minimize chaos, reduce stress, and improve relationships. One other important point to note is that nonfinite and ambiguous losses may comingle with losses that occur from death. For example, one client who sought counseling for support after her husband died came initially to share her grief over the loss of her husband. Later on, the grief was more about the loss of herself when she married her husband, who had been a very controlling and abusive person at times in the marriage. The initial consultation was for a death-related loss, followed by another layer of her grief that was both nonfinite and ambiguous in nature.

Name and Validate the Loss

Many nonfinite and ambiguous losses and losses that involve an ongoing, chronic process are disenfranchised in nature. Recognizing and naming these losses was cited by Doka (1989) and Boss (1999, 2006) as the first step in offering support to individuals who have experienced disenfranchised grief from loss experiences that are not recognized. The ability to name the experience and its unique effects that are often unacknowledged by others can provide a powerful source of strength to those who experience ambiguous loss and chronic sorrow. Clients who begin to understand the nature of these losses and receive validation for them often experience relief and improved self-concept almost immediately (Roos, 2002). In a study of infertile women, Harris (2009) reported that recognition of the ongoing intense grief response to their infertility allowed participants to spend less time attempting to receive validation for their experiences and more time focusing on activities that supported active problem solving within the confines of their situation. You may wish to talk about the assumptions that have been broken or shattered from the client's assumptive world and the significant work involved in rebuilding that world after it has been shattered through these kinds of losses.

Foster Realistic Expectations

The more success-oriented a culture is, the more difficult it is to accept losses that do not have a defined closure (Boss, 1999, 2002, 2006). There is also the romanticized ideal of "overcoming" adversity that may be highly unrealistic for individuals who are facing nonfinite and ambiguous losses. The focus of counseling is to identify the strengths and resilience that are present, while understanding that there are realistic limitations to one's tenacity and capacity. Clients learn to control what they can and to let go of what they cannot control. This letting go is not something that is easily done, and there are very few role models in Western society to demonstrate acceptance of limitations instead of overcoming all odds through insurmountable difficulties—a message that readily becomes an expectation, reinforced through popular media, but which rarely occurs in real life. Relationships get redefined, and modalities that focus on awareness and acceptance of ambiguity, such as meditation, yoga, and mindfulness, may take on new meaning. Often, there is a redefining of the self that occurs, along with new interests, hobbies, and connections to others who understand experiences that are surrounded by ambiguity and uncertainty.

Reconstruct Identity

Patricia's personal identity changed quickly from that of a woman who was embarking on an exciting new phase of her life to that of a woman whose life as she once knew and anticipated it would be was shattered as she became the caregiver to a man who now seemed much older than her. Janice was overwhelmed with sadness at the realization that the family she had always dreamed of having was not a source of safety and comfort, but a means whereby she was essentially made invisible and irrelevant to the people she loved the most in her world.

One's personal identity changes in the presence of these types of losses. The work of counseling will involve redefinition of one's identity in a way that is consistent with reality and that also allows for the recognition of the person as an individual with unique abilities, skills, and strengths that may need other avenues for validation and expression. Patricia will need to find value and worth in herself outside of her work, with a new network of friends who can accommodate her limitations, and she will need outlets to channel her needs for expression and meaning.

Normalize Ambivalence

It is not unusual to have mixed emotions when you do not know whether someone you love is here or not here or whether a situation that seems intolerable will ever end. Patricia sometimes fantasized about James dying and then felt tremendous guilt when she would realize where her thoughts had taken her. She felt guilty for being angry that she was tied down, that James required so much attention and care, and that she was not free at her age to do what she pleased. Eventually, she realized that she felt both love and resentment for James, which was very difficult, and she was alone in these feelings because she did not think anyone in her circle of friends would understand her ambivalence. Janice often pondered just walking away from her family, wondering if they would even miss her if she was gone—at least, until everyone got hungry and realized that nobody had made dinner! However, she also loved them deeply and felt trapped in a situation where she loved them, but could not engage with any of them on a meaningful level. It is important for counselors to normalize these conflicted feelings and to allow for the presence of opposing thoughts and emotions that will naturally arise from such situations. Although not how they may have perceived themselves in the past, it is important to recognize that it can be a normal reaction to resent others who seem unaffected by the same kind of losses or who seem protected from adverse events in life (Harris, 2009; Harris & Daniluk, 2010).

Identify Resources

Helping clients with information about community resources and other supports is a high priority. Identifying potentially damaging triggers (both external and internal) and implementing strategies to reduce the effects of these triggers can be very useful. Emphasizing the highly individualized nature of grief helps to reduce self-criticism. It is also important to be aware that approaches to some conditions are inappropriate and may worsen responses to losses that are ambiguous or ongoing in nature (i.e., pushing for closure or resolution). In this regard, counselors need to understand that these individuals may have already had destructive experiences with prior professionals or well-meaning but uninformed helpers (Harris, 2010). As these types of loss experiences become more commonplace in our current society, it is vitally important for helping professionals to develop a basic understanding of these phenomena in order to avoid inadvertently pathologizing a normal response to these very difficult types of losses.

Identifying resources may also involve personal resources that are available to the client. For example, one of our clients whose husband had advanced Parkinson disease spent a session describing the intolerable situation she was in, being essentially homebound with a man whose declining mental capacity and functionality overwhelmed her strength and patience. The session turned into an opportunity to brainstorm how one of her husband's friends could organize all of his other friends and extended family members to regularly come for "shifts" to do something with him at the house so that she could plan to do the things she wanted to do on her own or with her own friends away from the home. In her sessions, she began to realize that she was initially trying to protect her husband from embarrassment about his condition by not inviting people to their home. However, she realized that the shame over his loss of functionality essentially trapped them together in the home, causing more tension and stress for each of them. In recognizing that they both needed the support of others, she found a solution that provided relief for both of them.

CONCLUDING THOUGHTS

Living losses occur with great regularity in everyday life. Some of these losses effect change in us in subtle ways, and the adjustments to our assumptive world is minimal. However, *living loss* experiences continually shift the sand where we are standing, resulting in an ongoing sense of disequilibrium and adjustment. Not only can we no longer be the same as we were before, but any ideas or dreams about what the future would hold get wiped out from our projections about what we hoped our lives would be like. Losses that are ongoing in nature require frequent accommodation and adjustment, and they provoke a profound grief response that is also ongoing and unpredictable in nature. When living losses require us to rebuild our assumptive world, counselors must be able to journey alongside a sometimes arduous and prolonged process, helping clients to see their deeper strengths and resilience as they grow and deepen in the midst of their ongoing grief and adjustment.

Glossary of Terms

Ambiguous loss loss that remains unclear, cannot be fixed, and has no closure. It can be physical or psychological. Present in losses where an individual may be psychologically present but physically absent or in losses where an individual may be physically present but psychologically absent.

Chronic sorrow an ongoing response to losses that are continual and unending in nature; the chronicity of the feelings and the ongoing nature of the loss set chronic sorrow apart from other forms of grief.

Living losses   losses that will remain as an ongoing presence in the life of an individual; the individual will continue to "live" with the loss experience. The ongoing nature of the loss will require continual adaptation and adjustment.

Nonfinite losses   loss experiences that are enduring in nature, usually precipitated by a negative life event or episode that retains a physical and/or psychological presence in an ongoing manner.

Separation distress   the presence of yearning, longing, preoccupation, and searching for the deceased individual after a death.

Questions for Reflection

1. Go back to the loss line exercise from Chapter 4. If you did not do this exercise before, complete it now. Once you are done, look at the losses that you have noted on your loss line. Which of these losses might be considered nonfinite losses—losses that forever changed you and that you continue to recognize in your life now? Can you think of any losses that were ambiguous in nature? How did you handle these losses? How did others respond to your experiences of these losses?

2. Why do you think nonfinite and ambiguous losses are often not recognized or acknowledged socially?

3. Think of some popular movies or television programs that provide examples of nonfinite and ambiguous losses. How were these losses portrayed in these films? Before you were aware of these concepts, how would you have viewed these kinds of loss experiences?

4. One of the biggest challenges for individuals who face nonfinite and ambiguous losses is the ongoing nature of the grief and the anxiety that accompanies the uncertainty associated with these losses. What are some of the social implications for individuals who experience these kinds of losses? Can you think of ways to offer support to individuals like Patricia from our case study in this chapter?

References

Boss, P. (1999). *Ambiguous loss.* Cambridge, MA: Harvard University Press.

Boss, P. (2002). *Family stress management.* Thousand Oaks, CA: Sage Publications.

Boss, P. (2006). *Loss, trauma and resilience: Therapeutic work with ambiguous loss.* New York, NY: W.W. Norton & Company.

Boss, P. (2007). Ambiguous loss: Challenges for scholars and practitioners. *Family Relations, 56*(2), 105–110. Retrieved from http://www.ambiguousloss.com/

Boss, P., & Couden, B. A. (2002). Ambiguous loss from chronic physical illness: Clinical interventions with individuals, couples and families. *JCLP In Session: Psychotherapy in Practice, 58*(11), 1361–1380.

Bowlby, J. (1988). *A secure base: Parent-child attachment and healthy human development.* New York, NY: Basic Books.

Bruce, E. J., & Schultz, C. L. (2001). *Nonfinite loss and grief: A psychoeducational approach.* Baltimore, MD: Paul H. Brookes.

Bruce, E. J., & Schultz, C. L. (2002). Nonfinite loss and challenges to communication between parents and professionals. *British Journal of Special Education, 29*(1), 9–13.

Burke, M. L., Eakes, G. G., & Hainsworth, M. A. (1999). Milestones of chronic sorrow: Perspectives of chronically ill and bereaved persons and family caregivers. *Journal of Family Nursing, 5*(4), 374–387.

Carroll, J. S., Olson, C. D., & Buckmiller, N. (2007). Family boundary ambiguity: A 30-year review of theory, research, and measurement. *Family Relations, 56*(2), 210–230.

Casale, A. (2009). *Distinguishing the concept of chronic sorrow from standard grief: An empirical study of infertile couples* (DD, New York University, Silver School of Social Work). Available from ProQuest Dissertations and Thesis Database (UMI No. 3353016).

Doka, K. (Ed.) (1989). *Disenfranchised grief: Recognizing hidden sorrow.* Lexington, MA: Lexington Books.

Harris, D. (2009). *The experience of spontaneous pregnancy loss in infertile women who have conceived with the assistance of medical intervention.* Retrieved January 25, 2011, from Proquest Digital Dissertations, http://search.proquest.com/docview/ 305169744/fulltextPDF/133A8C6EF0F1A5CDECB/1?accountid=15115 (UMI No. 3351170).

Harris, D. (2010). *Counting our losses: Reflecting on change, loss, and transition in everyday life.* New York, NY: Routledge.

Harris, D., & Daniluk, J. (2010). The experience of spontaneous pregnancy loss for infertile women who have conceived through assisted reproduction technology. *Human Reproduction, 25*(3), 714–720.

Jacobs, S., Mazure, C., & Prigerson, H. (2000). Diagnostic criteria for traumatic grief. *Death Studies, 24,* 185–199.

Janoff-Bulman, R. (1992). *Shattered assumptions: Towards a new psychology of trauma.* New York, NY: Free Press.

Jones, S. J., & Beck, E. (2007). Disenfranchised grief and nonfinite loss as experienced by the families of death row inmates. *Omega, 54*(4), 281–299.

Lindgren, C., Burke, M., Hainsworth, M., & Eakes, G. (1992). Chronic sorrow: A lifespan concept. *Scholarly Inquiry for Nursing Practice, 6,* 27–40.

Olshansky, S. (1962). Chronic sorrow: A response to having a mentally defective child. *Social Casework, 43*(4), 190–192.

Parkes, C.M. (1996). *Bereavement: Studies of grief in adult life.* London, UK: Routledge.

Prigerson, H., Horowitz, M., Jacobs, S., Parkes, C., Aslan, M., Goodkin, K., . . . Maciejewski, P. K. (2009). Prolonged grief disorder: Psychometric validation of criteria proposed for the *DSM-V* and the *ICD-11. PLOS Medicine, 6*(8). Retrieved February 10, 2011, from http://www.ncbi.nlm.nih.gov/pmc/articles/ PMC2711304/pdf/pmed.1000121.pdf/?tool=pmcentrez

Roos, S. (2002). *Chronic sorrow: A living loss.* New York, NY: Brunner-Routledge.

Roos, S., & Neimeyer, R. (2007). Reauthoring the self: Chronic sorrow and posttraumatic stress following the onset of CID. In E. Martz & H. Livneh (Eds.), *Coping with chronic illness and disability* (pp. 89–106). New York, NY: Springer.

Tedeschi, R. G., & Calhoun, L. G. (2004). Posttraumatic growth: Conceptual foundations and empirical evidence. *Psychological Inquiry, 15,* 1–18.

Teel, C. S. (1991). Chronic sorrow: Analysis of the concept. *Journal of Advanced Nursing, 16*(1), 1311–1319.

Tubbs, C.Y., & Boss, P. (2000). Dealing with ambiguous loss. *Family Relations, 49*(3), 285–286.

Weiner, I. (1999). *Coping with loss.* Mahwah, NJ: Lawrence Erlbaum.

CHAPTER 8

Working With Emotions—
Yours and Theirs

*P*robably one of the biggest concerns for counselors who begin to work in the area of bereavement is how to work with strong emotions as they arise in clients. Although we have earlier shared that not everyone will grieve through the sharing and expression of their feelings, many clients will experience strong emotions as part of their grief. In this chapter, we wish to look at the role that emotions might play in the grieving process, and how counselors can help their clients to benefit from working constructively with their feelings.

Many bereaved clients will feel overwhelmed by their feelings, and they will come to counseling in hopes of learning to contain their feelings. The good news is that clients can often learn how to manage their feelings, but the hard part is that they learn to do this by first having to focus on them. In their everyday world, bereaved individuals are often given much advice and receive many messages that minimize their experience, probably with the intent of helping them to manage their feelings. However, in the counseling process, we often do just the opposite, and a lot of time is often spent exploring and gaining insight from feelings rather than trying to avoid or minimize them. Thus, what may occur is that we might, at first, intensify the feelings because we pay attention to them, and even focus on them instead of trying to diminish and contain them for the sake of social propriety. The identification of and work with feelings can be very rewarding and empowering for clients, ultimately moving them into deeper work that allows them to recognize their strengths and potential for growth.

There is some discussion about the difference between feelings and emotions. Typically, feelings are viewed as faster than emotions in terms of response (the response time of the feeling; how fast it responds to real world stimulation), and it takes someone less time to recognize feelings because they are instant reactions to stimuli that occur in the present moment. Emotions tend to be viewed as a longer-term effort, after an individual has had an opportunity to reflect upon feelings that have surfaced, and meaning or significance has therefore been assigned to the felt experience. Feelings are closer to sensory stimulation; thus, if you touch something, you feel it almost instantaneously, which is a fast reaction. An emotion could represent a deeper experience because it might affect more of you, and you may become more invested in it because you have delved into and reflected upon the experience more, but that is only because it is now also attached to your cognitions and interpretations more. For example, depression will have more of an impact upon you than just an isolated feeling of sadness. We find these distinctions are mostly academic, though, and for the purposes of this chapter, we will use these two terms interchangeably, as both feelings and emotions are important in our discussion, and the work with feelings and emotions in the counseling setting is going to involve the same process.

THINKING CRITICALLY ABOUT FEELINGS

Individuals who live in Western society tend to think of feelings as primitive, irrational, weak, pathetic, and an indication that someone is out of control. Stop and think for a moment about how many derogatory terms and phrases there are to describe someone who readily expresses emotions and what these phrases imply:

> "He lost it."
> "She was hysterical."
> "He went nuts."
> "You need to get a grip."

The implication is clear: if you express strong emotion, you are out of control, and you need to regain your composure quickly. Stoicism and rationality are espoused as true virtues—for example, "He's holding up so well" or "She is staying strong for the kids." Individuals who deny their emotions and function solely from an analytical, rational perspective are seen as smarter, more competent, and desirous. Feltham (2010) ventured to address the issue of emotion in counseling by stating that the most effective counselors tend to be those who are more naturally intuitive and emotionally responsive, both characteristics that are more acceptable to feminine socialization patterns. He concluded that most counseling theory is generated by men, and placed cognitive processing at the top of what is most desirable in counseling practice. He also stated,

> there is a prejudice against raw emotion and direct knowledge, and a demand for theoretical justification. Crying remains an uncomfortable phenomenon and is rare in public and in educational institutions, as is expressed anger. Direct, heartfelt responses to the common human experiences of loss and heartache receive relatively little attention in counselling training. (p. 184)

We have previously discussed the importance of the counselor's focused and compassionate presence within the counseling relationship. Genuine caring and compassion are feeling-oriented, and clients are very likely to "know the difference between a counselor who really cares deeply and one who either struggles to do so or who is primarily cognitively rather than emotionally oriented" (Feltham, 2010, p. 184). This statement is not meant to indicate that counselors who are more cognitively focused will be ineffective, but to emphasize the importance of being able to access your own feelings and intuition in order to respond in kind to clients' feelings and emotion states. As counselors, we will be touched and moved by the pain and suffering of our clients, and we do share a common human lived experience with them. However, showing emotions, especially openly with clients, is often seen as a sign of weakness or lack of professionalism (Curtis, Matise, & Glass, 2003). It is important to place feelings into the appropriate social and cultural context—and in most modern Western societies, feelings are devalued and stigmatized, so it is important to look critically at how intellect and cognition are privileged, and emotions and intuition are devalued—and yet *both* of these entities are important aspects of the whole human experience.

FUNCTIONAL FEELINGS

In the therapeutic setting, feelings can be seen as valuable indicators of what is most important to the client's process. They give an indication of what Gendlin (1978) referred to as the "felt sense" of the client in a situation, and when you are able to identify and focus on the client's feelings, you are probably working very directly with the places of most concern and difficulty to the client. You may recall our earlier discussion of the use of immediacy in the counseling process in Chapter 5. Immediacy includes working in the here and now, with the feelings that are currently arising in the session. Yalom (2002) stated that working in the here and now, noting feelings that are present in the client during the session, enables the most potential for insight, growth, and change in clients.

In the counseling session, it is important to help clients learn to befriend their feelings and try to learn from them. Although not everyone experiences strong feelings in response to significant life events, when intense feelings are present and we try to block them, we can end up feeling more anxious. Suppressing strong feelings takes a lot of energy, and it can "backfire" when the defenses that function to contain the feelings are overloaded in some way, and the suppressed feelings can end up being released in a flood that can be overwhelming to the person and to those around him or her. We need to be able to experience feelings appropriately—in a way that is constructive, in the proper environment, with the ability to reflect upon them as well. It is important to connect compassionately with the feelings that are present in order for defenses to soften in a safe environment, and thus lessen the anxiety that they may cause. Feelings tend to "live" in our bodies, and we often experience a physical sensation when strong feelings are present. Sometimes, clients will experience a "charge" with an emotion, which can be described as a strong physical association with a certain feeling. We interpret this "charge" as the feeling attempting to get your attention that something important is happening and needs your focus. People often remark about feeling nauseous or their stomach being upset, jittery or shaky, hot or cold, clammy, or heavy in their chest. You may have heard of the "fight–flight" response to stress, which is the way our bodies respond when we feel acutely stressed, frightened, or threatened. There is a direct link between how we feel and how our bodies respond, and we can often use our bodies to help us identify our feelings and to channel them in ways that are healthy and constructive. In many ways, it is much easier to be "in our heads," but experiencing life from a cognitive orientation alone means we are denied the full and rich depth of being a complete person, which involves an integration of our thoughts, feelings, and physicality.

EMOTIONAL INTELLIGENCE

For the past century, we have become very focused on developing our intellectual abilities. With the introduction of the Stanford-Binet Intelligence Test in 1916 (SB5) (Fancher, 1985) and the Wechsler Intelligence Scales (the WAIS in 1939 and the WISC for children in 1949) (Frank, 1983), people focused on "IQ" as an indicator of who was smart, who was most likely to succeed, and who would be revered socially. Although Wechsler especially tried to look at more global capacities, such as the ability to solve real-life problems and to navigate successfully within one's environment, the focus was still mostly upon rationality and cognitive reasoning. Emotional components of the human experience were seen as mostly irrelevant to the measure of cognitive potential that was present in each individual.

The value placed upon cognitive and rational problem solving have become globalized to expectations about a person's character, ability to navigate social situations, and a general belief that people who are "smart" by these standards are those who should be revered, emulated, and given social deference. However, in reality, these expectations do not exactly work out in terms of personal success, social integration, and in the cultivation of compassion and empathy with others. We can all think of individuals in various professions who would be considered brilliant in terms of their intellectual capacity, academic accomplishments, and rational problem-solving abilities, who, nonetheless, have a great deal of difficulty managing their personal relationships, getting along with others, or who are not able to work with others in settings that require teamwork. So intellectual prowess is admirable, but it leaves something missing in terms of relating to others. The example of Dr. Gregory House in the television show *House* (Egan & Alexander, 2005) would provide a good illustration of someone who is intellectually brilliant, but socially crippled and unable to successfully navigate his relationships with his colleagues and individuals who try to be his friend. Although this television show is meant to be entertaining, it is a good example of how our social emphasis upon intellectual intelligence and cognitive processing are not the measures of a person who is successful in life.

The point to this discussion is that we live in a society that highly prizes intellectual capacity while dismissing social and emotional capacities, which are not only important, but also necessary assets for a person to live in harmony with others, and to be able to engage in relationships that are meaningful and reciprocal. Most of our relationships with others are predicated upon our ability to care, to empathize, and to respond to others in a meaningful way. Most attachment behaviors are also demonstrated through emotionally mediated behaviors. Grief is often viewed as a wound to our attachment system, and the responses to separation and a broken attachment are often emotional ones.

The first use of the term "emotional intelligence" is usually attributed to a doctoral thesis entitled *A Study of Emotion: Developing Emotional Intelligence* (Payne, 1985). Other authors later explored the concept of "emotional intelligence" (sometimes referred to as either EI or EQ) (Goleman, 1995; Mayer, Salovey, & Caruso, 2008). Instruments were developed to measure various aspects of EI, including the emotional competence inventory, which was created in 1999, and the emotional and social competency inventory, which was created in 2007. There are also several self-report and self-assessment scales available to the public via the Internet (Bradberry & Greaves, 2009; Mayer, Roberts, & Barsade, 2008).

Goleman's (1995) exploration of EI is probably the best-known and is popular because of the publication of his popular book of the same name and the release of a secondary book entitled *Social Intelligence* (Goleman, 2006). According to Goleman, to be successful requires the effective awareness and understanding of yourself, including your feelings, intentions, and responses, as well as the ability to understand the feelings and responses of others. The awareness of EI and its cultivation are important in grief counseling because it is very important for both counselors and their clients to develop a capacity to work with emotions that fosters competence rather than flooding because of emotional overloading. Working intelligently with emotions that arise with clients is a process that involves assisting clients to:

1. identify the primary emotion(s) that is/are currently present,
2. be able to name and/or describe the intensity of the emotion(s),
3. find a way to work with emotions in a healthy manner, and
4. seek to understand the message or meaning that comes from the emotion(s).

It is amazing to realize how little attention has been paid to the emotional content of our experiences and how readily we try to suppress or deny feelings rather than learning to work with them constructively. Many clients do not really know how to begin identifying their feelings and readily get stuck when asked what they are currently feeling. For example, a counselor might see a client clenching his fist, tightening his jaw, and becoming red in the face, only to find the client will respond to question about how he is feeling with, "I don't know . . . just upset, that's all." Learning to identify feelings may involve some education for our clients regarding how to accurately describe what they are feeling and what to do with the feelings that they do recognize in themselves. A good place to start might be to share with clients a "feeling vocabulary list" to help them to learn to identify what they are feeling (see Figure 8.1). We often try to simplify things by suggesting that there are four basic feeling states: sad, mad, glad, and scared. You can then brainstorm different words that could be used to describe varying aspects of each of these feeling states. We often suggest you begin with words that describe the least intense sensation of that feeling "cluster" and gradually progress to the most intense description of that feeling. For example,

Abandoned	Demoralized	Frustrated	Left out	Rotten
Abused	Depressed	Furious	Lonely	Run down
Accepted	Desolate	Futile	Lonesome	
Affectionate	Despair		Longing	Sad
Afraid	Desperate	Glad	Loved	Satisfied
Agitated	Despised	Glorious	Loving	Scared
Alarmed	Despondent	Good	Lousy	Selfish
Alienated	Destroyed	Grand	Low	Sensual
Alone	Discontented	Grateful		Serene
Amazed	Discouraged	Gratified	Mad	Sexy
Amused	Discredited	Great	Maligned	Shaky
Angry	Disgraced	Guilty	Miffed	Shocked
Anguished	Disinterested		Miserable	Sickened
Annoyed	Disliked	Happy	Mistreated	Skeptical
Anxious	Dismal	Hateful	Misunderstood	Slandered
Appreciative	Displeased	Hatred		Spiteful
Ashamed	Dispassionate	Helpful	Needed	Startled
At ease	Dissatisfied	Helpless	Negative	Surprised
Awful	Distressed	Hesitant	Neglected	Suspicious
Awkward	Distrustful	Hindered	Nervous	Swamped
	Disturbed	Hopeless	Numb	
Baffled	Done for	Horny		Tearful
Battered	Doubtful	Horrible	Obsolete	Tense
Belittled	Downhearted	Humble	Offended	Terrible
Belligerent	Downtrodden	Humiliated	On edge	Terrified
Below par	Dread	Hurt	Oppressed	Threatened
Bewildered	Dreadful	Hypocritical	Optimistic	Thrilled
Bitter			Ostracized	Tormented
Blue	Ecstatic	Ignored	Outraged	Transcendent
Bored	Elevated	Ill at ease	Overlooked	Trusting
Bottled up	Embarrassed	Impaired	Overwhelmed	
Branded	Empty	Impatient		Uncertain
Broken	Enraged	Impotent	Panicky	Uncomfortable
	Enthusiastic	Imprisoned	Passionate	Uncooperative
Calm	Envious	Inadequate	Perplexed	Underrated
Capable	Euphoric	Incapable	Pleased	Understood
Cast off	Exalted	Incompetent	Powerless	Uneasy
Cheapened	Excited	Ineffective	Pressured	Unhappy
Cheerful	Excluded	Inept	Proud	Unimportant
Competent	Exhausted	Inferior	Put down	Unloved
Confident	Exhilarated	Inflamed	Puzzled	Unqualified
Conflicted	Exposed	Insecure		Unsatisfied
Confused		Insignificant	Reborn	Unsure
Constrained	Fantastic	In the dumps	Rebuked	Upset
Contented	Fearful	Intimidated	Regretful	Uptight
Criticized	Fine	Irritated	Rejected	
Crushed	Fit		Rejuvenated	Wanted
	Foolish	Jazzed	Relaxed	Warmhearted
Debased	Forlorn	Jealous	Relieved	Washed up
Defeated	Forsaken	Jilted	Resentful	Whipped
Deficient	Frantic	Jittery	Restless	Worried
Deflated	Friendly	Joyful	Revengeful	Worthless
Dejected	Frightened	Jumpy	Ridiculed	Worthy
		Laughed at	Ridiculous	

FIGURE 8.1

Feeling Vocabulary List.

feeling words to describe *mad* might include *irritated, annoyed, frustrated, angry, enraged,* and *furious.*

There are different ways to help clients to work constructively with their emotions. Sometimes, just naming the feeling and talking about it can be enough for a client to address what is being brought to the surface by that emotion. As mentioned in the previous section, emotions sometimes carry a "charge" with them that we experience physically. Clients can sometimes feel intimidated by this intense sensation, afraid that in exploring their emotions, they will lose control over them, or they will say or do something that is not congruent with how they view themselves. Choosing a way to work constructively with different emotions needs to be based upon the client's personality and comfort level with the counselor, and this process can be facilitated by drawing from the strengths and interests of the client, that is, if the client likes to write, draw, paint, listen to music, and so on. We will discuss more specific ideas later on in our chapter that explores various therapeutic modalities. The following are some ideas about helping clients to identify and work constructively with their feelings:

- Help clients express feelings—invite them to explore their feelings, talk about their feelings, and give an affirmation about their right to have feelings.
  "That must have been a very stressful time for you. As you remember the events, how do you feel about what happened?"
- Alert the client to the importance of nonverbal clues as indicators of feelings:
  "You tell me you are pretty well over it, but I notice your eyes are full of tears."
- Help clients to begin identifying feelings and their intensity when they are in the sessions with you:
  "You have said that you were a bit upset by what happened, but as I watch the expression on your face, I wonder if you are really pretty angry."
- Help clients to sort out confused or conflicted feelings.
  "If I were to draw a chart of how you are feeling, what percentage of your feelings would be angry, what part hurt, and what part afraid?"
- Help clients to gain an understanding that they can have more than one feeling at a time, and that it is normal to have dichotomous feelings occurring at the same time (i.e., happy and sad, excited and scared, etc.).

"In the midst of feeling devastated by what has happened since your
   husband's death, can you think of some people and activities that
   would be positive for you now?"
- Use feelings to help reconnect clients with the deceased person(s),
   if that would be beneficial.
   "Pretend that you are your wife and I will pretend to be you.
   Can you think of what she might be feeling if she were with you
   right now?"

Once a client has identified how he or she is feeling and explored
the feeling in the session, there is usually a "message" that is behind
the feeling. It may be simple, such as anxiety that results from realizing
that you are now alone at night after your spouse died and you need to
do what is necessary to feel safe and connected to others when you are
home. Or, it might be that what is happening has brought up experiences that have left you feeling abandoned or highly vulnerable, and
you need to be in touch with someone from your past to work these issues through, if possible. As a counselor, remember that you are always
listening with your intuitive "rabbit ears" (Yalom, 2002), both for the
content that is being said in words and the experience that is occurring
through the nonverbal cues and emotional tone of what the client is
saying.

WORKING WITH DIFFERENT EMOTIONS

Important guidelines for counselors to have in place are that they need to be
aware of their emotions when they come to the surface, to have cultivated
an ability to work constructively with their own emotions, and to apply the
same "rules" about honoring emotional content and material in their lives as
they expect from their clients. These things will affect how a counselor will
be able to facilitate emotional work and process with clients.

When you begin to sense that there is a lot of emotion present in
the client, you may try to slow the session down. Empathic responses or
immediacy may be used depending upon what the client is experiencing.
The client may only stay with the feelings for 5 seconds, but in staying
with these feelings, even if for a very brief time, there is often a sense of
competency and relief afterwards. Emotions are often intensified in the
sessions, and the client is invited to go to a deeper level, closer to his or
her core feelings. Stay with the feelings as long as the client tolerates it

and stays connected to them in the session. Once the client begins to shift out of the feelings, talk about what he or she felt and put it into a context. A good suggestion for follow-up with clients after they have gone deeply into emotional work is to first validate that it is hard work, and then to ask what the experience was like for them. Often, working in this way with emotions brings a sense of exhaustion, but also a sense of clarity. After exploring feelings, a shift may occur in the client's perceptions, although it may not be apparent right away.

If your client is struggling with intense emotions, try to normalize the feelings and assure him or her that these feelings will not continue with this same intensity and magnitude forever. One helpful statement might be "It is very difficult and intense right now for you, but it will not always be this way down the road." If the client has attempted to keep emotions under control by suppressing them for a long time, initially experiencing the emotions may carry the fear that he or she will be overwhelmed, or rendered nonfunctional or paralyzed by these feelings. Remind your clients that they have the choice about how they want to handle their emotions, and provide modeling in the session that allows them to focus on the emotions, and then get some distance from them in alternating waves. Normalize clients' concerns that the feelings can be scary and that this is difficult work.

As we discussed earlier in the section on resistance, you must be respectful of people's defenses, and your goal is not to insist that people emote, but to recognize when clients need your assistance in working constructively with the emotions that are present. You, as the counselor, need to be able to help the client find what she or he needs both internally for control and externally for release of the emotional material. There are times when clients need help in containing their emotions (different from suppression), especially when they are overwhelmed or feeling unsafe (Kennedy-Moore & Watson, 2001). We will explore the issue of containment further when we discuss trauma and grief overlaps. We will also discuss some specific therapeutic modalities that may help clients to work constructively with their emotions later on. We recognize that once clients begin to focus on their story and what has brought them to counseling, feelings often rise to the surface readily. It is hoped that this chapter will help you, as the counselor, to be open to your clients' experiences of emotional material and be able to facilitate your client's process with quiet confidence and compassion. Remember that most people want a deeper connection with their inner self and that usually occurs by working with emotions.

SUGGESTIONS FOR SPECIFIC EMOTIONS

As we believe that feelings/emotions serve a purpose, it might be helpful to look at some of the ways that feeling states might be reinterpreted as informative and positive to clients and their experiences, and to also provide some practical suggestions for counselors in working with emotions.

- *Fear*—functions to help in self-protection, and it often arises when we do not feel safe. It is important to sort out old fears from what has happened in the past versus anxiety about what is happening in the present, and listen to what has happened in the past about how the fear is being interpreted in the current situation. For example, if a client has had a difficult situation with other helping professionals, the anxiety that is present in the session may be related to fear of how you might respond rather than to something more general in his or her life experience. It is important to remember that you get afraid for a reason and the first consideration when a client is fearful is to ensure that she or he feels safe, first with himself or herself, then with you in the session, and then in his or her environment and experiences. There is a difference between fear and generalized anxiety. Fear is usually associated with something specific, even if the trigger for the fear may seem elusive at first. Anxiety tends to be more generalized and does not usually have a specific focus, although the anxiety may transfer to various situations when it is intensified.

    When people are afraid, they may have a sense of "going cold" inside and their hands and feet may also feel cold or numb. Some people are agitated by fear and others are paralyzed by it, so people may speak very fast and seem keyed up, or they may actually come across as very contained and shut down. It is only with time and gentle exploration you may have a deeper understanding of the source of the fear or the background to the anxiety that your client is experiencing. Breath is associated with fear, and you will often notice that when a client becomes more anxious, breathing may become more rapid and shallow, or the person may actually hold his or her breath without even realizing it. It can sometimes be helpful for the counselor to breathe along with the client as he or she shares his or her story, and if the counselor notices that he or she is not getting enough air when following the client's breathing pattern, it might be an opportunity to say something like, "let's just take a deep breath together and slow things down a bit, OK?"

When clients feel anxious, they often have a hard time hearing you or taking in what you are sharing with them, and they may not remember much of what has been said in the session. Keeping things slow and calm and repeating things that are said a few times might be helpful. Be very clear when you speak, and make sure the client is able to hear and understand what you are saying by checking in several times during the session. People who are habitually in fear often dissociate, meaning they are physically in the room, but seem to have become absent psychologically and/or emotionally. The task then is for them to stay with it, work gently and quietly at the source if possible, and reframe the experience as necessary. Frequent dissociation in the sessions may mean that the client has a history of trauma, and unless you are trained as a therapist in this area of work, you could risk more harm than good if you push a client who is reexperiencing traumatic material as a result of the sessions. We will discuss this issue in greater detail later on, but this would be a time when you as the counselor need to be able to identify if a client's needs may be beyond your professional scope or abilities.

If you sense that your client is feeling overwhelmed by anxiety, you may also wish to help the person become more grounded in his or her body or in the room with you, so first start with the breath, maybe counting breaths together for a minute to start. You can then go through a "body scan" with the person, identifying feeling the feet on the floor, their weight in the chair, their arms on the chair or in their lap, feeling the tips of the fingers, and the sensation of breath from their nose, and then suggest that the client look around the room and name out loud several things that they see, such as the lamp, chair, picture, and so on. You can repeat this process as needed to help your client feel safe and supported by you and to help the client to feel physically and emotionally present in the session. Once the client is feeling more grounded, you can take the opportunity to talk about what you just did and why—and offer it as a tool that he or she can use if the anxiety returns and is overwhelming when not in a session. Relaxation tapes and CDs may be of help for clients to use when they are trying to go to sleep at night or at times when they are on their own and feel intense anxiety or panic. It might be a good idea for you to be familiar with specific relaxation tapes and CDs that you can recommend to your clients, especially ones that involve progressive relaxation and engage the body with the relaxation imagery or instructions.

- *Anger*—serves the purpose of a warning light and gives energy to get past blocks. Anger tells you that something is wrong, and it often comes up when a person feels that she or he has been violated or treated unfairly in some way. It can also be protective when a person feels threatened or vulnerable. It is very important that clients understand that anger is okay and that it is a natural part of the grieving process for many people. If you think of being robbed of something that is precious and irreplaceable to you, one of the first reactions you might experience would be anger toward someone who could do such a thing. Grief is no different, as when you lose someone you love or when you experience a significant loss, there is often a feeling of being robbed, being deprived, and a constant reminder of the unfairness in how events have unfolded—and anger would be a natural response to any of these scenarios. Care must be taken to disentangle anger from violence, and if your client has experienced violence associated with anger in the past, this emotion might be a scary and difficult experience.

  A good image of constructive anger is to describe it as a life force that can be empowering and highly informative of when a client needs to attend to what is happening in a very conscious way. Anger is like the mushroom that pushes through the concrete in the sidewalk—we sometimes need this energy in order to get through the blocks that are present and preventing us from moving forward. Constructively channeling anger is what has been at the core of some very well-known advocacy groups and support organizations, such as Mothers Against Drunk Driving, so it is important to understand that a person can experience anger and have it be a positive experience.

  Anger sometimes looks like fear because people may shut down out of fear of their anger. Often, the person who is angry turns red in the face, clenches fists, tightens the jaw, and may physically shake. The counselor can help to facilitate an understanding of where the anger is coming from and help the client direct it and focus it in order to release it. Verbal expression of angry feelings may be enough. Sometimes, however, it is helpful to engage the body to physically release the anger in order to clear it to get to the underlying issues. People often feel better afterwards. Writing or scribbling in a journal with heavy strokes, throwing paint at a canvas, breaking eggs with your hands in the sink, kneading and pounding bread dough, digging vigorously in the garden, hitting pillows, tearing paper, or yelling into a pillow may also help release it (these are all suggestions that have come from our clients!) The release is only really helpful if the client can

then talk about the feeling and what is underneath it afterwards;
physical release without meaning being attached to the activity may
not provide the client with the clarity and understanding that is
needed afterwards. Use of language is very important with anger
as well. We have smiled as some of our most prim and proper
clients chose very strong language to express some of these feelings,
knowing that they would never talk like this outside of the session!
Using strong language can be a form of release as well, so be aware
of the possibility of expanding your feeling vocabulary in ways you
might not have expected as a grief counselor!

- *Sadness*—is often more socially acceptable than anger, especially
  for women. In sadness, a person tends to retreat inside; sometimes,
  clients seem to "melt" into themselves when they express their
  sadness. It might be helpful for the client to have something to
  hold, such as a pillow, a small blanket or throw, or a stuffed animal.
  If clients experience deep, intense sadness, they may begin to sob
  heavily and rock back and forth. You are the supportive witness to
  their experience, and the importance of your presence should not be
  underestimated. Most people are very self-conscious when they are
  crying in front of another person, so rather than staring at the person
  when they are crying, we would suggest that you drop your gaze
  a little from their face to their shoulder or knees and wait patiently.
  You can breathe with the person silently. You can gently let the client
  know it is okay to cry and okay to feel this much. Let people breathe
  deeply and let the sadness out. Beginning counselors may feel a
  great urge at a time like this to jump in and "rescue" the person, but
  this may be the only time and place that the client can actually enter
  fully into the sadness without having to worry about what someone
  else thinks or feels as a result of the expression of such profound
  emotional pain.

  After experiencing deep sadness, the client may want contact,
  and it is very important to be clear about what the client wants and
  needs (not what the counselor wants and needs!) In my (D.L.H.)
  client office, I keep a chenille throw over the back of my chair. If a
  client goes into a place of deep sadness, I will sometimes take the
  throw and wrap it around their shoulders as a gentle form of contact
  that is nonintrusive to the client's process. There is a tendency
  to come out of this type of expression slowly. It is important to
  reassure clients that they will have time at the end of the session to
  "regroup" before finishing the time together. It is also the counselor's

responsibility to ensure that the client has returned to a sense of normalcy before leaving the office and driving a car. Some of our clients choose to go for a brief walk to regroup after an intense session before getting into their car and driving away.

One final suggestion for clients when they are experiencing strong emotions outside of the sessions is to find ways for them to recognize their feelings and work with them, but to also be able to contain them and bracket their feelings when necessary. Clients can have "grief drawers" in their homes, where they store pictures, music, memorabilia, and linking objects. When clients realize that strong feelings are arising, they can open the drawer and use these items to facilitate some of their process. Some clients may light candles when they are actively involved in this work—when the candle is lit, they focus their attention and emotional energy on the contents of the drawer and the associated feelings that arise from going there. Clients may choose to write about this experience in a journal and share it with you when they come for their next session. When they are done, they can blow out the candle, and put the things back in to the drawer, and close it shut. Clients can use music to do something similar—when a particular song is done, or the CD is finished, they actively move away from the emotional processing and consciously move into another room as a form of bracketing the experience.

Clients need to know that they can enter deeply into their emotional experiences with competence and feel empowered by their emotions rather than crippled by them. Learning how to go deeply and then to come back out of the intensity is a valuable skill that can be helpful in this process.

WHAT ABOUT THE COUNSELOR'S FEELINGS?

Our students often ask us if we have cried with our clients and how we feel about the counselor sharing his or her feelings with the client. On the surface, there is generally a perception that crying in professional settings is an indicator of lack of professionalism or a sign of weakness on the part of the counselor. The answer may be that it can be a good thing and can also be an indication of the counselor's need to attend to personal issues that may need to be addressed (Curtis et al., 2003). As counselors, we are human beings, and we connect with our clients at a deep and empathic level. To hear stories of pain, suffering, and deprivation and not be affected would be highly unrealistic, and sometimes as we fully enter our clients' world we will be deeply moved by their stories and experiences (Yalom, 2002). A normal human reaction might involve tears that fall as we listen to a client's painful story, and these tears simply validate the depth of the client's experience and our shared human connection. Problems occur if the client's story triggers an area of vulnerability within the counselor, and the feelings that come to the surface for the counselor are not those in resonance with the client, but a personal reaction to the client's material that is based on the needs and unresolved material in the counselor. Counselor's feelings that take the focus of the session away from the client could be damaging to clients, and the counselor could inadvertently use the client to process his or her own unresolved emotional material, which is highly unethical. We will later discuss the role and value of supervision for counselors, which provides a safe place for the counselor to work through personal issues that arise in sessions with clients.

To summarize, we have explored how feelings and working with emotions in the counseling process can be a very important and empowering aspect of counseling bereaved clients. Counselors must have an understanding of their own feelings and experiences, and be comfortable working with clients when they enter into deeply intense emotional states, and be able to facilitate the constructive processing of these emotions as part of their work with grieving clients.

Glossary of Terms

Emotional intelligence   the level of an individual's ability or skill in the identification, assessment, and management of the emotions of oneself, and to the reactions of the emotions of others.

Feeling vocabulary   ability to accurately identify and name a particular emotion in terms of its intensity and application to a given situation.

"Felt sense"   term identified by Gendlin to describe an unclear, preverbal sense of something significant as that "something" is experienced in the body. It is not the same as an emotion, as it is typically *unclear* and vague; and it is always *more* than any attempt to express it verbally.

"Fight–flight" response   also referred to as the acute stress response; bodily response to a perceived threat or acute stressor with a discharge of the sympathetic nervous system, priming the animal for fighting or fleeing in response to a threat.

Questions for Reflection

1. What were you taught about emotions when you were growing up? How has this learning in your formative years influenced how you handle your emotions and the emotions of others?

2. Think of the four main domains or emotions (sad, mad, glad, and afraid) and look over the feeling vocabulary that was posted in this chapter. Which of these emotions is the most difficult for you personally? Which is most difficult for you to handle from someone else? How might your reactions to emotions affect your interactions with your clients?

3. What do you think is the difference between containing/bracketing emotions and suppressing emotions in the context of counseling?

4. Go to the following Web link to access an online test for emotional intelligence (EI) and take the test: http://testyourself.psychtests.com/testid/2092. What were your thoughts and feelings as you took the online self-test? Can you think of examples in day-to-day functioning where EI would be valuable?

References

Bradberry, T., & Greaves, J. (2009). *Emotional intelligence 2.0*. San Francisco, CA: Publishers Group West.

Curtis, R., Matise, M., & Glass, J. C. (2003). Counselling students' views and concerns about weeping with clients: A pilot study. *Counselling and Psychotherapy Research, 3*(4), 300–306.

Egan, D. (Writer), & Alexander, J. (Director). (2005). Failure to communicate [Television series episode]. In D. Shore (Executive Producer), *House.* New York, NY: Fox Broadcasting.

Fancher, R. E. (1985). *The intelligence men: Makers of the IQ controversy*. New York, NY: Norton.

Feltham, C. (2010). *Critical thinking in counselling and psychotherapy*. Thousand Oaks, CA: Sage Publications.

Frank, G. (1983). *The Wechsler enterprise: An assessment of the development, structure, and use of the Wechsler tests of intelligence*. Oxford, UK: Pergamon.

Gendlin, E. T. (1978). *Focusing*. New York, NY: Everest House.

Goleman, D. (1995). *Emotional intelligence*. New York, NY: Bantam.

Goleman, D. (2006). *Social intelligence: The new science of human relationships*. New York, NY: Bantam.

Kennedy-Moore, E., & Watson, J. C. (2001). How and when does emotional expression help? *Review of General Psychology, 5*(3), 187–212.

Mayer, J. D., Roberts, R. D., & Barsade, S. G. (2008). Human abilities: Emotional intelligence. *Annual Review of Psychology, 59*, 507–536.

Mayer, J. D., Salovey, P., & Caruso, D. R. (2008). Emotional intelligence: New ability or eclectic traits. *American Psychologist, 63*(6), 503–517.

Payne, W. L. (1985). A study of emotion: Developing emotional intelligence; self integration; relating to fear, pain and desire. *Dissertation Abstracts International, 47*, 203A (UMI No. AAC 8605928).

Yalom, I. R. (2002). *The gift of therapy*. New York, NY: Harper Collins.

CHAPTER 9

When Grief Goes Awry

With there being so much broad variation in what is considered "normal" grief, how do you know when something is wrong, or when a bereaved individual needs more specific professional help? When does grief become complicated and how do we recognize it? This is a question that continues to challenge theorists and clinicians alike. In the previous chapters, we have discussed how grief is a multifaceted experience and its manifestation between individuals is highly unique and dependent upon many interacting factors. But how can you tell when the bereaved cross that "imaginary line" from normal to complicated grief (CG), and what are the implications of grief going awry? Most bereaved individuals find that the acute grief symptoms gradually diminish over time through a natural integrating process. However, approximately 10% of bereaved people experience grief that is ongoing and often debilitating for a long period (Shear, Boelen, & Neimeyer, 2011).

Recently, there has been a great deal of research that focuses on this group of bereaved individuals that experience unabated grief for a prolonged time, negatively affecting their ability to function and cope. In some instances, the bereaved individual may fear that if she or he stops grieving, the connection with the deceased person will be lost. Another aspect or type of grief is that the person loses a part of himself or herself with the death of the deceased person and, as a result, feels completely lost. Being bereaved may also be a new defining role and identity for the grieving individual, as he or she now defines himself or herself by the loss and the role of being "left behind." In these examples, being bereaved is experienced as a loss of self and identity.

In this chapter, we will review some of the terminology that is often utilized in the discussion of grief that has veered away from what would be considered a normal trajectory. We will also describe some of the main features of CG, as postulated by prominent researchers in this area. As this book's focus is upon clinical work with bereaved individuals, we will also explore some of the clinical implications for CG and for grief that is intermixed with exposure to traumatic events. Finally, we will provide an overview of the current treatment modalities that are being proposed for therapeutic work with individuals who are experiencing CG.

WHAT IS COMPLICATED GRIEF?

The terminology that is used to describe grief that has gone wrong somehow can be confusing. Grief that has gone awry is sometimes referred to as complicated grief (CG), prolonged grief disorder (PGD), or traumatic grief in the published literature, although the loss itself may not be associated with a traumatic death (Worden, 2009). These terms are often used interchangeably; their origin and association vary slightly depending upon the backgrounds of the researchers who first proposed the discrete criteria for what we would call "difficult grief." This difficult CG involves prolonged acute grief symptoms, and situations in which the bereaved are unable to rebuild a meaningful life without the deceased person. Current consensus regarding the criteria for CG states that it may be present after any loss that is extremely personally devastating and,

> The devastation can derive from sudden, unexpected death; from the quality of the relationship to the deceased; and/or personal predispositions. (Tolstikova, Fleming, & Chartier, 2005, p. 295)

In regard to the relationship to the deceased, CG is often thought of as a traumatic separation from the person who died, with pronounced separation distress and difficulties adjusting to life without the deceased being markedly pronounced (Gray, Prigerson, & Litz, 2004).

Typical CG symptoms include persistent feelings of intense yearning or preoccupation with the deceased, shock, disbelief, and anger about the death, difficulties with trust, and engagement in behaviors and activities to try to either avoid reminders of the loss or to feel closer to the deceased (see Figure 9.1). People with CG often ruminate or obsess over the various circumstances of the death, their relationship with the deceased person, or over the events since the death and their feelings and reactions since that time (Boelen, van den Bout, & van den Hout, 2003, 2006; Nolen-Hoeksema, McBride, & Larson, 1997; Stroebe et al., 2007). Prigerson and her associates (2009) have proposed criteria for the diagnosis of PGD (see Figure 9.2). It is important for counselors to be familiar with these criteria

Acute grief symptoms that persist for more than 6 months following the death of a loved one, including:

1. Feelings of intense yearning or longing for the person who died—missing the person so much it is hard to care about anything else.
2. Preoccupying memories, thoughts, or images of the deceased person that may be wanted or unwanted and that interfere with the ability to engage in meaningful activities or relationship with significant others; may include compulsively seeking proximity to the deceased person through pictures, keepsakes, possessions, or other items associated with the loved one.
3. Recurrent painful emotions related to the death, such as deep, relentless sadness, guilt, envy, bitterness or anger, that are difficult to control.
4. Avoidance of situations, people, or places that trigger painful emotions or preoccupying thoughts related to the death.
5. Difficulty restoring the capacity for meaningful positive emotions through a sense of purpose in life or through satisfaction, joy, or happiness in activities or relationships with others.

FIGURE 9.1
Clinical Features of Complicated Grief.
(From Shear, 2010)

in order to know when a client may need more intensive assessment and therapeutic support.

Risk factors for CG can be grouped into three main categories. The first of these includes *personal psychological vulnerability*, such as a personal or family history of mood or anxiety disorders (Gamino, Sewell, & Easterling, 2000), insecure attachment style (van der Houwen et al., 2010), and history of trauma or multiple losses (Gamino et al., 2000). This category can also include the bereaved individual's relationship to the deceased, as some relationships tend to be associated more with difficulties in bereavement, such as parental loss of a child, followed by the loss of a spouse, sibling, and a parent (Clerien, 1993). A second category concerns *circumstances of the death* itself, such as untimely, unexpected, violent, or seemingly preventable death (Currier, Holland, & Neimeyer, 2006; Currier, Holland, Coleman, & Neimeyer, 2008; Gamino et al., 2000). And finally, a third category of risk factors focus on the *context in which the death occurs*, such as social support that is inadequate or that is problematic in some way (Wilsey & Shear, 2007), or concurrent stresses such as financial concerns or other hardships (van der Houwen et al., 2010). It is important to be able to recognize when clients are experiencing CG, as it is a source of significant negative impact upon health and quality of life (Germain, Caroff, Buysse, & Shear, 2005; Hardison, Neimeyer, & Lichstein, 2005; Latham & Prigerson, 2004; Monk, Houck, & Shear, 2006;

A. Bereavement (loss of a significant other).
B. Separation distress—chronic and persistent yearning, pining, longing for the deceased, reflecting a need for connection with the deceased that cannot be satisfied by others. Daily, intrusive, distressing, and disruptive heartache.
C. Cognitive, emotional, and behavioral symptoms: The bereaved person must have five or more of the following symptoms experienced daily or to a disabling degree:

   1. Confusion about one's role in life or diminished sense of self (i.e., feeling that part of oneself has died)
   2. Difficulty accepting the loss
   3. Avoidance of reminders of the reality of the loss
   4. Inability to trust others since the loss
   5. Bitterness or anger related to the loss
   6. Difficulty moving on with life (i.e., making new friends and pursuing new interests)
   7. Numbness (absence of emotion) since the loss
   8. Feeling that life is unfulfilling or meaningless since the loss
   9. Feeling stunned, dazed, or shocked by the loss

D. Timing: Diagnosis should not be made until at least 6 months have elapsed since the death.
E. Impairment: The disturbance causes clinically significant impairment in social, occupational, or other important areas of functioning (i.e., domestic responsibilities).
F. Relation to other mental disorders: The disorder is not better accounted for by MDD, generalized anxiety disorder, or PTSD.

FIGURE 9.2

Diagnostic Criteria for Prolonged Grief Disorder.

(From "Prolonged Grief Disorder: Psychometric Validation of Criteria Proposed for *DSM-V* and *ICD-11*" by H. G. Prigerson, M. J. Horowitz, S. C. Jacobs, C. M. Parkes, M. Aslan, K. Goodkin, . . . P. K. Maciejewski, 2009, *PLoS Medicine, 6*, p. e1000121.)

Prigerson et al., 1997) and, therefore, requires treatment that may go above typical grief counseling and support.

CG is more prevalent in individuals who have attachment difficulties or whose models of the self or of the world do not allow for the accommodation and integration of significant life events into how they view themselves, others, and the world (Davis, Wortman, Lehman, & Silver, 2000; Prigerson et al., 2009). Who we are shapes how we grieve, and who we are is very much associated with how we relate to others. When we are highly bonded and possess a significant amount of attachment anxiety, there is a higher tendency toward CG. The outcomes of CG can be very serious, and intervention is required to assist these individuals to preserve their health, their lives, and to counteract the potential negative sequelae that can result from its impact upon the lives of these individuals. As counselors supporting bereaved individuals, we cannot afford to be naive and journey alongside people in their grief without awareness of this issue.

According to Prigerson et al. (2009), controlling for depression and anxiety, CG is associated with the following:

- Myocardial infarction ("heart attack") and congestive heart failure
- Immune system dysfunction, placing individuals at higher risk of colds and illness to cancer-related illnesses
- Substance use and abuse
- Essential hypertension
- Functional impairment
- Reduced quality of life
- Suicide attempts

On a more practical level, we often begin to consider a client to be experiencing a CG response when (a) the intensity of the grief worsens instead of improving or the individual's ability to compensate for the loss(es) begins to crumble after a certain lapse of time, (b) the individual's ability to function on a day-to-day basis is compromised, and (c) there is a sense of being completely "stuck" in a deep and unrelenting place of grief and trauma over the course of many months' duration.

OVERLAPS BETWEEN GRIEF AND TRAUMA

To some extent, all grief is traumatic, as significant losses require us to rebuild our shattered assumptions about the world that no longer exists as we once thought (Janoff-Bulman, 1992). When we lose someone whom we love, we also lose significant aspects of ourselves. Our world is never the same. We may feel frightened, powerless, and void of meaning. As mentioned earlier, the term "traumatic grief" is often used interchangeably with the term "complicated grief" because of the mechanism of psychic overload that prevents adequate coping and stress management in the bereaved individual, and the resemblance to the models of traumatic stress disorders that are described in the *Diagnostic and Statistical Manual of Mental Disorders* (*DSM*; American Psychiatric Association, 2000; Tolstikova et al., 2005). In fact, many comparisons have been made between complicated/traumatic grief and posttraumatic stress disorder (PTSD), even in the absence of a traumatic event to cause the death, because of the frequent reported disturbances in sleep, concentration, intrusive images of the deceased person, and the avoidance and estrangement noted in some bereaved individuals (Simpson, 1997). However, the main distinction between these two concepts is that the exposure to a threat that is described in the criteria for PTSD in the *DSM* is a very different experience from losing a close relationship, so traumatic grief is seen as a different diagnostic entity from PTSD (Neria & Litz, 2003).

It is important to note that traumatic experiences are subjectively assessed by individuals, and how a loss by traumatic means is perceived by an individual will vary, dependent upon the meaning that the individual attaches to that event and the nature of the relationship to the lost person (Neria & Litz, 2003). As counselors, it is important to remember that traumatic material and overlay is interpreted by the client's perception of the event and not by whether the counselor believes the event to be traumatic in nature or not. Because this discussion can be confusing, let us make some distinctions between some of the terms that are commonly used. A *traumatic loss* (death that occurs as a result of an event that would be seen as traumatic, such as a violent act, car accident, or an event where there may be mangling of the body) is not necessarily going to lead to traumatic grief, although it can. Using the term *traumatic loss* places the focus of the bereaved individual's experience on the events and the stressors that occurred around the loss and not necessarily on the response of the bereaved individual. The term *traumatic grief* delineates the degree of the separation anxiety and assault to the assumptive world that is experienced by the bereaved individual. In other words, this term focuses on the experience and response of the bereaved person, and not upon the events surrounding the death itself.

The clinical presentation of an individual with CG is often anxiety based, whereas in normal grief, the presentation is usually typically sadness or anger. It is important to note that symptoms of trauma are very similar to the symptoms that are described in CG—avoidance, intrusion, anxious arousal, depression, dissociation, and anger/irritability are often present in individuals with CG as well as in individuals who are exposed to traumatic experiences (Jacobs, Mazure, & Prigerson, 2000). Some researchers have compared normal grief with the *DSM* criteria for PTSD and found parallels between these two descriptions, indicating that experiencing a significant loss (whether or not it is the result of a traumatic event) can challenge a person's ability to accommodate what has happened into his or her assumptive world (Rando, 1997; Simpson, 1997). The common thread between traumatic grief and a traumatic response to an event is found in the propensity for psychological overload that is demonstrated in the similarities between the two responses. This distinction can be very confusing, but for practicalities' sake, if your client describes feeling highly anxious or unsafe, or tends to focus on the events surrounding the loss rather than the person, you are probably dealing with traumatic overlay of some sort. What mainly separates PTSD from complicated/traumatic grief is the presence of separation distress, including intense yearning for the deceased person and intrusive thoughts of, or pangs for the lost person (Horowitz et al., 1997; Prigerson et al., 2009).

The presence of complicated/traumatic grief presents the counselor with the need to assess whether or not his or her training and background is appropriate for working with individuals whose lives are so deeply compromised and whose health and well-being may be at stake. If you are not trained in therapeutic techniques that require skill at both clinical assessment and the processing of traumatic material, a referral should be made to someone with more advanced training in work with grief and trauma. Some of the clinical implications for complicated or traumatic grief are now discussed.

The Experience of Loss and Death Can Trigger Old Traumatic Experiences to Come to the Surface

The common denominator in experiences of grief and trauma is loss of control. When we lose something of value or someone whom we love, the overarching feelings often center on powerlessness, helplessness, and feeling robbed. Of note is that the core features of trauma also revolve around these same feelings. Profound, significant losses may lead to an intensification of feelings of vulnerability and anxiety. In clients with a history of trauma, a significant loss might cause reentry into the traumatic material and the anxiety associated with feeling unsafe (Crenshaw, 2006–2007; Siegel, 1999). In the diagnostic descriptions that were listed in the beginning of this chapter, a history of trauma would be seen as a form of preexisting personal vulnerability in the bereaved individual (Gamino et al., 2000). Counselors must recognize when clients' former traumatic experiences are "doubling" onto the current loss experience and normalize this recurrence for clients, while assisting clients to learn how to contain the traumatic material while exploring the grief related to the current loss.

There Is Often a "Dance" That Occurs When Trauma and Grief Coexist

An important rule to keep in mind is that traumatic material will tend to overshadow the grief-related symptoms at first because clients who are experiencing symptoms related to trauma will not be able to focus on other aspects of their experience until they feel safe, are able to trust the counselor (which may take some time), and they have a semblance of control over what to share and how to share it with you. Clients must feel safe and know there is a "container" for the traumatic material in place before they can do any form of process work, which is the basis for the work with most bereaved individuals. This principle is frequently described in literature related to trauma from abuse and terrorism (Herman, 1997) and in childhood traumatic grief experiences (Cohen, Mannarino, & Deblinger, 2006).

Traumatic material is mediated by more a primitive (primary) system of the brain than grief (Crenshaw, 2006–2007; Perry, 2005). This primary system controls the fight–flight response, which drives individuals to seek safety and security quickly when activated. In his work with childhood traumatic grief, Perry (2005) stated,

> The key to therapeutic intervention is to remember that the stress response systems originate in the brainstem and diencephalon. As long as these systems are poorly regulated and dysfunctional, they will disrupt and dysregulate the higher parts of the brain. All the best cognitive-behavioral, insight-oriented, or even affect-based interventions will fail if the brainstem is poorly regulated. (pp. 38–39)

Clients who are dealing with trauma will often have a sense of unease, and they will often feel vigilant and anxious, but they may not be able to tie these feelings to a specific event, thought, or feeling because the trauma response does not primarily work on cognition, but more on instinct. Counselors can keep in mind that emotional paralysis or an angry demeanor in a client may serve as a protection for a client who is feeling highly vulnerable and unsafe emotionally. Pushing or going too deeply before a client feels a sense of containment or control in the sessions may cause the client to emotionally flood, resulting in dissociation[1] or the person feeling violated within the therapeutic setting.

Grief is primarily mediated through the attachment system, and is tied into cognition, which is related to attributing meaning to events and sequencing events in a certain order (Parkes, 2006). Thus, grief is usually

---

[1] Dissociation occurs when an individual is overwhelmed by stimuli or information. Although the person remains physically present, there is a sense that emotionally and/or cognitively the person is absent. The continuum may run from daydreaming to actual amnesia about events or conversations. When dissociation occurs in a therapeutic context, it may signal that the person has either been triggered regarding previously traumatic material or is overwhelmed by what is happening in the session. Because it is seen as a protective response, when you are aware that your client is dissociating, it is important to slow things down and gently refocus the client into the room with you, offering the ability to reengage with you in a way that feels safe and nonthreatening.

experienced in a more linear way than traumatic events in isolation (Davis, 2001; Shaver & Tancredy, 2001; Weiss, 2001). Clients who are experiencing grief will often be able to name the feeling(s) and tie the feeling(s) to an experience or experiences directly related to their grief, and they will usually be able to share about their loss experience in a mostly linear and cohesive fashion. You will often hear of the importance of bereaved clients being able to "tell their story," which involves the ability to describe events in this way. Keep in mind that grief is not always expressed as sadness—there is often profound anger at feeling robbed or deprived as a result of a loss, as well as the myriad of other emotions that have been described previously. Bereaved individuals often go into their grief very deeply, and it is often helpful for the counselor to facilitate this deep exploration, which often involves emotional catharsis. Although we have discussed in an earlier chapter that not all bereaved individuals need to deeply explore their emotional responses to loss and "work them through," it can probably be assumed that the majority of bereaved clients who seek grief counseling would tend to be self-selected as more representative of those individuals who would find this way of working with grief to be beneficial. This being said, attention to individual differences in client experiences, responses, and expressions is of paramount importance, which has been discussed previously as well.

The "dance" between trauma and grief is obvious. If you try to engage in deep processing of grief-related material when the client is feeling traumatized, you risk the client shutting down, dissociating, or feeling more out of control and anxious—with the results being that the client may feel worse instead of better afterwards. If you try to offer a means of containment to a client who needs to deeply explore his or her grief, you risk suppressing the experience and encouraging the client to remain superficially engaged or avoidant of grief that may need to be attended at that time. Most likely, effective counselors know when containment is needed, while also having the ability to gently explore and help the client to work through the raw grief when it surfaces.

CLINICAL IMPLICATIONS FOR TRAUMA AND GRIEF

Counselors Need to Focus on Their Client in Order to Know How to Best Proceed

Listen carefully. If your client is sharing more about the event that happened or images of how the person's body looked or was imagined to look, or seems highly anxious or uncomfortable, go slowly and provide stopping points to check in with the client in the session. Feelings of anxiety and vigilance indicate to you that your client is feeling unsafe and unsure. You may have clients describe nightmares about what happened to their loved one. These kinds of dreams may involve the context of an event where the griever felt powerless and the loved one suffered harm, mutilation, or death, or where the person hears or sees the loved one, but there is an ominous overtone or a sense of something being terribly wrong.

There is often an obsessive quality to what is shared by the client when the grief is complicated or traumatic in nature. Although most people who are in the grieving process yearn for contact with their deceased loved one, those whose grief is complicated are often obsessed by what happened and the details surrounding the death, and they are often consumed by feelings of anger, rage, fear, or powerlessness. They may have intrusive thoughts that focus on what happened, or they may relive the event(s) over and over in their minds. They may experience bodily symptoms either from the stress they are under or similar to those that might have been experienced by the lost person. They may be unable to go to the place where the event happened or find themselves avoiding similar sites (certain roads, certain types of cars, certain buildings or types of buildings). There is also often fear of being triggered by outside stimuli—TV programs, songs on the radio, and exposure to a similar event, and they may have an aversion or avoidance pattern in their daily functioning, such as a refusal or reluctance to drive through certain intersections or go near certain buildings. They may also feel a sense that they will die soon or have a sense of fatalism about life. In addition, their level of everyday functioning is usually profoundly affected, and many of these individuals are just getting by in regard to their work functioning and in their everyday routine, which adds another tremendous stress on top of their process.

The Grieving Process May Be Stunted by the Trauma That Is Present

The trauma and the feelings of being traumatized—feeling violated, powerless, angry, and out of control—must first be recognized and validated, and the individual needs to feel a sense of control—even if the control is how he or she chooses to disclose details or not, or how the sessions may proceed. Counselors must be clear in working with individuals who are feeling unsafe and anxious that initially they only need to know what the client needs to share with them. Pushing for details and content when clients are hesitant or pushing back may be experienced by clients as intrusive and further increase feelings of anxiety. Attempts to minimize or even reframe the magnitude of the client's feelings or to act as if the client's anxiety and hesitancy are not an important issue will only demonstrate to the client that he or she cannot be open about feelings, thoughts, and difficulties with you. In families and certain groups where there has been a suicide, there are higher rates of suicide in the remaining members, so feelings about wanting to continue living and possible thoughts of suicide should be taken seriously and not dismissed (Crosby & Sacks, 2002; Jordan & McIntosh, 2011).

Treatment Modalities

One important aspect of working with individuals who are experiencing traumatic overlay is the need to slow the process down and not to push the person to go deeper into feelings that could lead to flooding with traumatic images and further traumatization. Slowly, allow the person to share about what happened. Focus on breathing, taking breaks, and maintaining a strong presence in the room. Being able to talk about small "chunks" of the bereaved individual's experience is sometimes referred to as "dosing" the experience—only dealing with small and selected segments of the painful and traumatic aspects of the client's experience at a time (Jordan & McIntosh, 2011). CGT has been proposed as a means to assist bereaved individuals by a series of interventions designed to address some of the specific and more problematic areas of CG (Shear et al., 2011). In CGT, clients are asked to maintain a grief diary, to engage in imaginal exercises that are designed to revisit the death, and situational revisiting exercises are used for avoided activities and situations. The revisiting portion of the treatment is similar to a form of exposure therapy that is used with the treatment of PTSD. (For more information on the clinical application of CGT, see Shear, 2010.)

Cognitive behavioral therapy (CBT) has also been proposed as a useful technique in working with CG, where the bereaved individual is invited to address negative cognitions that have formed around the loss experience and to reframe these cognitions in a more realistic and meaningful way. According to Boelen et al. (2007), the goals of CBT in CG include,

> (a) integrating the loss with existing autobiographical knowledge, (b) changing unhelpful thinking patterns, and (c) replacing unhelpful avoidance strategies by more helpful actions and coping strategies. (p. 151)

Meaning reconstruction therapy has also been proposed as a way to reduce some of the debilitating acute grief symptoms, providing clients with the opportunity to address their losses, relationships, and purpose in life in the context of the narrative of their life's story with the deceased individual and without that same person (Neimeyer, 2001). The specific goals of meaning reconstruction therapy include,

> (a) finding a meaningful place for the *event story* of the death in the client's ongoing self-narrative, (b) reviewing and revising the *back story* of the relationship with the deceased, both to address residual concerns and to reconstruct the attachment bond with the deceased in a way that does not require his or her physical presence, (c) "re-visioning" life and fostering creative problem solving, and (d) reinforcing dedicated action through legacy work. (Shear et al., 2011, p. 154)

It is important to remember that these descriptions are a very condensed overview of each of these therapeutic approaches, and each of these treatment modalities requires specialized training in the context of being a skilled and experienced therapist. These approaches are briefly described here for you to keep in mind if your client is struggling with the basic interpersonal counseling approach to grief that we have described in this book so far.

The Use of Medication in Complicated Grief

The use of medication is often a complex issue for bereaved individuals. Medication may or may not be used, and many clients will have strong feelings about the use of medication during this time. The counselor's role at this time is to suggest referrals for medication assessment when indicated and to help clients to explore their feelings about the use of various medications during this process. For instance, I (D.L.H.) worked with a client whose son died suddenly. Her grief was indeed very complicated and debilitating. Because of her inability to sleep and her descriptions of difficulties functioning in her daily activities almost a year after her son died, I suggested that a referral to a medical specialist might be of benefit. However, when I discussed this referral with her, she became very upset, associating the use of medication with her experiences of her mother, who was severely depressed and required hospitalization for severe depression when she was a child. After we discussed her concerns and she was able to separate her mother's depression from her CG response over the death of her son, she did agree to seek this assessment and agreed to a course of antidepressant medication, after which she then seemed to have more energy to address some of the unfinished and unresolved issues that surrounded her son's death in the therapy sessions.

For individuals with ongoing depressive symptoms that impair their functionality or sleep patterns over a longer period, or for those individuals whose anxiety is interfering with daily functioning, medication may be of benefit while the traumatic themes are being worked through in counseling. Important to this discussion is that CG often co-occurs with major depressive disorder (MDD) and PTSD (Shear, Frank, Houck, & Reynolds, 2005). It is generally thought that the use of medication in individuals with a normal, acute grief reaction is not indicated and that in these situations, medication may actually prolong the grief response rather than assist in its resolution (Worden, 2009). However, in a study that was spearheaded by Shear and her colleagues (2005) with individuals who were identified with CG symptoms, bereaved individuals with depressive symptoms who were taking antidepressant medications demonstrated a slightly better response to therapy than those individuals with similar symptoms who were not placed upon medication, which is consistent with other studies related to this topic. For the purposes of this chapter, it is suggested that counselors pay attention to the level of functionality of the client, along with descriptions of sleep habits and patterns of thinking that tend to "spiral downward" without the client being able to recover in between times of deeper despair and despondency. For clients who, over many months, have been unable to develop more regular sleep patterns, who do not tend to oscillate between grief symptoms and daily functioning, and who fall into the diagnostic criteria for MDD or PTSD, assessment for medication may be of benefit, and the counselor would be remiss in not recommending such a referral in these situations.

Social Support and Stigma in Complicated Grief

In clients whose grief is complicated or prolonged, it is important to keep in mind that individuals who would normally be the main sources of support to your client may be overwhelmed or frightened by the severity, intensity, and duration of your client's reactions. In addition, individuals suffering from CG symptoms may find that navigating through a maze of social service agencies and the courage and energy it takes to find appropriate help to be daunting. This may cause further isolation and a deeper sense of loss and despair for your client. Thus, counselors could be of great benefit to these clients by keeping abreast of the local resources, programs, and supports that may be available to clients in specific situations (Dyregov, 2004). As in normal grief, social support is a key component to the healing process in CG. Individuals who are experiencing non-CG often feel that their friends and family members do not fully understand the depth of their experience. You can then consider how much more an individual who is experiencing CG might feel this way.

Advocacy and Empowerment in Complicated Grief

Advocacy is often an important way for the individual to feel that what has happened may have some meaning to it. Advocacy can be thought of as a form of "therapeutic activism" (Jordan & McIntosh, 2011, p. 32) and as a means to try to change things that have surfaced as inequities, injustices, or causal elements in the event that has happened. It is also a means for regaining a sense of personal power after experiencing an event where one felt powerless or helpless. It may also be a way to channel the intense emotions that have arisen as a result of being traumatized, besides being a way for individuals who have experienced a similar event to support each other through identification with the common cause. The group Mothers Against Drunk Driving was begun by women who lost their loved ones because of drunk drivers, and this organization has provided a powerful presence to lobby for stricter laws and penalties for driving while under the influence of substances. Many suicide prevention groups are formed by individuals who have been personally affected by the suicide of a loved one. The popular television show "America's Most Wanted" was hosted by John Walsh to help families find and convict perpetrators of violent crimes after his 6-year-old son was abducted and murdered. Meaning-making through advocacy serves to integrate a traumatic event into one's existing assumptive world, and it also creates a legacy for the deceased individual.

FINAL THOUGHTS

Currently, there is a great deal of research and interest in the description, diagnosis, and treatment of CG. The amount of research and written literature on this topic in the past few years alone is daunting. Counselors need to stay informed as new research findings are released and to keep current on present-day thinking regarding the identification of grief that requires professional, focused intervention to prevent life-altering and potentially life-limiting sequelae. What is of most importance is not to focus on fitting a client's experience into a diagnostic category. In fact, there are many concerns that are raised by clinicians that diagnostic criteria can place labels upon clients that would further stigmatize them. So, we reiterate that the focus of this chapter is to provide you with a means to recognize when a client may need further assessment and intervention beyond what you, as a grief counselor, may be able to provide alone. The ability to support bereaved clients from a therapeutic stance is only possible if the client is able to engage in therapeutic work fully, without risk of being further traumatized by the process, while being given every possible and necessary consideration to function as fully as possible in the face of a crippling loss event. Counselors need to be able to identify when grief has gone awry and to assist clients to find the best and most appropriate supports available to meet their needs. Counselors must also keep their focus on the bereaved person as a fellow human being who is struggling with a very painful experience. We are reminded that our goal is to be fully present to that person's experience, while also being professionally informed and aware of the times when further support in other ways may be indicated for the client's best interests.

Glossary of Terms

Complicated grief   involves prolonged acute grief symptoms and situations where the bereaved are unable to rebuild a meaningful life without the deceased person; there is currently a movement toward the development of consensus criteria for complicated grief because of confusion over differing terminology to refer to difficult grief such as CG, traumatic grief, complicated mourning, and PGD.

Dissociation   although the person remains physically present, there is a sense that emotionally and/or cognitively the person is absent. The continuum may run from daydreaming to actual amnesia about events or conversations.

Posttraumatic stress disorder   the presence of a prescribed set of symptoms and behavioral manifestations that are described in the *Diagnostic and Statistical Manual of Mental Disorders* that occur after exposure to a traumatic event and that remain present for at least 2 months after the event. Symptoms may include frequent reported disturbances in sleep, concentration, intrusive images of the event or the deceased person, avoidance, and vigilance.

Trauma   a deeply distressing or disturbing experience, or a situation that involves a threat of death, serious injury, or significant potential harm to an individual. Trauma may be experienced directly or vicariously.

Traumatic grief   it delineates the degree of the separation anxiety and assault to the assumptive world that is experienced by the bereaved individual. Some losses are traumatic because they focus on the experience and response of the bereaved person, and not necessarily upon the events surrounding the death itself. For example, a palliative death of a very close attachment figure in certain circumstances may lead to traumatic grief if the loss causes the bereaved individual to feel unsafe, threatened, or highly vulnerable.

Traumatic loss   places the focus on the events and the stressors that occurred around the loss, which are usually sudden, unexpected, violent, disfiguring, or very much out of the normal expectation.

Questions for Reflection

1. List and describe client scenarios that would indicate a need to refer a client to a clinician with specific training and expertise in dealing with complicated grief or medical assessment. How would you know when you are "over your head" with a particular client?

2. What differentiates the experience of PGD from chronic sorrow that accompanies nonfinite losses?

3. Individuals with complicated grief are often identified and diagnosed as depressed by some professionals. What are some of the ramifications for making this diagnosis in individuals with complicated grief?

4. It has often been said that "all grief is complicated." Explore this statement, using the information you have read in this chapter.

References

American Psychiatric Association. (2000). *Diagnostic and statistical manual of mental disorders* (4th ed., text rev.). Washington, DC: Author.

Boelen, P. A., De Keijser, J., Van den Hout, M. A., & Van den Bout, J. (2007). Treatment of complicated grief: A comparison between cognitive-behavioral therapy and supportive counseling. *Journal of Consulting and Clinical Psychology, 75*(2), 277–284.

Boelen, P. A., van den Bout, J., & van den Hout, M. A. (2003). The role of negative interpretations of grief reactions in emotional problems after bereavement. *Journal of Behavior Therapy and Experimental Psychiatry, 34*(3–4), 225–238.

Boelen, P. A., van den Bout, J., & van den Hout, M. A. (2006). Negative cognitions and avoidance in emotional problems after bereavement: A prospective study. *Behaviour Research and Therapy, 44*(11), 1657–1672.

Clerien, M. (1993). *Bereavement and adaptation: A comparative study of the aftermath of death.* Washington, DC: Hemisphere.

Cohen, J., Mannarino, A., & Deblinger, E. (2006). *Treating trauma and traumatic grief in children and adolescents.* New York, NY: Guilford Press.

Crenshaw, D. A. (2006–2007). An interpersonal neurobiological-informed treatment model for childhood traumatic grief. *Omega, 54*(4), 319–335.

Crosby, A. E., & Sacks, J. J. (2002). Exposure to suicide: Incidence and association with suicidal ideation and behavior: United States, 1994. *Suicide and Life-Threatening Behavior, 32*, 321–328.

Currier, J. M., Holland, J. M., & Neimeyer, R. A. (2006). Sense-making, grief, and the experience of violent loss: Toward a mediational model. *Death Studies, 30*(5), 403–428.

Currier, J. M., Holland, J. M., Coleman, R. A., & Neimeyer, R. A. (2008). Bereavement following violent death: An assault on life and meaning. In R. G. Stevenson & G. R. Cox (Eds.), *Perspectives on violence and violent death* (pp. 177–202). Amityville, NY: Baywood.

Davis, C. (2001). The tormented and the transformed: Understanding responses to loss and trauma. In R. A. Neimeyer (Ed.), *Meaning reconstruction and the experience of loss* (pp. 137–155). Washington, DC: American Psychological Association.

Davis, C., Wortman, C., Lehman, D., & Silver, R. C. (2000). Searching for meaning in loss: Are clinical assumptions correct? *Death Studies, 24*(6), 497–540.

Dyregov, K. (2004). Strategies of professional assistance after traumatic deaths: Empowerment or disempowerment? *Scandinavian Journal of Psychology, 45*(2), 181–189.

Gamino, L. A., Sewell, K. W., & Easterling, L. W. (2000). Scott and White Grief Study—phase 2: Toward an adaptive model of grief. *Death Studies, 24*(7), 633–660.

Germain, A., Caroff, K., Buysse, D. J., & Shear, M. K. (2005). Sleep quality in complicated grief. *Journal of Traumatic Stress, 18*(4), 343–346.

Gray, M., Prigerson, H., & Litz, B. (2004). Conceptual and definitional issues in complicated grief. In B. Litz (Ed.), *Early intervention for trauma and traumatic loss in children and adults: Evidence based directions* (pp. 65–86). New York, NY: Guilford.

Hardison, H. G., Neimeyer, R. A., & Lichstein, K. L. (2005). Insomnia and complicated grief symptoms in bereaved college students. *Behavioral Sleep Medicine, 3*(2), 99–111.

Herman, J. (1997). *Trauma and recovery: The aftermath of violence—from domestic abuse to political terror.* New York, NY: Basic Books.

Horowitz, M. J., Siegel, B., Holen, A., Bonanno, G. A., Milbrath, C., & Stinson, C. H. (1997). Diagnostic criteria for complicated grief disorder. *American Journal of Psychiatry, 154*, 904–910.

Jacobs, S., Mazure, C., & Prigerson, H. (2000). Diagnostic criteria for traumatic grief. *Death Studies, 24*, 185–199.

Janoff-Bulman, R. (1992). *Shattered assumptions: Toward a new psychology of trauma.* New York, NY: Free Press.

Jordan, J. R., & McIntosh, J. L. (2011). *Grief after suicide: Understanding the consequences and caring for the survivors.* New York, NY: Routledge.

Latham, A. E., & Prigerson, H. G. (2004). Suicidality and bereavement: Complicated grief as psychiatric disorder presenting greatest risk for suicidality. *Suicide and Life-Threatening Behavior, 34*(4), 350–362.

Monk, T. H., Houck, P. R., & Shear, M. K. (2006). The daily life of complicated grief patients—What gets missed,what gets added? *Death Studies, 30*(1), 77–85.

Neimeyer, R. A. (Ed.). (2001). *Meaning reconstruction and the experience of loss.* Washington, DC: American Psychological Association.

Neria, Y., & Litz, B. T. (2003). Bereavement by traumatic means: The complex synergy of trauma and grief. *Journal of Loss and Trauma, 9*, 73–87.

Nolen-Hoeksema, S., McBride, A., & Larson, J. (1997). Rumination and psychological distress among bereaved partners. *Journal of Personality and Social Psychology, 72*(4), 855–862.

Parkes, C. M. (2006). *Love and loss: The roots of grief and its complications.* New York, NY: Taylor & Francis.

Perry, B. D. (2005). Applying principles of neurodevelopment to clinical work with maltreated and traumatized children: The neurosequential model of therapeutics. In N. B. Webb (Ed.), *Working with traumatized youth in child welfare* (pp. 27–52). New York, NY: Guilford Press.

Prigerson, H. G., Bierhals, A. J., Kasl, S. V., Reynolds, C. F., III, Shear, M. K., Day, N., . . . Jacobs, S. (1997). Traumatic grief as a risk factor for mental and physical morbidity. *American Journal of Psychiatry, 154*(5), 616–623.

Prigerson, H. G., Horowitz, M. J., Jacobs, S. C., Parkes, C. M., Aslan, M., Goodkin, K., . . . Maciejewski, P. K. (2009). Prolonged grief disorder: Psychometric validation of criteria proposed for *DSM-V* and *ICD-11. PLoS Medicine, 6*(8), e1000121.

Rando, T. (1997). Foreword. In C. Figley, B. Bride, & N. Mazza (Eds.), *Death and trauma: The traumatology of grieving* (pp. xv–xix). Washington, DC: Taylor & Francis.

Shaver, P. R., & Tancredy, C. M. (2001). Emotion, attachment, and bereavement: A conceptual commentary. In M. S. Stroebe, R. O. Hansson, W. Stroebe, & H. Schut (Eds.), *Handbook of bereavement research: Consequences, coping, and care* (pp. 63–88). Washington, DC: American Psychological Association.

Shear, K. (2010). Complicated grief treatment: The theory, practice, and outcomes. *Bereavement Care, 29*(3), 10–13.

Shear, M. K., Boelen, P. A., & Neimeyer, R. A. (2011). Treating complicated grief: Converging approaches. In R. Neiemyer, D. L. Harris, H. R. Winokuer, & G. F. Thornton (Eds.), *Grief and bereavement in contemporary society: Bridging research and practice* (pp. 139–162). New York, NY: Routledge.

Shear, M. K., Frank, E., Houck, P. R., & Reynolds, C. F., III. (2005). Treatment of complicated grief: A randomized controlled trial. *Journal of the American Medical Association, 293*(21), 2601–2608.

Siegel, D. J. (1999). *The developing mind: How relationships and the brain interact to shape who we are.* New York, NY: Guilford Press.

Simpson, M. (1997). Traumatic bereavements and death-related PTSD. In C. R. Figley, B. E. Bride, & N. Mazza (Eds.), *Death and trauma: The traumatology of grieving* (pp. 3–16). Washington, DC: Taylor & Francis.

Stroebe, M., Boelen, P. A., van den Hout, M., Stroebe, W., Salemink, E., & van den Bout, J. (2007). Ruminative coping as avoidance: A reinterpretation of its function in adjustment to bereavement. *European Archives of Psychiatry and Clinical Neuroscience, 257*(8), 462–472.

Tolstikova, K., Fleming, S., & Chartier, B. (2005). Grief, complicated grief, and trauma: The role of the search for meaning, impaired self-reference, and death anxiety. *Illness, Crisis, and Loss, 13*(4), 293–313.

van der Houwen, K., Stroebe, M., Stroebe, W., Schut, H., van den Bout, J., & Wijngaards-de Meij, L. (2010). Risk factors for bereavement outcome: A multivariate approach. *Death Studies, 34*, 195–220.

Weiss, R. (2001). Grief, bonds, and relationships. In M. S. Stroebe, R. O. Hansson, W. Stroebe, & H. Schut (Eds.), *Handbook of bereavement research: Consequences, coping, and care* (pp. 47–62). Washington, DC: American Psychological Association.

Wilsey, S. A., & Shear, M. K. (2007). Descriptions of social support in treatment narratives of complicated grievers. *Death Studies, 31*(9), 801–819.

Worden, J. W. (2009). *Grief counseling and grief therapy* (4th ed.). New York, NY: Springer Publishing Company.

CHAPTER 10

The Clinician's Toolbox: Therapeutic Modalities and Techniques in the Context of Grief

*I*n this chapter, we will explore some therapeutic "tools" and techniques that may be helpful in working with bereaved individuals. We offer these ideas and suggestions with the recognition that there are diverse ways for bereaved individuals to share their thoughts, feelings, and stories, and these ideas might help to facilitate this aspect of your work with clients. It is highly apparent that there is no such thing as "one-stop shopping" in grief counseling. Some clients will talk nonstop in a session for almost the entire time, whereas others will say very little and have a great deal of difficulty expressing themselves. Some clients will readily talk about their feelings and will be highly self-reflective in their encounters with you, whereas others may focus more upon events outside of themselves and be quite analytically oriented. Your job as a grief counselor is to facilitate the client's process in a way that is most congruent with that person's way of being in the world and with his or her needs and goals. In this chapter, we will describe some therapeutic adjuncts or differing ways of working with clients and their grief. Some of these modalities require specific additional training, and we will specify suggestions for additional resources and training opportunities for these modalities at the end of the chapter for your interest. This chapter is by no means an exhaustive review of counseling strategies for adaptation to loss. We have provided descriptions of these modalities because they are the ones in which we are most familiar. If you are interested in a deeper exploration of various exercises and strategies for working with bereaved individuals, we would refer you to Keren Humphrey's book *Counseling Strategies for Loss and Grief* (2009).

Before introducing work with clients that strays from a classical talk-therapy orientation, we go back to a foundational point in counseling: The relationship that you have with your client is what is most important. We would never encourage a counselor to try an intervention or strategy with a client unless there is a sense of comfort in the relationship, where the client trusts the counselor, and the counselor feels that he or she has a solid grasp of the client's concerns, values, and sensitivities. Remember, the relationship comes first, as the therapeutic alliance is the foundation to all the work that occurs. The client must have a good sense of trust in you, engagement with the process, and motivation to work before you can introduce an exercise or different ways of working together in the sessions. We have found that the well-timed introduction of a therapeutic adjunct can have quite dramatic results with some clients, often providing a catalyst for greater awareness, self-understanding, and reflection in the session and afterwards. Thus, we wanted to share some of the things we keep in our "counselor's tool kit" for you to consider in your work with clients as well.

RITUALS AND LINKING OBJECTS

Rituals usually involve an action that is initiated on the part of the bereaved individual to give a symbolic expression to certain feelings or thoughts (Lewis & Hoy, 2011). Romanoff and Terenzio (1998) stated that rituals "facilitate the preservation of social order and provide ways to comprehend the complex and contradictory aspects of human existence within a given societal context" (p. 698). Rituals can provide a way for clients to both express and contain strong feelings, and they often give a sense of order and control within a situation where an individual has felt very out of control and impotent. They can be created privately by a client, cocreated by a client with a counselor, or culturally established through family and social contexts (Romanoff & Thompson, 2006). They often offer an opportunity to create meaning from what has happened (Neimeyer, 1999). In addition, rituals often provide a means of connection to the individual who is now gone, as the symbolic nature of the ritual often ties in to the continuing bond that may exist with the deceased loved one, and it may nourish a sense of the deceased's presence that is ongoing in some way with the client.

Probably the most common ritual in North America is the funeral, which serves many purposes: honoring the deceased individual's life, providing a structured opportunity for social support to be offered to the family and close friends, reaffirmation of values and beliefs, and reintegration of the family into the community without the deceased individual. However, the funeral is a time-limited ritual and does not afford an opportunity to be revisited by the bereaved as the grieving process unfolds (Castle & Phillips, 2003). Certainly, the presence of a grave or marker for a deceased loved one can provide an opportunity for ongoing visitation by loved ones and possibly a sense of connection with the deceased individual or to a higher power. However, in the absence of an avenue for expression, this visitation alone may not actively engage the bereaved individuals into that process. That being said, we might suggest that a bereaved person complete a "rubbing" of a cemetery marker or plaque to bring to the session as a means of sharing this experience with you. For clients who do not live in the same city as where their loved one is buried, or who have difficulties with transportation, a rubbing might be a good way for them to "visit" their loved one's memorial when they wish to do so, but they are unable to travel to the site. Rubbings are made by placing tracing paper or thin paper over the marker and then "rubbing" a crayon, pastel stick, or chalk over the surface. The lettering and images of the marker are then transferred onto the paper. Pictures of the marker are often helpful as well, but the physical task of making the rubbing is often therapeutic for the bereaved individual.

Ritual activities may include visiting the grave, displaying photographs of the deceased, showing photos and speaking about the loved one to others, taking up an interest the deceased enjoyed, writing letters to the loved one, watching a particular TV program that evokes memories, creating something, wearing or interacting with something that belonged to the deceased, attending a particular event because the loved one would have attended it or honoring the loved one by attending an event (such as a memorial), creating a memorial of some kind, lighting a candle in honor of the deceased person on specific dates and times, creating a memorial trust in the name of the deceased person, and planting a tree or special plant in honor of a loved one (Lewis & Hoy, 2011). There are as many rituals possible as there are individuals on the earth, and these are just the more common examples that we see in our practices.

Keep in mind that rituals can also be used for losses that are not death related and for rites of passage, as the use of ritual provides a symbolic avenue for recognizing significance and to attach meaning to an event where the individual may feel a loss of parts of himself or herself or of something that is highly significant but not necessarily related to a death.

Perinatal Loss/Reproductive Loss

It is becoming more common for hospitals and health professionals to recognize the significance of the loss of an unborn child. Many clinics and emergency departments offer chaplain support services to women who miscarry or deliver a stillborn baby. These spiritual care providers may offer a blessing for the baby and the family, say prayers for the baby and the family, and their presence highlights the recognition by others that a loss of significance has occurred (Kobler, Limbo, & Kavanaugh, 2007). Other rituals that are now commonly used in this type of loss include taking footprints of the baby and placing them on a card, providing parents with a "memory box" that contains items that were related to their baby, such as any clothing used, baby bracelets, footprints or handprints, and photos taken (if possible). Many of my (D.L.H.) clients have brought these memory boxes into their sessions and painstakingly gone through each item with me, with the presence of something tangible providing a means to physically touch the same materials that were in contact with their baby, or that held significance to them.

Another example of the use of ritual in reproductive loss comes from the work of a client who had gone through several years of unsuccessful infertility treatment. After one of her counseling sessions, she made a clay model of her uterus. She then formed several small balls of clay that represented each of the embryos that were transferred into her body during the various infertility procedures. She initially placed all of the "embryos" into the clay uterus, told them that she loved each of them, and then she took each of them out of the clay container, one by one, saying goodbye to the children that she would never bring into the physical world with her. She then buried each of these clay balls to symbolize her desire to recognize the significance of the loss of her children after these treatments were unsuccessful.

Commemorative Jewelry and Personal Belongings

Grieving clients often use special items as a means of maintaining a connection with what they have lost. More than simple keepsakes, these items are often imbued with a great deal of symbolic meaning to a person, relationship, situation, or a part of themselves. Often referred to as "linking objects," clients frequently take items that they associate with their loved one and attach significance to them as reminders or as a means of feeling connected to their deceased loved one (Neimeyer, 1999; Volkan, 1981). Common examples of these items are clothing, photographs, personal items (such as a pet's collar, a child's stuffed toy, and a lock of hair), items associated with a place of significance, such as where someone died or was given the news, and letters and gifts that were from a significant person. These objects are often worn or carried by the bereaved individual throughout the day.

One example of this type of object was shared by a client who wore a locket that her deceased husband had given to her before he died. She also confided that she had placed a very small pinch of his ashes in this same locket so that he was "always with her." One client chose to place her prescription lenses into her deceased husband's glasses and she then wore them herself. Clients will often wear jewelry that belonged to their loved one or have jewelry made that represents something that is significant to them. For example, one client whose mother died took her mother's wedding ring to a jeweler and added her mother's birthstone as well as the birthstone of herself and her sister to it and wore it every day as a reminder of the love her mother gave to her family. Many clients will wear the deceased's clothing, use everyday objects that the deceased regularly used (like coffee mugs or pens), and keep specific objects on display that remind them poignantly of their deceased loved one, and this will often provide a sense of comfort and meaning for them.

It is often helpful to ask clients if they have any objects of connection that they find meaningful and, if so, to have them bring these objects to their sessions. It can be very powerful for the counselor to validate the existence and value of these objects with the client, and can often lead to a deepening of the therapeutic alliance as the client explores the meaning of the objects with the counselor (Humphrey, 2009).

Letters, Journals, and Electronic Communication

Several of our clients have written letters to their deceased loved ones, talking with them in ways that are similar to how they might interact with them if they were still alive. Often, writing letters helps the bereaved individual to feel connected to the deceased person, although processing the implications of their absence. In essence, the deceased person "hears" about the grieving process from the bereaved individual, who would most likely share this process verbally with the same person if he or she were still alive. There are numerous Web sites that allow bereaved individuals to post online memorials and notes to their loved ones, including their pets. Several of our clients have stated that these online memorials are very comforting to them, and that they have an added bonus of being readily available at all times, and do not require transportation or venturing into a public place when privacy is desired.

More recently, electronic media is becoming a more common form of expression for bereaved individuals. Several clients have shared that they have created a memorial site for their loved one, often using the individual's social media site to do so. Thus, a Facebook page that belonged to a deceased loved one may turn into a memorial page for that same person. A uniquely creative client established an e-mail account for his deceased wife and wrote to her regularly using this e-mail address. Intermittently, he would go into the account he had created for her and read what he had written, and then reply back to his own e-mail account what he thought his wife would say to him in response to what he had shared.

Use of Ritual With Conflicted Relationships

In relationships where there has been ambivalence or negativity, rituals can still be useful to work through some of the unfinished business that remains after death. In addition to writing letters to the deceased person to explore and express feelings toward the deceased individual, there are other possibilities. One client came for grief counseling after the death of her mother. In the course of counseling, it became obvious that the relationship she had with her mother had been very conflicted, and that she had been subjected to verbal and emotional abuse from her mother for most of her life. When the client's sisters were going through her mother's things, they set aside her mother's dark navy suit for her to have, saying that she was the same size as their mother. The client brought the suit to one of her sessions and talked about the memories she had of her mother wearing this suit, including a particularly painful time when her mother berated her in front of many people at church. Two sessions later, the client came in and said she felt "so much lighter." When asked to explain, she stated that she chose to take a seam ripper and tear the suit apart at the seams. She then tried to burn it but found it only melted because it was polyester, so she then chose to bury it along with a picture of herself from the time she had a memory of a particularly negative event when her mother had worn this suit. After she did this ritual, she described feeling that she was "finally free" from her mother's oppression.

WRITING AND NARRATIVE AS THERAPY

Many current bereavement researchers and practitioners argue that meaning reconstruction is the central process involved in grief (Neimeyer, 1999). In this approach, human beings are seen as the "weavers of narratives that give thematic significance to the salient plot structure of their lives" (Neimeyer, 1999, p. 67). When a significant loss occurs, the assumptions that one has made about life can be dramatically shaken at their very core. When these assumptions are violated, or shattered by the death of a loved one or a significant loss event, the life narrative of the person becomes fragmented and incoherent. Significant losses require individuals to rewrite the narrative of their lives in a way that allows for an explanation of what has occurred within a context of personal meaning and congruence with how they now see the world, others, and themselves. Thus, approaches that focus on the person's story of his or her life and the loss that has occurred may assist in creating a new, more meaningful self-narrative that emerges from the loss experience itself (Parry, 1991).

There are several possibilities to assist clients to tell their story, and to begin to identify where their self-narrative has become fragmented as a result of a shattered assumptive world view. We will briefly discuss a few of the narrative strategies that may be of benefit in helping clients rewrite their life narrative in the context of grief counseling.

Clustering

Clustering is a form of brainstorming that may be useful for clients who feel very stuck, or who need to sort through many different competing thoughts and feelings. Initially, ask the client to think of a central point or aspect of their experience. Write that word in the middle of a sheet of paper and circle it. Then, begin to brainstorm about all of the different tangents that may extend from that central point—draw lines from the central point to a word that represents each tangent or feature of the central point and circle these words separately. You can then expand further upon these secondary tangents as needed.

Clustering is often very helpful to assist clients to process a great deal of material in a short time, in a way that is manageable. This is especially useful when a client feels overwhelmed, is having difficulties staying on track with his or her thoughts, and when there are multiple and convoluted tangents to the client's descriptions. Putting thoughts and feelings like this onto paper will often help clients to see their issues in a very condensed, but complete form. In the example that is provided (see Figure 10.1), we have asked Mary to cluster her experiences related to the loss of her husband. Mary's primary, core experience is the loss of Sam, her husband of 23 years. She then explores the major issues that surround this loss and then focuses on some of the key aspects of each of these issues in secondary and tertiary clusters. Once complete, a client can look at a cluster drawing and often will feel a stronger sense of clarity in regard to what is most important and what aspect of the loss needs his or her primary attention at that time. It might also be helpful to have clients complete a cluster of their lives before the loss experience and compare it with the cluster they have completed in their present situation.

FIGURE 10.1

Clustering.

*The above example was a cluster that was completed with a
client after her husband died from a sudden illness 2 years ago.
The main circle in the page started with the death of her husband,
then the most important issues that were on her mind as a result
of losing her husband. She then went to each of these issues and
explored each further with more clustering.*

Life as a Book

In this exercise, clients are advised to think of their life as a book. In setting up this experience, you might ask clients to think about what the elements of a good book are—such as the plot, the twists and turns, the characters, and what the book has to offer to the reader. Then, you ask the client to think of what the title of his or her "life book" might be. When going to the "text" of the book, you can ask clients to think of specific times or events in their lives as separate chapters of the book. This may take some time and reflection, so we often find it helpful to make this suggestion to a client in the session and to begin the process with them, with the counselor scribing for the client. When the session is nearing its end, you can then turn your written page(s) over to the client and ask that the client continue to reflect upon the exercise and fill it in more before the next session. Clients often find this exercise to be a powerful way to reflect upon their lives and experiences, and it may be a useful tool to place the current grief-laden portion of their lives in the context of their entire life experiences.

Use of Metaphor and Story

Metaphors invite clients to capture the "essence" of an experience or feeling through the use of descriptive imagery and symbolism. One suggestion for the use of metaphor is to ask the client to think of their loss, their grief, or their present life situation in terms of an image or an object. For instance, one client described his current situation as feeling like he was in a car that was out of control without a driver, while he was strapped so tight in the seatbelt in the back seat that he could not breathe. Descriptions such as this provide a rich source of material to explore with the client that can offer meanings on different levels (Humphrey, 2009; Neimeyer, 1999).

Another exercise that utilizes a similar method is the virtual dream story, which is a story that is told in figurative language (see Figure 10.2) (Neimeyer, Torres, & Smith, 2011). This exercise may help clients to work with "core" issues, while using the figurative language to have some distance from the personal aspects of their experience that may be overwhelming or too intense to discuss directly. In this exercise, clients are assigned a set of six elements (settings, figures, and objects) of the virtual dream and are instructed to write a story that includes these elements, adjusting them to relate to their loss experience. For example, a client may be asked to write a story with a violent storm, an unearthly light, a dove, a strong man, a mask, and a closed door. After the client finishes writing, ask the client to read

Situations/Settings	Figures/Voices	Objects
A wasting illness	A wise woman	A rose
A violent storm	A mysterious stranger	A burning fire
A troubled sea	A booming voice	An ancient chart
An early loss	A choking sob	An ambulance
A long journey	An angel	A mask
A secret room	A dove	An empty bed
A cool book	A serpent	A closed door
An unearthly light	A wrinkled elder	A coffin
A precipice	An overheard song	A naked sculpture
A cave	A strong man	A treasure box

FIGURE 10.2

Virtual Dreams.

Clients are told to use two elements from each box (settings, figures, and objects) and to create a story that includes them, tailoring the elements to their own experience. Above are some sample virtual dream elements.

(With permission from "The Virtual Dream: Rewriting Stories of Loss and Grief" by R. A. Neimeyer, C. Torres, and D. A. Smith, 2011, *Death Studies, 35,* pp. 646–672.)

the story out loud to you, and then explore the various elements and their relevance to the client's current situation. This exercise may take some time and a little bit of coaching, but it can be a powerful catalyst for exploration and meaning-making by the client.

Letter Writing

There are different forms and variations of this exercise. In its simplest form, clients may be asked to write a letter to the lost person (may not be a loss from death only) to share their thoughts and feelings with that person. The letters typically focus on the expression of thoughts and feelings about the loss and their grief. If the letter is being written to someone who is still alive, it is important to emphasize that it is being written for the client's purposes, and not for the purposes of the other individual, and that the letter should not be sent. Letter writing can also be a very process-oriented exercise, with clients writing letters to themselves in the past, perhaps forgiving themselves, or speaking with the voice of experience now to a younger and more naive version of themselves at an earlier time. Clients can write letters to their past or future selves as well, providing a way to work on past painful events or reminding their future self about a time in their lives that they will remember forever. In some cases, a ritual to dispose of the letter, such as ripping it up, burning it, or burying it, may offer a sense of resolution to the client regarding issues that have been "hanging" in the client's mind as unfinished or unresolved issues (Humphrey, 2009).

ENERGY-BASED THERAPIES ("POWER THERAPIES")

We include a brief section here to familiarize you with energy-based modalities and how they have been used with bereaved individuals. Each of these techniques requires highly specialized training and supervision, so you would not be able to incorporate them into your practice without first immersing yourself into the understanding and use of each under the direct supervision of certified trainers/practitioners. However, because these modalities are often mentioned in both the scholarly literature and in popular venues, we think it is a good idea for you to have a basic understanding of them and to know when they may be appropriate for clients in the event a referral to another practitioner might be considered or a client brings these topics up for discussion with you. Commons (2000) referred to these therapies as "power therapies" because of their ability to rapidly assist some clients who are paralyzed by traumatic images and material.

Eye Movement Desensitization and Reprocessing

Eye movement desensitization and reprocessing (EMDR) was initially introduced with a controlled study of Vietnam veterans and victims of sexual molestation (Shapiro, 2001). It was found that with the use of this procedure, clients could quickly desensitize traumatic memories, and restructure irrational thoughts and negative self-assumptions, and there was a significant reduction in debilitating symptoms (Solomon & Shapiro, 1997). Solomon and Rando (2007) discussed the use of EMDR with bereaved individuals to assist them in processing and reframing highly disturbing and/or painful material that has been stored in association with their memories of the deceased individual. Their research has demonstrated that using EMDR with clients who are experiencing symptoms of trauma and distress reduces the debilitation that can occur when the client's functionality is affected by intrusive grief symptoms (Solomon & Rando, 2007). EMDR is an eight-stage treatment method that involves elements of psychodynamic, interactional, and body-oriented therapies along with cognitive behavioral elements. It is thought that the multimodal approach of EMDR elicits an ability to process traumatic and distressing material at an accelerated pace. It is very important to recognize that EMDR training is an intensive process for counselors who are already very skilled clinicians. EMDR should not be attempted without completion of the training and demonstrated competence in the method under supervision. We offer this brief description as a possible consideration for referral in clients with whom talk therapy does not seem effective or where talk therapy tends to heightens anxiety.

Thought Field Therapy

Thought field therapy (TFT) was introduced as a treatment for distressing psychologically related symptoms. Callahan and Callahan (1996) concluded that the control mechanism of the emotions and all physiology of a person are accessible through the energy systems of the body that are utilized in acupuncture called meridians. By stimulating meridian treatment points (sites where the acupuncture needles or pressure are applied in Chinese medicine), TFT makes subtle changes in the emotional and physiological systems of the person. Different types of disturbances involve tapping different meridians and pressure points on the body. In the TFT treatment, clients focus on the emotional pain that is most disturbing to them in the grieving process. The TFT therapist asks the client to become attuned to the targeted emotion, and while experiencing these feelings, the therapist directs the client through a specific set of tapping procedures on specified pressure points on the body. The procedure is usually brief. Afterwards, subjective distress is reassessed and the procedure is repeated until the client describes a reduction in the distress level. Training for practitioners involves learning the correct procedures for different client presentations.

This procedure is not without its detractors. Many mainstream therapists and researchers cite lack of outcome evidence as problematic in the recommendation of the use of TFT. Proponents cite it as one of the "power therapies" that is beneficial for clients with severe and intractable distress (Commons, 2000; McNally, 2001). We have heard of several clinicians who work with clients who have debilitating symptoms of trauma and complicated grief describe many benefits of this modality with their clients, so we have included a brief description of it here. We suggest that you investigate this modality and the recent literature on implementation and efficacy of TFT if you are interested in its application to bereaved individuals.

Emotional Freedom Technique

The emotional freedom technique (EFT), developed by Craig (1995), takes TFT a step further using a single comprehensive procedure, thus eliminating the need for a complicated diagnosis and specific treatment protocols. Supporters of EFT allege that, by tapping on all the meridian points, problems associated with the misdiagnosis of underlying emotional distress because of poor or ambiguous definitions are eliminated. Craig stated that successful treatment of patients, even when the order of the tapping was changed, is proof that the diagnosis of a particular disorder is unnecessary and even problematic for treatment effectiveness. During EFT, persons are instructed to focus on their fear while they tap different meridians on various parts of their body. It is thought that focusing on fear while tapping is akin to imaginal exposure and distraction, respectfully. EFT incorporates the same fundamental components as systematic desensitization and distraction. Therefore, a decrease in subjective units of distress ratings by group EFT may be because of a combination of exposure and distraction, rather than on account of the specific tapping locations.

USE OF PERSONALITY AND TEMPERAMENT INVENTORIES

Although we do not usually recommend the use of measures and instruments as part of grief counseling practice, we often find that clients who embark upon a process of trying to sort themselves out might benefit from the self-exploration that can be facilitated by the completion of self-scoring personality questionnaires. We often find it helpful, at times, to think of how clients process information and generally prefer to interact with their everyday world so that our way of being with them is consistent with their needs and preferences. Most of the inventories that we will discuss in this section are available as free online versions (we will list the Web sites at the end of this chapter), which allows clients to complete them at home and to read about their results and absorb the information on their own before doing so with the counselor. In addition to assisting clients to develop a deeper awareness and understanding of themselves, working together on the material that has surfaced as a result of completion of these inventories can assist the counselor to choose language, imagery, interactional style, and therapeutic suggestions that might be more congruent with the client's values, beliefs, and strengths.

The Myers-Briggs Type Indicator (MBTI) was developed as a personality measure based upon Jung's theory of psychological types (Myers, McCaulley, Quen, & Hammer, 1998). The authors, Isabel Myers Briggs, and her mother, Katharine Briggs, built upon Jung's theory of personality types when they designed the measure. The MBTI sorts psychological differences into four opposite pairs, or *dichotomies*, with a resulting 16 possible psychological types. None of these types are *better* or *worse*; however, Myers-Briggs theorized that individuals naturally *prefer* one overall combination of type differences (Myers, McCaulley, Quenk, & Hammer, 1998). In the same way that writing with the left hand is hard work for a right hander, so people tend to find using their opposite psychological preferences more difficult. The MBTI is not a tool to assess psychiatric diagnoses or personality disorders. Rather, it is used to help individuals to better understand themselves and how they perceive the world around them. It is broken down into four different indices that reflect individual preferences in these various areas.

- *Extraversion/introversion*—How a person is energized and where their focus is (not necessarily if they like people or not)—does the person prefer time alone to recharge or does he or she get energy from being with others? Do you tend to "think out loud" or like to work and reflect privately?
- *Sensing/intuition*—What do you pay attention to? How do you "take in" information? Do you tend to focus on your five senses and be more concrete in your thinking or do you pay more attention to your "gut instinct" and things that are more in the realm of your imagination?
- *Thinking/feeling*—How do you make decisions? How do you come to a conclusion? Do you tend to organize and structure choice in a logical and objective way or do you prefer to organize and structure information in a more personal, value-oriented way?
- *Judging/perceiving*—What kind of lifestyle do you prefer? How do you deal with the world? Do you tend to make lists and plan your schedule or do you prefer to "wing it" and leave your options open?

If you look at these four areas, there are conclusions you might be able to make regarding a person who is grieving based upon their type. People who are introverted may need some "down time" to process their grief. Extraverted individuals may find attending a support group where there are others who are sharing and interacting with them to be highly beneficial. People who tend to score higher on the thinking portion of the scale may have difficulty dealing with strong emotions that arise or they may feel uncomfortable with others who express emotion. These individuals may also struggle with others who attempt to get them to emote in order to "feel better." Individuals who tend to be stronger in sensing scores may have difficulty if they did not get a chance to see the body after death, whereas highly intuitive individuals may be more prone to engage in a deep quest for existential meaning after a significant loss. Individuals who tend to score higher on the judging portion of the scale tend to appreciate organization and routine; obviously, the disorganization and chaos that is often a part of grief has the potential to be especially distressing for them.

These generalizations, of course, have to be checked out with the person to make sure they are right. However, just thinking about it in terms of individual preferences and differences takes away the language of grieving a "right" or "wrong" way and helps understand where there may be some difficulty and where there may be strengths. These differences may also be a source of stress in family members who are grieving differently because of their personality type. The Keirsey Temperament Sorter (Keirsey, 1998) is very similar to the MBTI, and it might offer a more simplified way for clients to understand personality typology and to see how knowing their preferences may assist them to find their own unique path through their grief. Other inventories we have used that may be helpful in client's self-discovery might be the true colors characterization (Kalil, 1998) and the Enneagram of Personality (Riso, 1996).

MINDFULNESS-BASED INTERVENTIONS

Although often associated with Buddhist thinking, mindfulness meditation does not require an individual to embrace Buddhist beliefs in order to practice mindful awareness. In therapeutic work, mindfulness practice incorporates elements into the client's experience that may be of great benefit, including learning to cultivate an intentional focus on the moment-to-moment experience as it is in the here and now, detached observation of thoughts, feelings, and sensations, and nonjudgmental acceptance of one's experience exactly as it is (Humphrey, 2009). The mindfulness practice that has been adapted to psychological work in the West is also sometimes referred to as insight meditation or Vipissana. Rather than teaching clients to shut out their experiences, thoughts, and feelings, the cultivation of mindful awareness allows clients to enter these experiences and states fully, but without being overwhelmed by them. Clients who engage in mindfulness practice often describe feeling that they are very in touch with their direct experiences, but that they no longer find these same experiences as distressing or distracting as they once were. Western therapies, such as Gestalt, psychodrama, and the internal family systems (IFS) model (which will be discussed in the next section), draw upon elements of mindfulness, bringing the client into a full awareness of the present experience in order to heal or work through experiences or issues from the past (Johanson, 2006).

There are numerous clinical applications for mindfulness practices. Levine (1989a, 1989b, 1989c, 1998) has written several books on the topics of death, dying, and grief and mindfulness. We also have found a book written by Sameet Kumar entitled *Grieving Mindfully* (2005) to be a good resource as well. The actual mindfulness-based stress reduction (MBSR) program was developed by Jon Kabat-Zinn at the University of Massachusetts Medical Center. The MBSR training involves an 8-week introductory program, which includes both didactic training and daily meditation practice (Kabat-Zinn, 1990; Sagula & Rice, 2004). Our chapter on therapeutic presence incorporates many aspects of mindfulness practice, so you might wish to review that section of the book to refresh the ideas that were presented for the counselor to practice in relation to the client, including breathing with clients and full awareness and attention on the client and the client's sharing during the session. The most common, basic techniques that are used are the body scan technique and following the breath.

Body Scan Technique

One of the first techniques learned and practiced in the MBSR program is the body scan. It seems that we have a tendency to neglect our body unless there is something wrong with it, which is unfortunate because what is called the "felt body sense"—awareness of body sensations, which are often quite subtle, can give us valuable insight into what is going on with our bodies and with our whole being as well. The body scan is a practice of devoting moment-to-moment attention to our body just as it is. Typically, the body scan is performed lying down, but can be practiced in any position. Clients are instructed to direct a broad, expansive attention to the body as a whole, then very focused attention in systematic fashion to various regions of the body and then once again an expansive awareness of the entire body. Through this process they will often discover a lot about how their body feels, its sensations, and their mental reactions to paying attention to various parts of our body. Clients are instructed to pay attention in this way, without trying to fix or change anything, in order to become less critical of their body's perceived imperfections and responses to the environment, and to cultivate greater acceptance and appreciation for their bodies at that very moment (Kabat-Zinn, 1990).

Following the Breath

In this practice, you are asked to find a comfortable sitting position and bring your attention to the sensation of breathing. Breathe in long and out long for a couple of times, focusing on any spot in the body where the breathing is easy to notice, and your mind feels comfortable focusing. This could be at the nose, at the chest, at the abdomen, or any spot at all. Stay with that spot, noticing how it feels as you breathe in and out. Do not force the breath or bear down too heavily with your focus. Let the breath flow naturally, and simply keep track of how it feels. Savor it, as if it were an exquisite sensation you wanted to prolong. Clients will often express that it is difficult to control their thoughts—that their minds wander a lot, and that they find it difficult to stay focused on their breathing. We let them know that this is normal and that if their mind wanders off, simply bring it back. We encourage them and tell them that if their mind wanders 100 times, simply bring it back 100 times. We emphasize being compassionate with themselves as they begin this process and to not be focused on whether they "did it" as much as they are doing it and learning it.

Many people do have a hard time with their thoughts, and they may get discouraged. We are so used to our hyperactive minds, that we barely notice the fact that they are usually churning with activity. So, we tell clients that when they first sit and meditate, they may be caught off guard by all the activity. Some people find it helpful to use a little imagination to help them meditate. For example, instead of counting or following your breath, they might prefer to imagine a peaceful scene, perhaps floating in a warm lagoon, until the noise of their mind quiets down. One especially useful image has been that of sitting on the edge of a fast-flowing river, where all of your thoughts, feelings, worries, and concerns are the water as it rushes by you, as you sit on the river bank and watch it.

Clients can experiment with different kinds of breathing. If long breathing feels comfortable, stick with it. If it does not, change it to whatever rhythm feels soothing to the body. They can try short breathing, fast breathing, slow breathing, deep breathing, shallow breathing—whatever feels most comfortable to them at that time.

GRIEF AND THE INTERNAL FAMILY SYSTEM
(SUBMITTED BY DEREK SCOTT, BA, RSW*)

The IFS model of therapy (Schwartz, 1995) is one in which treatment is based on an understanding that the personality exists as a system of parts to which compassionate curiosity may be brought in order to facilitate healing. The "parts" in this model may be understood to be autonomous aspects of the personality that have specific roles. Schwartz defines one of these parts as the "exile" or "protector." The exiled parts hold extreme feelings and/or beliefs about themselves, which may threaten to "blend" (i.e., overwhelm and define the system). When this occurs, an individual may identify solely as the blended part (e.g., "I am sad" or "I am ashamed"). When these vulnerable parts get triggered, other parts jump up to distract us from them and these reactive protective parts are termed "firefighters." Common firefighter distractions might include using TV, sleep, alcohol, drugs, sex binging, food binging, rage, and so on to keep the system occupied until the agitating energy of the vulnerable parts is no longer present. The other group of protectors in the system are referred to as "managers," and they seek to ensure that the vulnerable exiles do not get triggered. They do this by attempting to manage the outside world and/or other people. For example, commonly in grief the decision not to visit the gravesite is manager-led; that is, seeking to avoid the inevitable triggering of the parts that are holding distressing affect.

In addition to the *parts* of the personality system, we also have a Self, and the salient aspects of the Self in terms of the therapeutic work are curiosity, compassion, and calmness. It is Schwartz's (1995) position that everyone has a Self and the work of the IFS therapist is to help the client's Self to respond to the parts of the system that are holding distress. Once these parts are compassionately witnessed in terms of the burdensome feelings and/or beliefs they are holding, their burdens may be released and they may choose a new role in the system, bringing great relief to the bereaved and helping the system to return to balance.

When working with grief, the IFS therapist will be sensitized to the typical burdens held by the cluster of parts connected to attachment and loss, which

* **Derek Scott, BA, RSW,** is a certified gestalt therapist and group leader and a registered social worker with a BA (honors) in psychology from Keele University in England and has worked in the field of counseling and therapy since 1981. He has experience with various insight-based holistic modalities including action-method psychodramatic work, gestalt two-chair and contact boundary work, body-focused awareness, cognitive therapy and reframing, chakra system and guided imagery, and the internal family systems (IFS) model. He currently resides in London, Ontario, Canada.

are typically parts that are holding depression, sadness, missing/yearning, protest (anger), guilt, powerlessness, and despair. Many of these parts hold burdens from unresolved losses in childhood, and they are activated by the present loss. Consequently, the feelings have the intensity of a child's response, and the protective system becomes engaged to prevent the person from becoming overwhelmed. By attending to the typical managing protectors, honoring their strategies of postponing, displacing, replacing, minimizing, avoiding, somaticizing, numbing, and shaming (which is particularly prevalent in disenfranchised losses), and reassuring them that the client's Self can hear the exiled pain without becoming overwhelmed, the protective parts of the system may then step aside and allow access to the burdened exiled parts.

This model is nonpathologizing; every part is recognized for its beneficent intent for the system. Proponents find it to be an efficient, effective, and inherently respectful therapeutic modality. For more information and to witness a role-play of working with complex grief, please see the Web links and resources listed at the end of this chapter.

SANDTRAY WORK

Sandtray therapy (or "sandplay") is a technique based upon practical, creative work in a sandtray. Use of sand as a therapeutic method was originally developed by Dr. Margaret Lowenfeld in the 1920s. She was influenced by H.G. Wells who wrote about observing his two sons playing on the floor with miniature figures and his realization that they were using these figures to work out their problems with each other and with other members of the family. After reading about Well's descriptions of his sons at play, she added miniature figures to the shelves of the playroom of her clinic. The first child to see them took them to the sandbox in the room and started to play with them in the sand. Dr. Lowenfeld felt she had found a method to help children express the "inexpressible." She eventually formalized the play with miniature figures, sand, and water in a blue-bottomed, aluminum container in her London-based play therapy clinic to work with children to help them to express and work through emotionally charged issues. One of the children with whom she worked stated that the tray gave her "a whole world to play with," which inspired Dr. Lowenfeld to call it the "World Technique" (Lowenfeld, 1979).

The current use of the sandtray with adults began with the work of Dora Kalff, a student of Carl Jung who later studied Lowenfeld's World Technique. She recognized that the archetypal content and symbolic process involved in this medium could make it readily adaptable to Jungian theory, and she used the term "sandplay" therapy to distinguish it from Lowenfeld's work (Kalff, 2004). As with the World Technique, sandplay therapy is now used with both adults and children. There is now an International Society for Sandplay Therapy and another organization called the Sandplay Therapists of America, and there is an extensive training and supervision process for therapists to become qualified in the formal modality of sandplay therapy.

Most clinicians who use sandplay therapy with adults still use figures as representational models of either intrapsychic processes or of situations that are brought up in verbal (talk) therapy prior to the work in the tray. Sand can be either dry or wet. Some clients talk as they work, and others remain silent. The meaning of the work emerges as the client experiences it and shares it with the therapist. For the client, working in a sandtray translates personal experience into a concrete, three-dimensional form. Just as a picture can say more than a thousand words, a figure or scene can express feelings, emotions, and conflicts that previously had no verbal language. Thus, sand-worlds that are created can offer a rich and highly personalized vocabulary for preverbal or nonverbal experience. Without having to depend upon words, clients can increase their capacity for expression through the tray. Often, clients experience a sense of awareness and clarity that was not possible in talk therapy alone.

Once some aspect of the self has been made tangible in the sandtray, the ability to experience it, share it with another, experiment with it, play with it, revise it, and learn from it is possible. Internal struggles and tensions can be "played out." Familiar "stuck" patterns may be loosened and the beginnings of new, more satisfying ways of being may emerge. There are two different ways of using sandtrays that we would like to share with you as possible adjuncts in working with bereaved individuals.

Hands in the Sand

Sand itself has many connotations for individuals. In her book *Healing and Transformation in Sandplay,* Ruth Ammann (1991) stated that "Sand is matter ground by the infinity of time. It makes one mindful of eternity. Sand is matter which has been transformed and has almost become liquid and spiritual" (p. 22). Sand in its dry form is almost like liquid. It is light and when we touch it with our hands, it feels soft. In this type of sandtray work, clients are simply asked to immerse their hands in the sand and to work with the sand in whatever way comes to them. The exercise is nonverbal; clients are asked to focus on their hands, the sensations that their hands experience, and what they are feeling as they do the exercise. They are usually given about 5 minutes to work the sand with their hands. When clients' hands enter the sand, deeper thoughts and feelings often come quickly to the surface. The tactile sensation of the sand may also remind someone of their desire to be touched and to gently touch someone else—something that may be missing in the loss of a loved one. For some, the act of immersing their hands in the sand or feeling it as they lightly touch the surface changes the tone of the session immediately, often intensifying it, and focusing it completely on the client's experience. The use of music during this time can help to foster the process of the client nonverbally. Music can be chosen by the client in advance, or the counselor can choose a piece that may fit the client's situation or mood. At the end of the session, we "debrief" the process, with the clients being able to integrate the affective and tactile experience with their own personal stories of loss.

Another use of the "hands in the sand" approach is to help clients remain grounded when there has been a tendency to dissociate in the session or the client begins to feel overwhelmed by the material brought up in the session. Several of my (D.L.H.) clients instinctively now reach for the tray in my office and keep it in their laps while we are in the session, often working their hands in the sand while they are talking as a means of feeling "grounded" and more present during the session. This way of using the tray is similar to grounding methods that help clients to remind themselves that the story they are recounting is not happening in the present, such as rubbing their feet on the floor or naming objects in the room as a means to stay connected in the present when talking about traumatic material (see Figure 10.3).

FIGURE 10.3
Hands in the Sand—Working the Sand
Nonverbally With the Hands.
Clients place their hands in the sand and work the sand as they feel drawn to do so, whereas the counselor remains silent and fully present to the client's work. Evocative music is often used in this process. After 5 minutes, the client is gently asked to complete the work, and the counselor asks the client to describe the thoughts and feelings that arose during this process.

The Tray as Metaphor

The other method that I (D.L.H.) use the sandtray is similar to how sandplay therapists use the tray—by having a client place representational figures into the tray to better visualize a situation or to better describe it. This method has been very helpful when clients remain "stuck" on a particular issue or situation. However, the use of such representational figures involves training in the use of the tray for that purpose, so we suggest the use of representational objects that are natural and more symbolic in nature, such as rocks, leaves, pictures, or objects that may be brought in by the client. Clients may choose a particular rock, shell, piece of wood, feather, or other item from a bowl that is kept near the tray, and they usually explain why they chose a particular object to represent a certain person or situation. The tray may be seen as their life, their loss, their family, or whatever topic is the focus of that session (see Figure 10.4).

The advantage of this method is that it allows clients to project their own interpretations onto the objects themselves and this becomes part of the "process" of the tray. Both ways of working in the tray often help to slow the session down, especially when there is a lot of anxiety or intense emotion present. The "hands in the sand" method is very tactile for clients who need touch to stay "connected" to their emotions. The tray as metaphor method allows clients to be "outside" of the situation or relationships that are being represented while having an opportunity to focus directly upon them. Often, subtleties in the situations that are being represented in the tray may not be readily accessible for the client in typical talk therapy, and the sandtray seems to give expression to words, events, feelings, and experiences in a way that might otherwise have been difficult for the client to name or describe.

GROUP WORK

Talking with others who have experienced loss can help clients to navigate their grief with supportive others who may uniquely understand what they are feeling. Grief support groups offer acceptance, information, connection with others, and an outlet for those who are a little further along their path to help others who are new to the grieving process. Grief is often viewed as a wound of attachment—we lose someone to whom we have a significant attachment, and there is often a gaping hole and sense of emptiness that is left behind. Being able to share about these feelings with others who understand

FIGURE 10.4

The Sandtray as a Representation or Metaphor.

(a) In this tray, the client used the four objects across the middle to represent the four seasons because her husband had died— the gray rock was winter, the silk flower was spring, the shell was summer, and the broken red leaf was fall. Below the four objects represented her life before her husband died—a shell with a deep purple interior, a pink quartz heart, a seed pod, and feathers. Above the objects represented her life after her husband died—a dark piece of flat slate, a piece of wood that looked like a "woman who was crying," and a broken piece of dried wood "which is what my life feels like now." The client worked in this tray off and on for several sessions. (b) This tray was made by a mother whose child had died in a car accident. She brought some of the cards that she had received from her daughter's friends, a few dried flowers from the funeral, a candle, and a poem that was also written by one of her daughter's friends. After working with the sand in the "hands in the sand" mode, she lifted her hands out of the sand and noticed that the pattern looked like a butterfly. She placed the items around the tray and took this picture when she was done. She described feeling that her daughter would like what she had done and that in doing the sandtray work, she felt closer to her daughter's presence.

and empathize relieves some of the emptiness and may foster a sense of hope in clients who feel the despair of going through this process on their own. Grief support groups can decrease clients' sense of isolation, help to normalize the grieving process and the significance of the loss that has been experienced, and provide opportunities for bereaved individuals to find ways to cope with the complexities associated with a significant loss.

Most grief support groups function on a self-help model, but some are professionally facilitated by an individual who is a counselor or a professional helper. It is beyond the scope of this book to explore all the intricacies of grief support groups. We strongly suggest that you obtain a list of grief support group resources and referrals in your community for your clients, so that you can make informed suggestions to clients who may benefit from being involved in a grief support group. Often there are groups for particular types of loss experiences, such as the loss of a child, a suicide survivors group, widow/widower groups, and groups for various ages, such as specialized children's groups or groups for seniors. Online support groups may be a good resource to some clients as well, especially if transportation or child care responsibilities interfere with attendance at a regular face to face group. However, there are no guarantees regarding the quality of these groups and typically there is no form of accountability or monitoring of these sites on a regular basis.

CONCLUSION

In this chapter, we have described some possible therapeutic techniques and adjuncts that you might find helpful either for your work directly with bereaved individuals or for your consideration as a referral for certain clients. Please keep in mind that no technique or modality can ever replace the healing potential of the relationship with that exists between the client and the counselor. Sometimes, clients need the opportunity to see their experiences through a different lens or to be able to process their material in a way that defies words. We hope you will use the resources, suggestions, and exercises at the end of this chapter to explore some of these ideas more thoroughly.

Glossary of Terms

Clustering   a form of therapeutic writing that calls for brainstorming and drawing to make connections between feelings and events in a concise manner.

Internal family systems (IFS) model of therapy   it is based on an understanding that the personality exists as a system of parts to which compassionate curiosity may be brought in order to facilitate healing. The "parts" in this model may be understood to be autonomous aspects of the personality that have specific roles.

Linking objects   items that individuals associate with their loved one and to which significance is attached; They may serve as reminders, or as a means of feeling connected to the deceased loved one.

Metaphor   literary figure of speech that uses an image, story, or tangible thing to represent a less tangible thing or some intangible quality or idea.

Mindfulness practice   it includes learning to cultivate an intentional focus on the moment-to-moment experience as it is in the here and now, detached observation of thoughts, feelings, and sensations, and nonjudgmental acceptance of one's experience exactly as it is.

Narrative   the telling of one's life story in such a way as to draw meaning and coherence into difficult events and circumstances.

"Power therapies"   so named because of their ability to rapidly assist some clients who are paralyzed by traumatic images and material; refer to EMDR, TFT, and EFT.

Ritual   usually involves an action that is initiated on the part of the bereaved individual to give a symbolic expression to certain feelings or thoughts.

Questions and Activities for Reflection

1. Complete one of the narrative exercises for yourself.

   After you have completed the exercise, think about how you felt as you were doing it. If there is someone with whom you feel comfortable sharing the exercise, talk about it with that person and discuss between yourselves what it was like to complete the exercise that you chose. Was there anything surprising? What clients and contexts of counseling do you think might benefit from completing one of these exercises? As the counselor, how would you use these exercises with clients?

2. Awareness exercise (contributed by Derek Scott, BA, RSW).

   The only time that exists is the present moment, yet we tend to spend much time ruminating about the past, which only exists as memory, or the future, which is fantasy. This exercise is designed to begin the practice of paying attention to the moment. We may consider that there are three "zones" of awareness: external sensory (the five senses), internal sensory (feelings), and internal cognitive (thoughts). We tend to spend a lot of time in the cognitive space, with our minds "cluttered" by various thoughts, analyzing our experiences, and thinking about the past and the future instead of directly experiencing these things.

   This exercise is done with a partner. Find a quiet space without the possibility of interruption. Face your partner and take 5 minutes to share what you are aware of by saying, "Now I am aware. . . ." Then switch. As your partner is sharing with you, simply nod and offer nonverbal encouragement.

After you complete this exercise, share with your partner what it was like to do this exercise. What were you aware of? Was there laughter? If so, what was it about? Did you find yourself censoring anything? If so, do you know why? You can also use this exercise with clients after you know them well and you believe they can tolerate focused attention with you in this way. Can you think of client situations where this exercise might be helpful in a session?

3. Touch and sensation exercise (to explore mindful awareness).

   The purpose of this exercise is to introduce the element of being in the here and now and cultivating awareness with clients (for the counselor), and for clients (guided by the counselor).

   Raisin exploration. Take a raisin and hold it in your hand. Begin by looking at it carefully, as if you have never seen a raisin before. Notice its texture, color, and the surface. Pay attention to any thoughts and feelings you have about raisins as well—liking, disliking, self-consciousness about doing this exercise. Next, smell the raisin. Notice any sensations that arise in your mouth or body as you smell the raisin. Then, bring the raisin to your lips. Notice your arm moving to bring your hand to your mouth, and the anticipation of eating the raisin. Place the raisin on your tongue. Roll it over in your mouth to feel the texture on your tongue. Finally, chew the raisin slowly, noticing the actual taste of this one raisin. When you are ready to swallow, notice the impulse to swallow as it comes up. Tune into your thoughts as you swallow. Are you anticipating another raisin? Does your mind or body begin to anticipate more? What did you experience as you did this exercise? (taken from Kabat-Zinn, 1990, pp. 27–28).

4. Video Clips from YouTube and the IFS Model.

   The following Web sites describe and demonstrate the IFS model. The first link demonstrates the use of the IFS model with a bereavement-related issue. The second link provides more information and demonstrations of the model in various applications through video clips.

   http://www.youtube.com/watch?v=ybRi78VzWTk

   http://www.yourtherapist.org/www/ifs-videos/

   1. Can you identify the "parts" that arise during the sample session with a grieving client?

   2. What did you like/dislike about how this model works with clients?

   3. Can you think of some of your own managers, firefighters, and exiles? How do these interact within your own system?

5. **Personality Inventories and Self-Assessments.**

The following are links to some very popular self-assessments that explore typology and preferences in people. Choose one of the links and take the self-assessment. Once completed and you have the results, explore how that particular inventory describes individuals with your (or other) types. Does it make sense to you? Did you feel it was an accurate description? If you know of other individuals who would be willing to complete the same inventory, would you think that their results are accurate? How can these inventories be used in your work, both with yourself and with your clients?

Myers-Briggs Type Indicator: http://www.humanmetrics.com/cgi-win/JTypes2.asp

Keirsey Temperament Sorter: http://www.keirsey.com/sorter/instruments2.aspx?partid=0

Enneagram: http://www.enneagraminstitute.com/dis_sample_36.asp?discover

References

Ammann, R. (1991). *Healing and transformation in sandplay: Creative processes become visible*. La Salle, IL: Open Court Publishing.

Callahan, R. J., & Callahan, J. (1997). Thought field therapy: Aiding the bereavement process. In C. R. Figley, B. E. Bride, & N. Mazza (Eds.), *Death and trauma: The traumatology of grieving* (pp. 249–266). New York, NY: Taylor & Francis.

Castle, J., & Phillips, L. (2003). Grief rituals: Aspects that facilitate adjustment to bereavement. *Journal of Loss and Trauma, 8*, 41–71.

Commons, M. L. (2000). The power therapies: A proposed mechanism for their action and suggestions for future empirical validation. *Traumatology, 6*(2), 119–138.

Craig, G. (1995). *Emotional freedom techniques: The manual*. Sea Ranch, CA: Author.

Humphrey, K. (2009). *Counseling strategies for loss and grief*. Alexandria, VA: American Counseling Association.

Johanson, G. (2006). A survey of the use of mindfulness in psychotherapy. *Annals of the American Psychotherapy Association, 9*(2), 15–24.

Kabat-Zinn, J. (1990). *Full catastrophe living: Using the wisdom of your body and mind to face stress, pain, and illness*. New York, NY: Bantam.

Kalff, D. (2004). *Sandplay: A psychotherapeutic approach to the psyche*. Cloverdale, CA: Temenos Press.

Kalil, C. (1998). *Follow your true colors to the work you love*. Laguna Beach, CA: Author.

Keirsey, D. (1998). *Please understand me II: Temperament, character, intelligence*. Del Mar, CA: Prometheus Nemesis.

Kobler, K., Limbo, R., & Kavanaugh, K. (2007). Moments: The use of ritual in prenatal and pediatric death. *American Journal of Maternal Child Nursing, 32*(5), 288–295.

Kumar, S. (2005). *Grieving mindfully: A compassionate and spiritual guide to coping with loss*. Oakland, CA: New Harbinger.

Levine, S. (1989a). *Who dies? An investigation into conscious living and dying.* New York, NY: Anchor.

Levine, S. (1989b). *Healing into life and death.* New York, NY: Anchor.

Levine, S. (1989c). *Meetings at the edge: Dialogues with the grieving and the dying, the healing and the healed.* New York, NY: Anchor.

Levine, S. (1998). *A year to live: How to live this year as if it were your last.* New York, NY: Bell Tower.

Lewis, L., & Hoy, W. G. (2011). Bereavement rituals and the creation of legacy. In R. Neimeyer, D. Harris, H. Winokuer, & G. Thornton (Eds.), *Grief and bereavement in contemporary society: Bridging research and practice* (pp. 315–323). New York, NY: Routledge.

Lowenfeld, M. (1979). *The world technique.* London: Allen & Unwin.

McNally, R. J. (2001). Tertullian's motto and Callahan's method. *Journal of Clinical Psychology, 57*(10), 1171–1174.

Myers, I. B., McCaulley, M. H., Quenk, N. L., & Hammer, A. L. (1998). *MBTI manual: A guide to the development and use of the Myers Briggs type indicator* (3rd ed.). Mountain View, CA: Consulting Psychologists Press.

Neimeyer, R. A. (1999). Narrative strategies in grief therapy. *Journal of Constructivist Psychology, 12,* 65–85.

Neimeyer, R. A., Torres, C., & Smith, D. A. (2011). The virtual dream: Rewriting stories of loss and grief. *Death Studies, 35,* 646–672.

Parry, A. (1991). A universe of stories. *Family Process, 30*(1), 37–54.

Riso, D. (1996). *Personality types: Using the enneagram for self-discovery.* New York, NY: Houghton Mifflin.

Romanoff, B. D., & Terenzio, M. (1998). Rituals and the grieving process. *Death Studies, 22,* 697–711.

Romanoff, B. D., & Thompson, B. E. (2006). Meaning construction in palliative care: The use of narrative, ritual, and the expressive arts. *American Journal of Hospice & Palliative Medicine, 23*(4), 309–316.

Sagula, D., & Rice, K. G. (2004). The effectiveness of mindfulness training on the grieving process and emotional well-being of chronic pain patients. *Journal of Clinical Psychology in Medical Settings, 11*(4), 332–342.

Schwartz, R. C. (1995). *Internal family systems therapy.* New York, NY: Guilford Press.

Shapiro, F. (2001). *Eye movement desensitization and reprocessing: Basic principles, protocols, and procedures.* New York, NY: Guildford Press.

Solomon, R. M., & Rando, T. (2007). Utilization of EMDR in the treatment of grief and mourning. *Journal of EMDR Practice and Research, 1*(2), 109–117.

Solomon, R. M., & Shapiro, F. (1997). Eye movement desensitization and reprocessing: A therapeutic tool for trauma and grief. In C. R. Figley, B. E. Bride, & N. Mazza (Eds.), *Death and trauma: The traumatology of grieving* (pp. 231–247). New York, NY: Taylor & Francis.

Volkan, V. (1981). *Linking objects and linking phenomena: A study of the forms, symptoms, metapsychology, and therapy of complicated mourning.* New York, NY: International Universities Press.

CHAPTER 11

Ethical Issues in Grief Counseling Practice

*E*xploring ethical issues in grief counseling is more than taking a look at complex cases that involve intriguing or confounding issues for the practitioner. To be a safe clinician, and to form a professional relationship with a client that is real, but clearly defined in regard to expectations and boundaries, is the foundation of competency and integrity in this work. Ethics is not something that we "tack on" to our practice, but something that comes from the core of how we practice and the choices and decisions (both small and large) that we make in regard to our clients and our profession. Gamino and Ritter (2009) stated,

> Ethical practice of grief counseling means helping clients and their families while operating from an internalized code of conduct and adhering to the highest level of professional standards and mores. To do so, the grief counselor must start from a position of personal integrity and responsibility and then be aware of and follow ethics codes, statutory regulations, and case law that pertain to their realm of practice. (p. 1)

We form relationships with clients who are dynamic, and who engage our personal feelings and reflections. Clients entrust us with their deepest feelings, thoughts, dreams, and fears, which then places them in a position of vulnerability with us. This concept of trust is essential for understanding the context of the therapeutic relationship. Inherent in that trust is the dynamic of a power differential, where the therapist has the power to betray or abuse the trust of a client, with serious implications for how that trust and power are handled. The training and perceived expertise of the counselor, and the willingness of the client to choose to open to the process with the hopes of improvement, imbue the counselor with a great deal of power and authority, no matter how much the counselor may ascribe to an empowerment-based or egalitarian person-centered approach. Therapeutic relationships are unique because they exist for the benefit of the client. Many bereaved individuals are at a vulnerable place in their lives, and our adherence to ethical standards of practice ensures that this vulnerability will be respected and protected within the therapeutic relationship that is established.

In this chapter, we will explore some of the ethical issues that are pertinent to the counselor, the therapeutic relationship with clients, and the profession of grief counseling.

COUNSELOR ISSUES

The Shadow Side of Counseling

Many authors have written about what we would refer to as the "human" side of helping professionals, and how these human aspects of the counselor can affect the therapeutic relationship and the counselor's everyday decision making and interactions with clients. Egan (2002) wrote about the "shadow side" of the helping relationship, describing the most common flaws of counselors to be manifest in (a) lack of knowledge of ethical practice standards, (b) being unaware of personal biases toward specific types of individuals, which will have an impact upon interactions with certain clients, (c) lack of reflection upon the therapeutic process and recognition of when there is a problem in the therapeutic alliance, (d) lack of self-awareness in their thoughts and feelings about specific clients, (e) lack of transparency and disclosure about the helping process with clients, which keeps the counselor in an elevated status as one who possesses "secret knowledge" and promotes client dependency rather than independence, and (f) rigid adherence to a specific approach in counseling without a willingness to assess whether this approach is actually appropriate or effective with a client. Page (1999) described the "shadow" of the counselor as those darker aspects of the counselor's personality, role, and experiences that emerge in the context of working with clients that may potentially affect the client in a way that can be harmful.

Gamino and Ritter (2009) referred to the presence of "blind spots," where the counselor "can get in a hurry, skip an important step, make an erroneous assumption, overlook a conflict of interest, neglect to consider a consequence, or rationalize an action as good for the client when it is really the counselor's own interests that are being served" (p. 3). These lapses in awareness can be the source of a great deal of harm to a client, and so we once again emphasize the importance of regular supervision and self-reflection for the counselor to protect the interests of the client. Pope and Vasquez (2011) cite many examples where breaches of the client's trust may occur as a result of treating the therapeutic relationship too casually, or of not maintaining rigorous standards of ethical practice. These authors discuss common breaches in ethical practice owing to lack of self-awareness, failure to recognize the influence and importance of the innate power differential in the therapeutic setting, lack of application of codes of ethics to client interactions, and failure of counselors to engage in ongoing professional development and training to maintain competency in practice.

The influence and impact of the personal issues and needs of the counselor are discussed in more detail in a later chapter. However, it is important to keep in mind that most individuals who enter the profession of counseling typically enjoy being with people and they wish to help others. As a result, there is often a very strong inherent desire to be liked by others, to be seen as helpful by clients, and to be respected by colleagues in the field. The shadow side of these good intentions is that if they are not placed in their proper perspective, they have the potential to lead to unhealthy and potentially damaging patterns, such as avoidance of difficult topics with clients, use of their work with clients to try to impress others, allowing perfectionistic tendencies and unrealistic expectations to drive the process and take over the needs of their clients, and setting up situations that could contribute to the misuse of the client–counselor relationship to fulfill unmet personal and social needs.

Counselor Self-Awareness

In order to practice with competence, counselors must know themselves and be familiar with their own needs, feelings, thoughts, behaviors, and sensitivities. If you do not have this awareness of yourself, you will have difficulties separating out your personal needs and feelings from your client, which could result in harm to your client. Counselors who are not self-aware will not have an understanding of how they may influence clients in ways that are unhealthy or even manipulative (Page, 1999). Often, these counselors' nonverbal responses to clients convey bias, judgment, or discomfort. They may avoid particular topics or may attempt to control the session in ways that prevent the client from exploring necessary topics or material, resulting in the client essentially being manipulated by the unconscious needs of the counselor. Table 11.1 provides an overview of how counselor self-awareness or lack of awareness can affect the client.

TABLE 11.1

Self Awareness

(Used with permission from Shebib, 2003)

Counselors With Self-Awareness	Counselors Without Self-Awareness
Identify and label their personal feelings	Avoid or are unaware of their feelings
Know where their feelings end and those of their clients begin	Project personal feelings onto clients
Recognize and accept areas of vulnerability and unresolved issues	Respond inappropriately because unresolved problems interfere with their capacity to be objective
Understand personal values and their influence on the counseling relationship	React emotionally to their clients, but do not understand why or how
Recognize and manage internal dialogue	Unconsciously use clients to work out their own personal difficulties
Understand and control personal defense mechanisms	Remain blind to defensive reactions
Know when and how clients are reacting to their style	Behave nonassertively (using excessive caution, placating behavior, etc.) because they are unaware of the limiting effects of self-defeating thought
Realize how they influence outcomes	Remain unaware of how their behavior influences others
Modify behavior based on reactions of clients	Behave based on personal needs and style rather than in response to the needs and reactions of clients
Set professional goals based on knowledge of personal skill strengths and limitations	Avoid or limit goal setting because they are unaware of personal and professional needs

ISSUES RELATED TO THERAPEUTIC RELATIONSHIP

Boundaries

The relationship between the counselor and the client is unique, although there are similarities to other types of relationships. Because of the unique boundaries and purpose of the counseling relationship, the process of counseling should be discussed with clients as you begin your initial sessions together. It is important for you to be transparent with your clients in regard to the therapeutic relationship. Clients need to understand how the process works, what the expectations are of them, what they can expect from you, and how the relationship parameters are defined. We cannot always assume that a client knows what the counseling process entails; therefore, it is important that it be explained and discussed as you begin your work together. The therapeutic relationship is very complex, and sometimes it is the relationship itself that forms some of the material of the counseling process (Yalom, 2002). Keep in mind that no matter what theory of therapy to which you subscribe or how many tools or interventions you use with clients, the therapeutic relationship itself is of paramount importance. Think of the things a client needs to know at the beginning and how you would explain the process to a client. Here are some possible examples of what might be helpful:

> "I believe deeply that you are the one who knows what is best for you."
> "My role is to help you understand what you want more clearly."
> "This is what you can expect from me . . ." (time, attention, availability . . .)
> "What I would hope is that you . . ." (can try to be as open as possible, attend to yourself and your needs, let me know if something does not feel right as we work together, be honest with me about how you think things are going in our sessions . . .)

Clients need to be able to understand that this is a real relationship and that the feelings, thoughts, and reflections that you share with them are genuine and real as well. However, clients often feel some confusion about this aspect of counseling. Are you like a friend that they are paying for services? Are you like a teacher who is imparting knowledge? Are you like a parent who gives advice and will comment on their behavior? The therapeutic relationship differs from other relationships in regard to the following:

- Boundaries—the relationship occurs within the context of the session times and professional settings.
- Purpose—the therapeutic relationship exists for the benefit of the client rather than for the needs of both individuals within it.
- Compensation—there is usually payment of some type given to the counselor for this time.
- Goals—the client's needs and vulnerability guide the process, not the counselor's agenda.
- Structure—there is a set time and place for the relationship to occur.

Below are some comparisons between the counseling relationship and other types of relationships that the client may consider to be similar.

Similarities and differences with respect to a friendship or an intimate relationship:

- Clients may feel that the counseling relationship is an intimate one because they share deeply of themselves with the counselor and often feel a sense of closeness with the counselor that they may not have experienced in their other relationships.
- The counseling relationship is one-way, oriented toward the client's needs, and not two-sided, as would be expected in an intimate relationship.
- Advice is given in friendships and in intimate relationships, but not in the counseling relationship.
- The counselor's personal feelings and needs would be out in the open in a friendship or intimate relationship, but shared in very limited amounts with a client for the purpose of therapeutic self-disclosure for the client's interests and not the needs of the counselor.
- The therapeutic relationship involves expectations of confidentiality that are not explicit in a friendship or an intimate relationship.
- The professional relationship has an ending—the goal of counseling is to end the relationship, which is different from the goal of a friendship or of an intimate relationship.

Similarities and differences with respect to a parent–child relationship:

- It is similar in that the client is sometimes seeking guidance in the counseling setting.
- The differential in terms of power and the goal of allowing the client to no longer need you is similar to a parent; however, in the counseling relationship, the counselor tries to equalize the power and give control over to the client.
- The unconditional positive regard of a counselor is similar to a parent's love for a child.
- It differs in that there is no ongoing relationship after the client–counselor relationship ends.
- The feeling of safety is common in both relationships.
- The counselor often provides mirroring to a client in a similar way that a parent might; in so doing, the client is better able to see who she or he really is, especially in clients with very poor self-image and who have never had a chance to know themselves well.
- The client takes the lead in the counseling relationship; whereas in a parent–child relationship, the parent directs the child.

- We do not tell clients what to do and do not impose rules upon clients as a parent might with a child.
- The goal of counseling is to teach the client to parent himself or herself if there have been deficits or inadequate parenting in the client's past.
- Although the counselor's values are often explicitly stated in regard to the process, the counselor's personal values are not imparted to the client in the way they are by parents, as the goal is for the client to become aware of his or her own values and to be able to respond in ways that are congruent with these values rather than those of the counselor.

Similarities and differences with teacher–student relationship:

- Often imparting knowledge is an aspect of both relationships.
- Modeling is a form of teaching, which can also occur in counseling.
- The client is not being judged or graded by the counselor as a student might by a teacher; you cannot do it "wrong."
- In the counseling relationship, the client is seen as the expert in his or her life, not the counselor, whereas the teacher is seen as being the expert in a particular area that is being taught.
- In counseling, the topic is the client's life and feelings, not an extraneous subject.
- Both relationships are structured and have boundaries that are different from friendships.
- Boundaries around a teacher–student relationship are probably not as rigid as those in a counselor/client relationship.
- The teacher–student relationship can lead to collegial relationships later on; however, the counselor–client relationship is a distinct relationship that will not evolve into another type of relationship.

We believe it is very important to think about how the counseling relationship can be confusing to some clients, and to be prepared when clients misunderstand the boundaries and the unique structure of the counseling sessions. A client may not understand why you do not accept his or her invitation to attend a social function, or may mistakenly believe that the intimacy of the counseling relationship indicates that your relationship is also one of friendship or another type of relationship. Because the counseling relationship involves a power differential, no matter whether the counselor attempts to equalize the power, there is the potential for abuse of that power, with the potential for harm to the client. The role of a counselor is one that involves a sacred trust, with clients willingly sharing their deepest selves and most personal vulnerability. This vulnerability and openness must be protected and safeguarded by the counselor.

Confidentiality

Probably one of the most important aspects of the counseling relationship is the trust that is established with the client through the knowledge that what is shared with the counselor will not be repeated to another person outside of the session. Because most clients are much more accustomed to having people share information with them and about them in everyday encounters, it is important to make the understanding and limitations of confidentiality explicit from the very beginning of the sessions. Essentially, confidentiality means that what is discussed within the confines of the session stays there—with the counselor. Unless you explain the nature of confidentiality, clients will often assume that you will share their information with your partner, your associates, or with others, and that assumption may limit their ability to share freely with you and to trust you with their deepest feelings and thoughts. Thus, it is important that you spell out specifically what confidentiality means, and what the limits of that confidentiality may be. For example, in a first session, we often begin by asking clients if they have any questions about us or how we work in our practices. After these questions have been answered, we will then describe that the counseling relationship is one that involves confidentiality, which means that what you say here will stay here and will not be shared with anyone outside of this room, with the following exceptions:

1. You ask me to share information with another professional, and you specify in writing what information is to be shared, with whom, and in what context.
2. I, or my records, are subpoenaed by a court of law for court proceedings.
3. If I have concerns for your safety or the immediate safety of another person that might involve life-threatening harm, I will have to share information about you for your protection or the protection of another person.
4. If in the process of your sharing I am given information that causes concern that a child under the age of 16 is in a situation where there is abuse or neglect, I am required to report these concerns to child welfare.

All jurisdictions in North America have legislation that requires counselors to report suspicions of child abuse and neglect to the appropriate authorities. We will also sometimes discuss how clients may wish to handle a scenario if they see us in a public place, offering that we would let the client decide if he or she wishes to acknowledge us and introduce us to others in their presence. Another aspect of confidentiality is the disclosure of supervision and how that is sought by the counselor. You do not need to identify the individual who functions as your clinical supervisor, but you may tell the client that you regularly seek supervision to discuss issues that occur in your practice where you feel it is best to obtain support, additional resources, and clinical recommendations. You should clarify that you do not share the client's name or identifying information with your supervisor, and that the supervisor is bound by the same constraints of confidentiality as you. Another important caveat to this discussion is the recognition that clients are not bound to the same adherence to confidentiality as the counselor. Thus, if you choose to self-disclose to a client because you believe that this disclosure may be beneficial to the client in some way, be aware that the client is not bound to confidentiality with you.

One additional aspect of confidentiality is the disclosure of how you keep your records, and who has access to these records/files. In most situations, you would be the only person who would have access to files, and they should be kept in a locked drawer. However, if you work on a team where other individuals have access to any information that you have written, or if you discuss client cases with other team members, then the client has a right to know that. Another place where confidentiality may become an issue is with phone and e-mail contact. Clients should be asked if they are comfortable with the counselor leaving a voice message for them if there is a need for contact or if they are returning a call made by a client, as not all clients disclose that they are seeing a counselor to other members of the household. In addition, if clients use e-mail to contact the counselor, then the counselor must use a secure e-mail address that is private and for which the counselor is the only one with the password to the e-mail account. Once again, clients should be asked if their e-mail address is private, and if they are comfortable with the counselor sending a reply to that e-mail account. Finally, the setting where the counseling sessions occur must provide privacy and be soundproof so that others who are outside the room where you are meeting with the client cannot hear what is being said. Calls to clients should not be returned in an area where others may overhear the conversations, and if there is any possibility that a client who is leaving your office may be familiar to another client in your waiting area, either provide an alternate exit for the client or adjust the scheduling of appointments so that these two clients

TABLE 11.2

Confidentiality Guidelines

- Explain what is meant by confidentiality in the counseling setting, including the limits of confidentiality. Ask clients about specific instances where confidentiality may be an issue for them (i.e., seeing the client at a public event, leaving phone messages, and replying to e-mail messages).
- Be aware of relevant legal statutes that may limit confidentiality (such as child abuse reporting and necessity of disclosure in the event of potential imminent harm to the client or another individual).
- Be familiar with codes of ethics in your professional association and adhere to these guidelines.
- Protect client records with secure filing systems and/or password protection on electronic files. Do not access phone messages or electronic messages in a place where they may be overheard or seen by others.
- Seek regular supervision with a trusted colleague or mentor in a private and formalized setting. Do not discuss client situations or information with anyone in a social gathering or in a public place.
- Ensure that the setting where you meet with clients is private and free from interruptions.
- Disclose to clients if you are working as a team with other professionals, and in that context, specify who will have access to information about them and what they share with you.

---

will not be placed in an awkward position of undesired disclosure. Table 11.2 provides a summary of confidentiality guidelines.

Many clients will describe complicating issues in their lives and in their relationships, such as secrets that they have long held close, situations that cause them embarrassment, or things they have said or done that cause them to feel a great deal of pain or discomfort. It is vitally important that the clients understand that you will not disclose these stories or situations to anyone else so that they will feel a sense of safety and trust in sharing such vulnerable material with you.

Dual Relationships

A dual relationship is one that involves both a counseling relationship and another type of relationship (i.e., friendship, business relationship, supervisory capacity, etc.). It places the client at risk by imposing another set of values that may not be congruent with the therapeutic relationship and where the needs of the client may not be foremost, which is one of the primary definitions of a therapeutic relationship. The client may be placed in a position of compromise with self-disclosure, negating the core conditions of safety and nonjudgment in the counseling relationship. In dual relationships, the counselor has a personal interest that may not be consistent with the client's interests. This alternate focus may lead to intended or unintended exploitation, harm, manipulation, or coercion of clients (Shebib, 2006). Although there are few specific guidelines in various codes of ethics in professional organizations and memberships, mostly all agree that any form of sexual contact between a client and a counselor is strictly prohibited and morally unethical, even after the client is no longer seeing the counselor for assistance.

The most common form of dual relationship that we encounter is that a former client may choose to take a course in which we are an instructor. Because the counseling relationship has revolved around a stance of nonjudgment and nonevaluation of the client's material, the immediate issue of duality is that the counselor is now placed in a position of having to evaluate a former client's learning, and that the instructor has very personal information about one student in the class that may place the client or the other members of the class at a disadvantage. In situations such as this, where no other faculty member is teaching the same course, we often meet with the student and suggest that another faculty member read and mark the assignments for that student, and we discuss concerns about the dual relationship to see what types of accommodation should be made for the client who is now a student.

Another relational conflict may arise if a counselor is asked to see another member of the same family, where disclosure by one member may compromise the therapeutic relationship that is established with the other family member(s). Some counselors may adamantly refuse to see members of the same family individually, whereas others may agree to do so, as long as there is an understanding between the family members regarding the sharing of common information. This can be a very tricky scenario to navigate, as even if the issue seems to be clearly identified by all the family members (such as the death of a family member), there are often secrets in families that are kept by members, and the counselor could be in a very difficult position of holding multiple confidences that are relevant to each of the clients who are being seen, without these individuals being aware of the counselor's knowledge. This "insider knowledge" could compromise the counselor's relationship with all of those individuals involved. For further reading about the complexities of dual relationships within therapeutic encounters, we refer readers to a book by Lynne Gabriel entitled *Speaking the Unspeakable: The Ethics of Dual Relationships in Counselling and Psychotherapy* (2005).

COMPETENCE IN GRIEF COUNSELING

We have stressed the importance of the counselor's self-awareness in working effectively and competently with clients. We now expand further upon the personal self-awareness of the counselor to include awareness of the ethical issues that may have an impact upon the profession of grief counseling. These issues include staying current with the research and literature in the field, knowing the limits of your scope of practice and training, and honoring the tangible limits that are present because of personal needs, family requirements, and physical demands. The following list was extracted from the codes of ethics for the Canadian Association of Social Workers (2005) and the Canadian Counseling and Psychotherapy Association (2007), and provides general guidelines for working with competence (Shebib, 2006):

1. Counselors should offer services that are within the limits of their professional competence, according to their level of education, training, and professional standards. Competent counselors know that the support and assistance of other professionals is necessary for issues that exceed their expertise and training.
2. Counselors should monitor their work and seek supervision, training, or consultation in order to evaluate their effectiveness. Continued professional development should be pursued in order to increase competence and to remain current with best practices, research, and literature in the field.
3. Counselors should not work in specialized areas of practice without proper training and acquisition of the specialized body of knowledge for that area.
4. Counselors should seek to base their work and practice on accepted theory and empirical knowledge (see discussion below).
5. When access to other professionals is limited or unavailable, such as in rural settings or in centers where there are long waiting lists, the substitution of other services that are not equal in comparison with access to a professional in a formal setting is not a viable or sound practice.
6. Counselors need to know when particular topics or problems are sensitive or delicate for clients. They need to be aware of when their clients' problems are similar to sensitive or difficult areas in their own lives. This knowledge is of paramount importance for counselors to know when to seek consultation or supervision, when to refer clients to another counselor, and when to enter counseling

to address their own needs. Clients have a right to expect that their counselor's judgment and abilities to work with them will not be impaired by unresolved personal problems or issues.

Issues that may interfere with counselors adhering to these guidelines can include lack of time or lack of available programs to engage in professional development that would enable the counselor to remain current in best practices, heavy caseloads that do not provide an opportunity to reflect upon counselor–client interactions and to have regular access to supervision and consultation, and inadequate training or preparation to work with a specific client or clientele.

In many of the previous chapters, we have discussed newer ways of thinking about grief and bereavement, based upon current literature and research. In her review of counselor practices, Breen (2010–2011) found that the majority of the grief counselors whom she interviewed based their practices on theories and research that were outdated and no longer considered relevant to the profession. Indeed, in the past 5 years alone, the amount of research and discussion on the topical areas of complicated grief, the efficacy of grief counseling, and the diversity of grief responses has dramatically changed what would have been considered sound and competent practice in the specialized area of grief counseling in the past. Although we think it is probably not feasible to always be able to provide evidence-based practice in a field where many of the constructs involved are not concrete and readily measured, it is unethical to continue to practice with clients in a way that may have been cautioned as potentially harmful in research that has been reported with this clientele. The only way to know how to identify when clients need additional resources and whether your work with clients is truly from a place of best practices is to remain current in the field, within both domains of counseling practice and bereavement research and theory.

CONCLUSION

Ethical practice as a grief counselor involves an ongoing commitment to self-awareness, self-care, and professional development in the areas of counseling and bereavement. It is important to protect the trust that our clients place in us, and to ensure sound and competent practice by our adherence to published ethical standards and guidelines in our professional association(s). Staying current in the research and literature in the field also helps to ensure that we engage in best practices when we meet with the clients who seek our support, as competency in ethical practice includes knowing what your scope of practice will include, being aware of effective interventions, and the ability to recognize when a client requires the skill of someone with different training or more experience with a particular issue. In essence, ethical practice includes both diligence and humility in the profession, in addition to the ability to be transparent with oneself as both a person and a practitioner.

Glossary of Terms

Boundaries   limits or guidelines that define the counseling relationship and denote the limits of acceptability in the therapeutic relationship. They outline the expectations in the therapeutic space and mark the point beyond which neither party is expected to go.

Competence in counseling   includes accurate representation regarding the limits of the scope of practice, involvement in ongoing and continuing education in the field, maintenance of accurate knowledge and expertise in practice, and the ability to address personal issues that could potentially hinder effectiveness.

Confidentiality   the ethical principle or legal right that a physician or other health professional will hold secret all information relating to a patient, unless the patient gives consent permitting disclosure; confidentiality can be broken in a number of circumstances including consent from the client, if the information is already in the public domain, when referring (with the client's consent), when the interest to protect another outweighs confidentiality, prevention of terrorism, instruction by a court, or during supervision.

Dual relationship   one that involves both a counseling relationship and another type of relationship (i.e., friendship, business relationship, supervisory capacity, etc.)

Questions for Reflection

1. Joanne, a client who comes to talk with you after the loss of her husband from a traumatic accident, discloses in her first session with you that not only did her husband die from a very tragic incident, but that his best friend, Steve, also died in this incident. When she tells you his best friend's name, you recognize that Steve was a client of yours in the previous year, and you did not know he had died. Joanne then proceeds to tell you that she knew that you had seen Steve for counseling, and that he spoke of you often to her husband. She then begins to ask you questions about Steve and details regarding his life and his relationship to her husband. How would you respond to this scenario?

2. You have been seeing Carol for about 6 months to help her as she grieves the loss of her son 2 years ago. Carol has good supports in place, and she is feeling better, although she still feels deep grief frequently. She

tells you that she thinks she is ready to finish her sessions with you. You review your time together and Carol shares that your assistance has been invaluable to her being able to get through this time, but she also says that she will miss the ability to keep in touch with you, and she asks if you could meet her for coffee sometime to catch up. How would you respond?

3. Think of the following personal needs that many people who are counselors have. As a counselor, look at each of these needs and think of how each could be potentially harmful to your clients:

   a. Need to be liked and to be helpful
   b. Need for status, prestige, or recognition from others
   c. Need for control
   d. Perfectionism
   e. Need for relationships/need for connection with others

4. Use the ethical guidelines that were posted in this chapter to discuss the following situations:

   a. A client who has been seeing you after the death of his wife asks you to talk to his adult daughter when he begins dating someone.
   b. You have just had a very difficult session with a client who is very depressed and angry. He directs some of his anger at you, saying that you really do not care about him and that you just see him because you are being paid to do so. After the session, you go into the lunchroom of the counseling center where you work. One of your colleagues is eating her lunch, and when she sees you says, "Wow, you look awful. What just happened in there?" How should you respond?
   c. Your client asks if you are in a relationship.
   d. You are invited by a friend to a dinner party. When you arrive, you are introduced to the other guests, including a man who is your client. How would you handle this situation?
   e. As your last client of the day leaves your office, it begins to rain and thunder. You know that she does not have a car and that she will be walking for blocks in the pouring rain to get to the bus stop. She asks if you could give her a ride to the bus stop. How would you respond?
   f. Your client shares a very moving story about her relationship with her deceased son. She is crying as she tells you this story, and you realize that you have tears spilling onto your cheeks as you listen.

5. The following questions are to help you to explore your values, beliefs, and sensitivities. You may want to work with a small group to discuss your answers to these questions.

   a. Do you think people are basically good or bad?
   b. What do you think motivates most people?

  c. Should people have the right to take their own lives?
  d. What kinds of clients would you like to work with the most (include information about age, gender, personality type, culture, religion, ethical background)?
  e. What kinds of people do you find most problematic for you personally?
  f. When you die, how would you most like to be remembered?
  g. Are some religions better than others?
  h. When should a counselor discuss religion with a client?
  i. Do you often feel responsible for the feelings, thoughts, or behavior of others?
  j. Imagine that you are a client. What would your counselor need to know about you in order to work effectively with you?

6. Write a two-page summary that answers the question "Who am I?"

References

Breen, L. J. (2010–2011). Professionals' experience of grief counseling: Implications for bridging the gap between research and practice. *Omega, 62*(3), 285–303.

Canadian Association of Social Workers. (2005). *Code of ethics.* Retrieved May 27, 2011, from http://www.casw-acts.ca/practice/codeofethics_e.pdf

Canadian Counseling and Psychotherapy Association. (2007). *Code of ethics.* Retrieved May 27, 2011, from http://www.ccacc.ca/documents/CodeofEthics_en_new.pdf

Egan, G. (2002). *The skilled helper: A problem-management and opportunity-development approach to helping* (7th ed.). Pacific Grove, CA: Brooks/Cole.

Gabriel, L. (2005). *Speaking the unspeakable: The ethics of dual relationships in counseling and psychotherapy.* London, UK: Routledge.

Gamino, L. A., & Ritter, R. H. (2009). *Ethical practice in grief counseling.* New York, NY: Springer Publishing Company.

Page, S. (1999). *The shadow and the counsellor: Working with the darker aspects of the person, role and profession.* New York, NY: Routledge.

Pope, K. S., & Vasquez, M. J. T. (2011). *Ethics in psychotherapy and counseling: A practical guide* (4th ed.). Hoboken, NJ: Wiley & Sons.

Shebib, B. (2003). *Choices: Interviewing and counselling skills for Canadians.* Toronto, ON: Pearson.

Shebib, B. (2006). *Choices: Interviewing and counselling skills for Canadians* (2nd ed.). Toronto, ON: Prentice Hall.

Yalom, I. R. (2002). *The gift of therapy: An open letter to a new generation of therapists and their patients.* New York, NY: HarperCollins.

CHAPTER *12*

Caregiver Issues for Grief Counselors

*E*very form of helping and caring is accompanied by its own unique emotional burden. For counselors, not only is caring a motivation or desire, but it is also a requirement in order to work effectively with clients. In essence, a counselor's livelihood is dependent upon his or her ability to profoundly engage with this capacity for caring and empathy without losing these abilities along the way. Grief counselors are especially prone to the accumulation of occupational stress and subsequent loss of their caring capacity on account of continually witnessing people's deep pain and despair, hearing clients' stories that highlight the unfairness of life events, repeatedly being exposed to the traumatic images and material that clients share, and the needs of their clients to process intense images and emotions with them. An additional drawback to the counseling profession is isolation. Even though you may be seeing clients all day, there is often a sense of seclusion that counselors describe in their work, as contact with other clinicians and colleagues is often limited by differing work schedules and the fact that most of the work occurs behind a closed door in private with your clients.

To many counselors, the "work" of counseling is a natural extension of who they are. In addition to typically being highly empathic and caring, most grief counselors closely identify with the choice to work in such an intense field. People who are drawn to grief counseling are usually not foreigners to the experience of loss and personal pain, and their desire to do this type of work is often a result of experiencing their own personal losses. Thus, it may be impossible to separate the person who is the grief counselor from the profession of counseling. This unique blending of who you are with what you do can be incredibly rewarding. However, it can also have unique drawbacks, as being so highly identified with your work can lead to difficulties with boundaries, a strong need to be validated in your work in order to feel validated as a person, and difficulties with balance in other areas of life if those other parts of your life are not consciously cultivated. Implicit in this statement is that some counselors will attach great value to their caring role, and when this role is impaired by stress or when there is frustration with one's work environment, significant damage can occur to the counselor's self-esteem and sense of meaning in the world.

SOURCES OF OCCUPATIONAL STRESS

In a study by Osipow, Doty, and Spokane (1985), three different dimensions were identified in the occupational stress of those engaged in helping professions:

1. internal stressors, including the internalized attitudes toward work and how problems are perceived and interpreted by the individual;
2. external stressors, which include the individual's perception and experience of stress in the work environment itself; and
3. coping resources available to counter the effects of the occupational stresses, and the individual's ability to draw upon these inner resources at various times.

Internal Stressors

Stresses that come from internalized sources may be the most difficult to identify, as they are often not readily apparent, are often not seen as problematic by the person, and the counselor may not necessarily be aware of their presence and influence upon his or her choices and experiences. Some of the more common internal stressors for counselors include having unrealistic expectations of themselves, or a need for this type of work to provide completion of unfinished business from the past. In grief counseling especially, a history of significant losses, personal death experiences, a high degree of emotional investment in clients without an opportunity to have time to pull back and be replenished, and feelings of powerlessness and lack of control in regard to life events can take a big toll over time. Caregivers also may struggle with self-induced stress, which can include tendencies toward perfectionism, fear of failure, and the need for approval. Counselors' needs for success and approval in the client setting may interfere with their being totally present and attentive to the needs of their clients. These needs are often manifest in the counselor having difficulties with boundaries. Signs that the counselor's needs are driving the process rather than the client's may include some of the following examples:

1. Excessive self-disclosure on the part of the professional caregiver, including detailed discussions of the counselor's personal problems or aspects of intimate life.
2. Beliefs in the indispensability of the counselor to the client that are perpetuated by the counselor.
3. Encouraging personal communication and dependence by the client upon the counselor, including the counselor giving out personal information.
4. Repeated or lengthy calls to clients outside of the session times.
5. Giving preferential treatment to a client to the detriment of others.
6. Buying gifts for or accepting gifts from clients that are more than token or symbolic gestures.
7. Lending money or personal belongings to clients.
8. Flirtatious behavior with a client or a member of the client's family.
9. Failure to seek supervision when a boundary has been crossed or is being "skirted" by the counselor (Sheets, 1999; Taylor, 1998; Wogrin, 2007).

It is these often unspoken, but very real issues that can cause the counselor to alienate himself or herself from others and not receive the needed peer support or supervision to ensure that the counselor's needs do not usurp the needs of the client or take advantage of a client's vulnerability.

Herman (1992) discussed the problem of unrealistic expectations in counselors, calling them "narcissistic snares." The most common snares include the aspiration and expectation of the counselor to heal all, to know all, and to love all. In addition, she discussed the concept of traumatic countertransference, where the counselor can become overwhelmed by bearing witness to the client's intense emotional experiences. She stated that any person who thinks he or she can work with people who have undergone traumatic experiences without having a good support system and time for personal care is setting up a very unrealistic scenario for doing this type of work over the long term.

Counselor self-awareness is a key component of the work of grief counseling. In fact, we think self-awareness and self-care are professional competencies that good counselors must cultivate and practice on a regular basis. Think about why you wanted to do this type of work. What draws you to this field? We mentioned earlier that the field of grief counseling tends to attract people with significant life losses and/or death experiences to enter into practice as the *wounded healer*, which can be a very powerful and effective place from which to work with the bereaved (Nouwen, 1996). However, it is important for counseling professionals to have examined the impact of the wounds from significant loss events and to experience a sense of healing from these wounds before attempting to participate in another individual's healing process. We have all known individuals who mean well and who truly wish to help others in this field, but who would be more aptly described as the "walking wounded" because their wounds are still readily apparent and need focused attention. Others, who take on the identity of being "damaged goods" as a result of their wounds, may continue to need others to feel better about themselves because of the overlay of shame onto their experience(s). These latter scenarios have the potential to bring harm upon potential clients, as it would be impossible to completely focus on the client's issues and experiences when wounds such as these in the counselor are still glaring and prominent (see Figure 12.1).

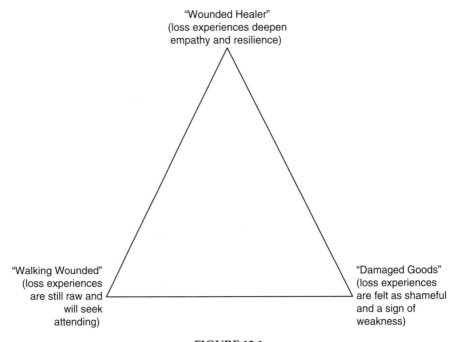

FIGURE 12.1
Differentiating How Personal Loss Experiences May Affect Counselors.

Worden (2009) stated that working with bereaved individuals may affect counselors by (a) making them more aware of their own losses, (b) causing them to be more "tuned in" to losses that they might fear (such as losing a child), and (c) heighten their awareness of personal mortality and existential anxiety. When working so closely with clients who are dealing with significant loss experiences, it is important for counselors to be very aware of their own loss history, and their attitudes about death and grief, and to be able to identify any topical areas that may present an especially difficult challenge because of personal experiences or vulnerabilities. This personal inventory for the counselor should also include whether the counselor can be fully present to the feelings of powerlessness, helplessness, and frustration that can arise in working with bereaved individuals, as we highlighted in an earlier chapter that you cannot take away the pain, you cannot bring back the loved one who died, and you cannot change what has happened. Counselors can be triggered into their personal pain when they witness the pain in their bereaved clients, and this discomfort can cause them to shut down emotionally, or, worse, attempt to shut the client down to stop this discomfort (Worden, 2009). Both Worden (2009) and Wogrin (2007) suggested that counselors complete a personal loss history (see Figure 12.2) and that they share this history with a friend or colleague to ensure that there are no "lurking shadows" that may impede their ability to work effectively with bereaved clients.

Ask yourself the following questions. Then take the time to review your responses with a trusted friend or colleague. Think about the ways that these losses and your responses to them might affect your interactions with bereaved clients or clients who are struggling with loss issues.

1. Complete a loss line of all the losses that you have had in your life (death and non-death related).
2. What are the most significant losses that you have experienced? How are these losses more significant to you?
3. How did you react to these losses? Do you tend to have similar reactions to loss experiences?
4. How did the people around you react to these losses and to you during these times?
5. What have you learned about death, grief, and life from your experiences?
6. What are your religious or spiritual beliefs about death? How about life events?
7. What are your cultural beliefs and assumptions about the expressions of grief, especially in regard to feelings and social obligations?
8. Based upon your own experiences, what do you believe people typically need from others as they attempt to cope with grief and loss?

FIGURE 12.2
Elements of a Personal Loss History.

External Stresses

Sources of stress that are external to the counselor can have a very big impact upon the counselor's effectiveness and ability to be fully present with clients. Some of the more common external stressors include the high demands placed upon individuals to see clients expeditiously even when their schedule is full, unrealistic expectations of the workload for counselors (especially when these counselors are in institutional and agency settings), limited or inadequate resources of clients to be able to afford counseling, and limited professional support and awareness of the intensity of the work by other professionals (Wogrin, 2007). On a more practical level, counselors in private practice often face the realities of the ebb and flow of people's lives, schedules, and financial reserves, which can lead to a wide fluctuation in income from month to month, causing difficulties in budgeting time and resources consistently. Choosing to practice in an agency or institutional environment may offer greater financial stability, but with a trade-off of the ability to have control over your time, schedule, and workload.

In her study of palliative care staff, Vachon (2004) found that the main sources of stress for caregivers were unrealistic workloads, low consideration of the input of caregivers in decision making, and little time for staff to offer support to each other. Previously, Vachon (1987) noted that much of the stress experienced by caregivers who worked with this population was related to their work environments and the unrealistic occupational expectations they felt from supervisors and administration rather than their work with individuals and family members who were terminally ill or bereaved.

Working environments that create a sense of depersonalization, demoralization, and moral distress can deeply challenge the assumptive world of those who work in such an atmosphere. In essence, work situations where there are unrealistic demands and expectations such as these can lead counselors to question the reasons why they entered this profession, whether the work they do really has any meaning or purpose, and whether they really do help others or not. It is almost impossible to be person-centered in your counseling practice if you, the counselor, are being objectified in the environment where you practice.

Coping and Internal Resources

The concept of coping implies some attempt at adaptation, either by the ability to reappraise stressful or negative experiences in some way or by reintroducing aspects of benevolence, meaning, and self-worth into situations that may otherwise challenge the existence of these values to an individual. Corr (2002) emphasized that coping is seen as a process of attempting to deal with challenges to one's assumptive world and situations that are perceived by the individual as stressful or even threatening, although coping strategies may or may not be successful. Perhaps the most important point to make about coping strategies in stressful work environments is the ability of the counselor to (a) identify the source of the stress, (b) explore if there is anything that can be done to either eliminate the stress or to change one's relationship to the stress, and (c) know when a situation has reached "critical mass," where ongoing attempts to grapple with a situation that is draining precious internal resources will eventually deplete the counselor of his or her ability to work competently and with a sense of integrity.

The ability to clarify how to respond to a stressful work environment requires the counselor to be comfortable recognizing when personal limits can be pushed and expanded, yet to also be realistic in regard to personal limits that should not be compromised. The difficulty here is that the longer you are exposed to ongoing stress and pressure in a situation, the more exhaustion you will experience, and this exhaustion can have a profound impact upon your ability to decide how you need to respond to the ongoing and significant stress in the work environment. Thus, a vicious cycle can be set up where you are chronically exposed to stress and become so depleted that you lose your ability to see yourself and the situation clearly, lessening your ability to know how to respond in a way that is congruent with your original intentions and values. Losing yourself in this way only adds more suffering to a stressful situation; thus, it is important to know yourself, that you are able to discuss issues and concerns with colleagues who are not in the same environment, and that you maintain a healthy and realistic view of your expectations of yourself and your workplace.

SPECIFIC MANIFESTATIONS OF OCCUPATIONAL STRESS

Many counselors enter the field with very good, but idealistic hopes about helping others and being successful in their chosen profession. Very few would probably even consider the possibility that they could experience negative repercussions from doing work that they have envisioned as highly rewarding. In fact, many individuals consider their profession of counseling as something akin to a "calling," which implies that a high degree of investment and sacrifice are expected as part of being a good counselor (Yalom, 2003). This desire to help others and to be so highly identified with the profession is both laudable and concerning, as a high degree of commitment and a deep capacity for empathy usually allow the counselor to be effective with clients, but these same attributes can set up the counselor for unique forms of personal harm that are insidious in nature. In this section, we will explore how exposure to certain stressful situations in counseling can deeply affect the assumptive world of the counselor, with the potential to harm the counselor personally and professionally. We will specifically discuss burnout and secondary traumatization (sometimes referred to as compassion fatigue).

Burnout occurs as a result of cumulative and ongoing emotional drain, trauma, and disappointments associated with an imbalance between the counselor's resources and the demands (both internal and external) placed upon him or her. It is seen as an evolutionary, cumulative process that starts with this imbalance and progresses to chronic emotional strain and exhaustion, depersonalization, and a sense of reduced personal accomplishment and satisfaction. The counselor who experiences burnout typically begins to cope with the emotional overload by distancing himself or herself from those who need help in order to feel more protected emotionally. What eventually happens is that the counselor can end up being and doing the very opposite of his or her primary motivation for entering the profession in the first place, and a devastating form of indifference and loss of human warmth begins to preside where there used to be compassion and concern. In addition, there is often personal shame and fear of others' judgment for this change in attitude to have occurred, which may prevent the counselor from being able to reach out and get the support and care that he or she needs from others. An unrelenting cycle can become established where the needs and expectations that the counselor has for himself or herself are added upon by the needs and demands of clients and/or the work environment, within a vacuum of resources for the counselor's renewal and energy, triggering the counselor to "try harder" to overcome the obstacles alone, but this effort only results in further, deeper depletion of the limited resources that are present.

Burnout is a state of physical, emotional, and mental exhaustion. The symptoms are caused by the stress that caring professionals experience in their careers, which is cumulative and often predictable (Maslach, 1982). It tends to be high when professionals experience a low level of control over decisions regarding how they will provide care, whether it is because of autocratic/bureaucratic factors, lack of input into how their workload and responsibilities are assigned, or being given more responsibility or a higher work volume than a person feels is possible to handle (Maslach, 1982). Recognizing and addressing burnout may involve looking at both internal and external factors. Professionals who are passionately devoted to their work often have a strong desire to be successful, and feelings of repeated disappointment or inadequacy may foster high stress and burnout. What is more common is an interaction between these factors, especially when high workload demands are in conflict with the time requirements and needs of people who are in emotional pain and crisis (Wogrin, 2007).

Secondary traumatization (also sometimes referred to as *vicarious traumatization* or *compassion fatigue*) refers to a state of tension and preoccupation with the individual or cumulative trauma of clients (Figley, 1995). Ironically, it is those counselors who have the greatest capacity for feeling and expressing empathy who tend to be at highest risk for compassion fatigue. Professional work that is focused on the emotional suffering of clients can include the counselor being exposed to information that is deeply troubling, which can also include absorbing suffering (Figley, 1995). In addition, the "work" of counseling involves the opening of one's self to another, which could increase the level of vulnerability of the counselor as he or she opens to the pain and suffering of others (Johnson, 1992).

The variety of symptoms associated with compassion fatigue include reexperiencing the client's story in a way that is intrusive, personally traumatizing, or overwhelming, a feeling of dread when faced with working with certain people, difficulty separating work from personal life, and guilt for being free of pain or suffering. Secondary traumatization implies a physical, emotional, and spiritual exhaustion with a decline in the ability to experience joy as the body becomes exhausted. Those who experience secondary traumatization may experience hopelessness, blame, anger, physical fatigue, and drug abuse. They may feel irritable and have great difficulty with sleep. Lack of sleep, along with the other symptoms, may put not only their job but also their client's well-being in jeopardy. Counselors who experience secondary traumatization are at a higher risk for depression, anxiety disorders, avoidance, and leaving the profession (Figley, 1999).

The type of stress encountered with secondary traumatization is different from what is experienced in burnout in that it is a result of vicariously experiencing the pain and trauma that your clients may share with you. Although secondary traumatization is detrimental to personal and professional functioning, it is preventable. If the counselor is highly self-aware, he or she will know when a client has shared something that is personally challenging or that leads to feelings of helplessness, hopelessness, and/or powerlessness. At these times, if the counselor readily addresses what has been taken in from the client and can process the material expeditiously with a supervisor or a trusted peer, the traumatic overlay is much less likely to occur.

SELF-CARE AS A PROFESSIONAL COMPETENCY

As our most important asset as counselors is our ability to care and to share in human compassion, it is of vital importance that these aspects of ourselves be nurtured, guarded, and protected so they will be available when we want and need them in our lives, both professionally and personally. We write this chapter with the assumption that in order for self-care to have any benefit, it must be recognized as a professional competency for effective counseling practice. It is not an option or something that you do when you have time. In the helping professions, there is always the need to establish a functional balance between taking care of others and taking care of self. Others' needs tend be apparent, insistent, and pressing and can easily overshadow the needs of the self. Rigorous self-awareness practices encourage the balance to remain level and may prevent the onset of burnout, secondary traumatization, and/or debilitating numbing/flooding (Pomeroy & Garcia, 2009).

Self-care for counselors and the regular seeking of peer support are imperative when your everyday practice involves an intense profession. Helping others to help themselves requires that the counselor accept his or her own needs as well as the needs of others. The greatest resource a counselor has is the ability to relate on a human level with his or her clients. In order to do this, the counselor must be comfortable with his or her own "humanness," which includes having needs and recognizing limitations. In fact, many counselors would say that the degree to which we take care of ourselves often reflects directly on our ability to foster the well-being of our clients. Preventing burnout requires that the counselor is self-aware of his or her own needs and is proactive in taking care of these needs in a healthy and constructive way. Unrealistic expectations, unmet needs, unfinished business, and the "need to be needed" must be addressed in an accepting and open way that allows the caregiver a chance to explore his or her own motivations and wounding in order to come to a place of healing and balance. Counselors need to cultivate a personal philosophy that will allow empathetic involvement with others while maintaining individuality and clear boundaries between the needs of self and the needs of others.

Professional peer support groups are an excellent resource for helping professionals to provide a place for the development of self-awareness, self-care, and interactions with others who are like-minded and share similar values. In one study of counselors, those who reported high occupational stress had lower levels of self-care and peer support than those who reported lower levels of stress (Sowa, May, & Miles, 1994). Being engaged in peer support with other clinicians counteracts the isolation and alienation that can occur from providing care to clients, and it also provides a place to receive much needed support and validation. Our society values the highly individualistic, self-sufficient "superman/superwoman" image. However, this image is completely unrealistic and denies our human need to both give and receive from others. Counselors must be able to see that being able to find support and receive it from others is in itself a strength that can be cultivated in the presence of a supportive network. Counselors also need to be able to find supportive persons in their lives who will allow them to ventilate feelings, share frustrations, find successful coping strategies, and observe positive role models in order to become empowered providers. The following are guidelines for counselors to assist them in engaging in reflective practice with necessary support and self-care strategies:

1. Recognize and honor your limitations; you are a human being whose capacity to care for others hinges upon your ability to care for yourself.
2. Have a place to go for support and debriefing that will respect the confidentiality of you and your clients.
3. Have regular supervision with someone who is experienced in this type of work.
4. Cultivate self-awareness of your issues, feelings, and values so that you will be able to separate them from those of clients.
5. Take advantage of professional development opportunities, such as workshops, courses, reading journals, and new materials.
6. Align yourself with a professional code of ethics and standards of practice within a counseling-related field.
7. Monitor your own health and well-being. Develop your private world in a way that is nurturing to you.
8. Give yourself permission to not always work well with everyone.
9. Monitor your working hours and time spent focused on client-related topics.
10. Recognize your own philosophy of life and how that impacts your work as a counselor.
11. Be aware of the unique signals from your body that may indicate you need to attend to work-related stress, such as disturbed sleeping patterns, changes in eating patterns, bodily aches and pains, and frequent illnesses that may indicate your immune system is being challenged.

CONCLUSION

Counselors are professionals who are also human beings. The profession of counseling relies upon the ability of the individual counselor to nurture and cultivate a capacity to care and connect with clients empathically. Counselors who work primarily with individuals who have faced painful losses, traumatic events, and the death of loved ones will be exposed to levels of human suffering and pain that can profoundly affect them at a personal level. Professionalism in counseling does not mean that the counselor will not be touched by this suffering; rather, being a professional in this field means that you have developed effective ways to take care of yourself and to find necessary support to explore your responses to clients' pain. Self-awareness is a key component of being able to identify when you need to attend to your personal feelings so that these responses do not interfere with your clients' process. Protecting your capacity to care may also involve an honest appraisal of your professional working environment and its impact upon your ability to be fully present to yourself and your clients. Having proficiency with the body of knowledge and completing a rigorous training program in this field are both very important. However, these factors will be of benefit to the client only if the counselor is able to connect with the client in a meaningful way. The relationship that forms between the counselor and the client is often stated to be the most important aspect of this work. Thus, attending to the personal aspects of the counselor is of paramount importance to maintain competency in this profession.

Glossary of Terms

Burnout it occurs as a result of cumulative and ongoing emotional drain, trauma, and disappointments associated with an imbalance between the counselor's resources and the demands (both internal and external) placed upon him or her. Burnout is seen as an evolutionary, cumulative process.

Coping the process of attempting to deal with challenges to one's assumptive world and situations that are perceived by the individual as stressful or even threatening, although coping strategies may or may not be successful.

"Narcissistic snares" unrealistic expectations by counselors to heal all, know all, and to love all.

Secondary traumatization (also sometimes referred to as *vicarious traumatization* or *compassion fatigue*) a state of tension and preoccupation with the individual or cumulative trauma of clients.

Traumatic countertransference also called vicarious trauma, where the counselor can become overwhelmed by bearing witness to the client's intense emotional experiences.

Questions for Reflection

1. After reading through this material, allow yourself to think of the following questions. If you have a trusted peer or colleague, see if you can answer these questions and review your answers with each other.

    -   How would you know whether you are burned out or too involved in your work?
    -   What are appropriate boundaries with others in this work?
    -   How much of yourself do you share that is personal in the professional setting?
    -   Why are you doing this work? What are you getting from it or what is in it for you?
    -   If you are an "innate helper," have you explored what may be the reason for you to be this way?
    -   Does your work give you a sense of belongingness or a sense of meaning?
    -   What "feeds" you in your life?
    -   Are you able to attach comfortably at times and also detach comfortably when you need to do so?

2. The Professional Quality of Life Scale (see pp. 210–212 in this chapter) was developed to measure compassion fatigue, burnout, and compassion satisfaction (Stamm, 2005). Fill out the scale and then score it. What do you think about this scale and the items that are listed on it? Are there areas where you are aware that you may have some vulnerability as an individual who works with individuals facing death, loss, and grief on a regular basis?

3. Awareness exercise.

    The only time that exists is the present moment, yet we tend to spend much time ruminating about the past, which only exists as memory, or the future, which is fantasy. This exercise is designed to begin the practice of paying attention to the moment. We may consider that there are three "zones" of awareness: external sensory (the five senses), internal sensory (feelings), and internal cognitive (thoughts). We tend to spend a lot of time in the cognitive space, with our minds "cluttered" by various thoughts, analyzing our experiences, and thinking about the past and the future instead of directly experiencing these things.

    In pairs, face your partner and take five minutes to share what you are aware of by saying, "Now I am aware . . ." Then switch. As your partner is sharing with you, simply nod and offer nonverbal encouragement.

    Debrief: How was that to do? What were you aware of? Was there laughter? If so, what was it about? Did you find yourself censoring anything? If so, do you know why?

4. Meditation exercise.

Becoming aware of the present moment, close your eyes and drop into your body with your breath. Let any places of tension leave your body on the outbreath. Remember that the only place is here, the only time is now, and you are safe. The only expectation is that you breathe.

After a while, start to imagine or feel energy coming into the center of your chest on the in breath. As you experience this energy say to yourself, "I am loved." Now with your outbreath, imagine it leaving your body from your perineum and going straight into the earth. As this energy flows from your body say the words to yourself, "I belong." Maintain this gentle, deep relaxed breathing for 5 minutes.

Gradually return your attention to the room, what you notice from your senses, the thoughts scurrying across your mind. As you open your eyes and return to the room, write down your experience of this exercise. If you have a trusted peer or colleague, ask this person to also do this exercise and discuss your experience with each other.

References

Corr, C. A. (2002). Coping with challenges to assumptive worlds. In J. Kauffman (Ed.), *Loss of the assumptive world: A theory of traumatic loss* (pp. 127–138). New York, NY: Brunner-Routledge.

Figley, C. R. (1995). Compassion fatigue as secondary traumatic stress disorder: An overview. In C. R. Figley (Ed.), *Compassion fatigue: Coping with secondary traumatic stress disorder in those who treat the traumatized* (pp. 1–20). New York, NY: Brunner Routledge.

Figley, C. R. (1999). Compassion fatigue: Toward a new understanding of the costs of caring. In B. H. Stamm (Ed.), *Secondary traumatic stress: Self care issues for clinicians, researchers, and educators* (2nd ed., pp. 3–28). Lutherville, MD: Sidran Press.

Herman, J. (1992). *Trauma and recovery*. New York, NY: Basic Books.

Johnson, C. (1992). Coping with compassion fatigue: Taking care of one's self while taking care of others. *Nursing, 22,* 116–121.

Maslach, C. (1982). *Burnout: The cost of caring*. Englewood Cliffs, NJ: Prentice-Hall.

Nouwen, H. J. (1996). *Ministry and spirituality: Creative ministry, the wounded healer, reaching out*. New York, NY: Continuum.

Osipow, S. H., Doty, R. E., & Spokane, A. R. (1985). Occupational stress, strain, and coping across the life span. *Journal of Vocational Behavior, 27,* 98–108.

Pomeroy, E. C., & Garcia, R. B. (2009). *The grief assessment and intervention workbook: A strengths perspective*. Belmont, CA: Brooks/Cole.

Sheets, V. (1999). Professional interpersonal boundaries: A commentary. *Pediatric Nursing, 25,* 657.

Sowa, C. J., May, K. M., & Miles, S. G. (1994). Occupational stress within the counseling profession: Implications for counselor training. *Counselor Education and Supervision, 34*(1), 19–29.

Stamm, B. H. (2005). *The ProQOL manual: The Professional Quality of Life Scale: Compassion satisfaction, burnout, & compassion fatigue/secondary trauma scales.* Baltimore, MD: Sidran Press.

Taylor, P. B. (1998). Setting your boundaries. *Nursing, 28,* 56–67.

Vachon, M. L. (1987). *Occupational stress in the care of the critically ill, the dying, and the bereaved.* Washington, DC: Hemisphere.

Vachon, M. L. (2004). The stress of professional caregivers. In D. Doyle, G. Hanks, N. Cherny, & K. Calman (Eds.), *Oxford textbook of palliative care* (3rd ed., pp. 992–1004). New York, NY: Oxford University Press.

Wogrin, C. (2007). Professional issues and thanatology. In D. Balk, C. Wogrin, G. Thornton, & D. Meagher (Eds.), *Handbook of thanatology: The essential body of knowledge for the study of death, dying, and bereavement* (pp. 371–386). Chicago, IL: Association for Death Education and Counseling.

Worden, J. W. (2009). *Grief counseling and grief therapy: A handbook for the mental health practitioner* (4th ed.). New York, NY: Springer Publishing Company.

Yalom, I. R. (2003). *The gift of therapy: An open letter to a new generation of therapists and their patients.* New York, NY: Perennial.

(See Professional Quality of Life Scale starting on the next page)

PROFESSIONAL QUALITY OF LIFE SCALE (PROQOL)

COMPASSION SATISFACTION AND COMPASSION FATIGUE
(PROQOL) VERSION 5 (2009)

When you *[help]* people you have direct contact with their lives. As you may have found, your compassion for those you *[help]* can affect you in positive and negative ways. Below are some questions about your experiences, both positive and negative, as a *[helper]*. Consider each of the following questions about you and your current work situation. Select the number that honestly reflects how frequently you experienced these things in the <u>last 30 days</u>.

| 1=Never | 2=Rarely | 3=Sometimes | 4=Often | 5=Very Often |

_____ 1. I am happy.
_____ 2. I am preoccupied with more than one person I *[help]*.
_____ 3. I get satisfaction from being able to *[help]* people.
_____ 4. I feel connected to others.
_____ 5. I jump or am startled by unexpected sounds.
_____ 6. I feel invigorated after working with those I *[help]*.
_____ 7. I find it difficult to separate my personal life from my life as a *[helper]*.
_____ 8. I am not as productive at work because I am losing sleep over traumatic experiences of a person I *[help]*.
_____ 9. I think that I might have been affected by the traumatic stress of those I *[help]*.
_____ 10. I feel trapped by my job as a *[helper]*.
_____ 11. Because of my *[helping]*, I have felt "on edge" about various things.
_____ 12. I like my work as a *[helper]*.
_____ 13. I feel depressed because of the traumatic experiences of the people I *[help]*.
_____ 14. I feel as though I am experiencing the trauma of someone I have *[helped]*.
_____ 15. I have beliefs that sustain me.
_____ 16. I am pleased with how I am able to keep up with *[helping]* techniques and protocols.
_____ 17. I am the person I always wanted to be.
_____ 18. My work makes me feel satisfied.
_____ 19. I feel worn out because of my work as a *[helper]*.
_____ 20. I have happy thoughts and feelings about those I *[help]* and how I could help them.
_____ 21. I feel overwhelmed because my case [work] load seems endless.
_____ 22. I believe I can make a difference through my work.
_____ 23. I avoid certain activities or situations because they remind me of frightening experiences of the people I *[help]*.
_____ 24. I am proud of what I can do to *[help]*.
_____ 25. As a result of my *[helping]*, I have intrusive, frightening thoughts.
_____ 26. I feel "bogged down" by the system.
_____ 27. I have thoughts that I am a "success" as a *[helper]*.
_____ 28. I can't recall important parts of my work with trauma victims.
_____ 29. I am a very caring person.
_____ 30. I am happy that I chose to do this work.

Based on your responses, place your personal scores below. If you have any concerns, you should discuss them with a physical or mental health care professional.

Compassion Satisfaction _____

Compassion satisfaction is about the pleasure you derive from being able to do your work well. For example, you may feel like it is a pleasure to help others through your work. You may feel positively about your colleagues or your ability to contribute to the work setting or even the greater good of society. Higher scores on this scale represent a greater satisfaction related to your ability to be an effective caregiver in your job.

The average score is 50 (SD 10; alpha scale reliability .88). About 25% of people score higher than 57 and about 25% of people score below 43. If you are in the higher range, you probably derive a good deal of professional satisfaction from your position. If your scores are below 40, you may either find problems with your job, or there may be some other reason—for example, you might derive your satisfaction from activities other than your job.

Burnout_____

Most people have an intuitive idea of what burnout is. From the research perspective, burnout is one of the elements of Compassion Fatigue (CF). It is associated with feelings of hopelessness and difficulties in dealing with work or in doing your job effectively. These negative feelings usually have a gradual onset. They can reflect the feeling that your efforts make no difference, or they can be associated with a very high workload or a non-supportive work environment. Higher scores on this scale mean that you are at higher risk for burnout.

The average score on the burnout scale is 50 (SD 10; alpha scale reliability .75). About 25% of people score above 57 and about 25% of people score below 43. If your score is below 18, this probably reflects positive feelings about your ability to be effective in your work. If you score above 57 you may wish to think about what at work makes you feel like you are not effective in your position. Your score may reflect your mood; perhaps you were having a "bad day" or are in need of some time off. If the high score persists or if it is reflective of other worries, it may be a cause for concern.

Secondary Traumatic Stress_____

The second component of Compassion Fatigue (CF) is secondary traumatic stress (STS). It is about your work related, secondary exposure to extremely or traumatically stressful events. Developing problems due to exposure to other's trauma is somewhat rare but does happen to many people who care for those who have experienced extremely or traumatically stressful events. For example, you may repeatedly hear stories about the traumatic things that happen to other people, commonly called Vicarious Traumatization. If your work puts you directly in the path of danger, for example, field work in a war or area of civil violence, this is not secondary exposure; your exposure is primary. However, if you are exposed to others' traumatic events as a result of your work, for example, as a therapist or an emergency worker, this is secondary exposure. The symptoms of STS are usually rapid in onset and associated with a particular event. They may include being afraid, having difficulty sleeping, having images of the upsetting event pop into your mind, or avoiding things that remind you of the event.

The average score on this scale is 50 (SD 10; alpha scale reliability .81). About 25% of people score below 43 and about 25% of people score above 57. If your score is above 57, you may want to take some time to think about what at work may be frightening to you or if there is some other reason for the elevated score. While higher scores do not mean that you do have a problem, they are an indication that you may want to examine how you feel about your work and your work environment. You may wish to discuss this with your supervisor, a colleague, or a health care professional.

WHAT IS MY SCORE AND WHAT DOES IT MEAN?

In this section, you will score your test and then you can compare your score to the interpretation below.

To find your score on **each section,** total the questions listed on the left in each section and then find your score in the table on the right of the section.

Compassion Satisfaction Scale:

3. _____
6. _____
12. _____
16. _____
18. _____
20. _____
22. _____
24. _____
27. _____
30. _____

Total: _____

The sum of my Compassion Satisfaction questions	So My Score Equals	My Level of Compassion
22 or less	43 or less	Low
Between 23 and 41	Around 50	Average
42 or more	57 or more	High

Burnout Scale:

*1. _____ = _____
*4. _____ = _____
8. _____
10. _____
*15. _____ = _____
*17. _____ = _____
19. _____
21. _____
26. _____
*29. _____ = _____

Reverse the scores for those that are starred.
0=0, 1=5, 2=4, 3=3, 4=2, 5=1

Total: _____

The sum of my Burnout Questions	So My Score Equals	My Level of Burnout
22 or less	43 or less	Low
Between 23 and 41	Around 50	Average
42 or more	57 or more	High

Secondary Trauma Scale:

2. _____
5. _____
7. _____
9. _____
11. _____
13. _____
14. _____
23. _____
25. _____
28. _____

Total: _____

The sum of my Secondary Traumatic Stress questions	So My Score Equals	My Level of Secondary Traumatic Stress
22 or less	43 or less	Low
Between 23 and 41	Around 50	Average
42 or more	57 or more	High

CHAPTER 13

Current Trends and Issues for Grief Counselors

*A*s we were starting to write this chapter, a book entitled *The Truth about Grief* (Konigsberg, 2010) was released. Written by a journalist who immersed herself into the theories and practices of grief counseling, this book has raised a considerable amount of controversy because of its critique of what the author calls the "grief counseling industry" in America. The writings of this author, along with some of the recent research studies in the field, deserve our attention, calling us to think critically about our work, our beliefs about how we practice, and how we seek to inform our way of practicing with factual and relevant information. We have already discussed the controversial issue of the efficacy of grief counseling in a previous chapter. We will now further the discussion regarding current or controversial issues in the field to provide a springboard to critically reflect upon the practice of grief counseling.

ONGOING IDENTIFICATION WITH STAGE THEORIES OF GRIEF

Stage theories of grief tend to focus on the need for bereaved individuals to progress through a series of distinct and time-limited psychological phases. Death educators and clinicians alike are often surprised to find that many professional training programs and many grief counselors in practice still tend to focus on the traditional stage theory as explicated by Kübler-Ross (1969). Those who are well-versed in research theory and current best practices in bereavement are highly aware that stage theories have very limited empirical support, that not all bereaved individuals experience a series of common stages in their grief, and what may have been described in the past as stages may actually be a conglomerate of various reactions such as disbelief, anger, and sadness that occur both simultaneously and in isolation at different points in time for different individuals (Prigerson & Maciejewski, 2008). It has been suggested that stage theories have been widely embraced by both popular culture and professional programs because the stages help to give some definition regarding expectations of what might be considered "normal," which would then provide ideas regarding what might also be considered "abnormal." Prigerson and Maciejewski (2008) stated that stage theories may "reflect a desire to make sense of how the mind comes to accept events and circumstances that it finds wholly unacceptable" (p. 435).

Important in this discussion is a caution for grief counselors to not look for a way to neatly package the experience of grief. Although stage theories are very popular and provide a reference point for some aspects of the grief experience, it is important to keep in mind that grief is a widely variable response that does not have a standardized trajectory, and there are many factors that determine how grief will be experienced, for how long, and the eventual outcome for a bereaved individual. In her book, Konigsberg (2010) described individuals who promote grief counseling as a set of prescribed steps, stages, and interventions, which she (rightly) challenges as simplistic and contradictory to what the current research identifies as potentially beneficial to bereaved individuals. Remember: meet clients where they are in their experience, not where you (or a theory) propose that they "should" be in their process.

WHEN IS GRIEF COUNSELING INDICATED?

As the overall conclusions of the recent research on the efficacy of grief counseling have indicated that the majority of bereaved individuals possess a good degree of innate resilience and do not require the intervention of a professional for support, how do we know when grief counseling should be sought? As stated previously, approximately 10% to 15% of bereaved individuals will experience symptoms of prolonged, ongoing grief that can be debilitating and cause significant health problems and that is related to higher mortality. Thus, it is very important for professionals whose counseling practice includes working with bereaved individuals to become very familiar with the symptoms of complicated grief/prolonged grief disorder (PGD) so that individuals who have this form of debilitating grief will be able to access intervention that is appropriate for their distress.

Most of the literature does not support preventive or proactive grief counseling, that is, offering unsolicited support and counseling services to those who may be newly bereaved but are not requesting professional support (Schut, Stroebe, van den Bout, & Terheggen, 2001). Individuals who seek counseling on their own, or who are referred by another clinician such as a family doctor, tend to benefit from therapeutic support, much in the same way that individuals with other issues benefit from interpersonal therapy (Larson & Hoyt, 2009). Of further interest is Altmaier's (2011) premise that empirical research cannot "capture" some of the variables in the therapeutic relationship that are dependent upon client and counselor attributes. She states,

> The background of best practices is important in selecting counseling approaches for a grieving client, keeping in mind that there is controversy over whether grief counseling is appropriate for everyone, only for the persons seeking treatment, or only for persons experiencing complicated grief. Moreover, though in general some counseling approaches may seem to be effective, research should not imply that the personhood of the counselor, the relationship of client and counselor, or the client's own self-healing processes are insignificant aspects of change. (p. 35)

In other words, she cautions about empirical studies that focus on client symptoms and effects of specific interventions without taking into account aspects that are relevant to the therapeutic relationship and the characteristics of both the client and the counselor in the process.

WHAT IS UNIQUE ABOUT GRIEF COUNSELING?

Although we discussed this issue previously, we will briefly return here to have another look at why grief counseling is a unique, specialized area of counseling practice. Counseling in general is seen as a form of support that assists individuals to adapt to events and issues that occur in their everyday lives, and of course, death and loss are events that do universally occur in the life of every human being. Thus, if counseling focuses on issues of adjustment and self-improvement, what makes grief counseling unique? The answer to this question lies in the understanding that grief is not a problematic response but an adaptive one. The goal of grief counseling is to assist the client to allow the adaptive aspects of grief to unfold without being misidentified as depression, anxiety disorders, or a traumatic stress reaction. Most grief counseling focuses on grief as a process that may enhance a person's ability to return to life rather than as something that needs to be treated. Grief counseling practice will be concerned with facilitating the recognition and engagement of the client's strengths, normalizing a response that is often pathologized and marginalized socially, and providing a safe place for the client to discuss the more troubling aspects of this time of disorganization and adjustment.

THE NEED TO FOCUS ON RESILIENCE INSTEAD OF NEGATIVE INDICATORS

There are several criticisms of the development of grief counseling as a unique area of specialization in clinical practice. At face value, it makes sense for clinicians who work primarily with bereaved individuals to have in-depth knowledge and understanding of the wealth of literature and research on bereavement that would be difficult for a generalist to achieve. It also would follow that a high degree of experience with bereaved individuals through a specialization in grief counseling would likely hone the skills of the counselor in working with the unique clinical features that may accompany grief in clients. However, the result of the development of grief counseling being identified as a unique specialization is the tendency to focus on the negative aspects of grief—those aspects that require intervention, or to see grief as something to be "treated," rather than an adaptive process that usually does not require professional intervention (Coifman, Bonanno, Ray, & Gross, 2007; Wortman & Silver, 1989).

The other side of the coin to the increased interest and research in bereavement is that this upsurge in information about grief may cause us to focus more on the negative aspects of grief. Most research focuses on problematic adaptation to loss and grief, and yet we know that this type of difficult grief occurs with the minority of bereaved individuals, thus skewing expectations of difficulties inadvertently onto individuals who are coping adequately with their loss. In addition, research measures that track the grief experience of participants are typically designed to identify problematic areas rather than good coping, growth, and resilience. Few, if any, grief measures will ask about laughter and moments of joy, but almost all of them will ask about sadness, crying, and loneliness (Bonanno & Keltner, 1997).

Even when clients contact a grief counselor for assistance because they are having difficulties with their grief, there are innate strengths and resilience that can be identified, and upon which the client can learn to draw upon in the counseling process. Grief counseling needs to be focused on the client's positive coping and inner resources, although recognizing that there are aspects to this experience that challenge the bereaved individual's view of the world and that do cause distress as well. It is very important to keep in mind that the majority of individuals who experience a significant loss will eventually continue with their lives in ways that will be fulfilling and meaningful.

RECOGNITION OF DIVERSITY WITHIN GRIEF AND GRIEF COUNSELING

It is important to keep in mind that the predominant views about grief and grief counseling come from research and literature that is published predominantly in the United States, followed by sources from mostly Western-oriented industrialized countries. The problem is that there is a tendency to apply the descriptions of grief and appropriate expectations and interventions related to grief to individuals in societies and cultures that may not share the same values and experiences. Konigsberg (2010) brought this point well to the forefront as she explored how individuals in Western society tend to view grief practices in non-Western cultures, implying that we "export" our grief theories and impose Western norms onto these cultures. Her descriptions are reminiscent of colonialist practices, where the invading group would claim dominance over the local culture and norms to establish a "better" and more "moral" life for the indigenous population. However, in the area of grief counseling, the "better" way is sometimes imposed upon the indigenous culture without acknowledgment that these cultures may have an effective way of approaching loss and grief; thus, the teaching of bereavement theory and practice in this way, without cultural awareness and sensitivity, has a distinctly narcissistic tone to it.

Many cultures do not see sadness or suffering to be things that an individual should rally against; rather, these experiences may be quietly accepted as just a part of life. Even within Western cultures, there is a great deal of diversity in regard to the expressions and rituals surrounding death. The Irish wake can be a celebration of the life of the individual who died, which can be punitively misinterpreted by outsiders as a grand form of denial and an excuse for a party, whereas the British emphasis on stoicism may be judged by others as a socially sanctioned form of suppression. For more detailed descriptions and explorations of religious and culturally mediated grief responses, readers are referred to several volumes that comprise the *Death and Bereavement Around the World* series edited by Morgan and Laungani, 2002 (Baywood Publishing).

In addition to cultural differences and variations, there is much written on the influence of gender socialization on the grieving process, which explores variations between how men and women grieve (see Doka & Martin, 2010; Golden, 2000; Lund, 2001; Staudacher, 1991). Although there is still strong gender socialization for men and women in Western societies in regard to the expression of affect and the cultivation of relationships, the changing roles of both women and men in the last generation in regard to work, education, and income means that there may now be more similarities than differences in grieving patterns and styles with both men and women. It is important to note that most of the research on grief is still influenced by the fact that more women than men tend to volunteer for research studies, and that the majority of bereavement research still draws heavily upon participation by individuals from middle class/upper middle class Western-oriented cultures.

What is most important to consider here is that our tacit understandings of what constitutes "normal" grief are often based upon descriptions and research from samples that cannot be readily generalized across cultures into a wide-ranging global context. As we have stated previously, the focus in grief counseling needs to be upon *congruence* for the individual—can this individual experience and express his or her grief in a way that feels consistent with his or her personality, beliefs, culture, and experiences?

THE SOCIAL CONTEXT OF GRIEF

An extension of the above discussion regarding diversity and grief is the exploration of the social context in which a bereaved individual lives and functions. There is often a tendency on the part of clinicians to focus on grief in terms of an individual's personal reactions to a loss. After all, the focus of most clinical work is upon the individual, either in private counseling or in small group work (sometimes referred to as "micro practice"; Wronka, 2008). And yet, we must recognize that these individuals exist within family systems, organizational systems, and even social and political structures that have an influence upon the interpretations of their experience of loss and the manifestation of their grief (referred to as "macro practice"; Kirst-Ashman & Hull, 2008). It is also important for the counselor to be keenly aware of any social expectations, cultural beliefs, and values that inform his or her practice so that these personal variables in the counselor are not inadvertently imposed upon clients who may not share the same beliefs and values.

Looking at these levels of intervention is very important, as the strict focus upon micro practice alone will not address the profound social influences under which an individual must live and function. The intrapsychic focus of counseling can have the potential to individualize social problems rather than identify that some problems may actually be the result of social norms that are in conflict with an individual's experience. Thus, working with a client's "self-talk" in a micro practice setting can become an exercise in identifying the social messages that have been internalized by a client about himself or herself. In this setting, it is possible to look at these internalized messages with a "macro lens," exposing the underlying social messages that have been adopted into the client's own values and self-judgments.

As most bereaved individuals seek grief counseling through one-on-one therapy or small group sessions, the broader issue becomes how to support clients in these micro practice settings, while maintaining awareness of how social rules and political policies shape the understandings of the individuals who seek therapeutic help and support. Lee and Hipolito-Delgato (2007) emphasized the need for clinicians to cultivate personal awareness of how they have been and are influenced by social and political forces, in order to be able to identify and disentangle the impact of these forces upon their engagement with their clients.

Grief counselors need to be aware of the social context of loss for their clients and be able to identify how social forces influence the process of adaptation to loss. We are social beings, and as such, we are all interconnected by our shared human experiences, with loss being one of these. We cannot define ourselves in isolation, and we all experience the dynamic interplay between our individual selves and the social and political structures in which we live. All of us experience many different types of losses, and we need the ability to recognize these losses and have the freedom to respond to them in ways that are congruent with our needs, free from the dictates of social rules that may deny or invalidate our deeply human experiences.

THE CONTROVERSY REGARDING DIAGNOSIS

With the advent of empirically derived criteria that more clearly define when grief poses a threat for potential harm and debility, there is now a great deal of controversy over whether this type of complicated grief should be included as a defined disorder in the next revision of the *Diagnostic and Statistical Manual of Mental Disorders* (*DSM*). PGD is now viewed as akin to but distinct from posttraumatic stress disorder and major depressive disorder, both of which are included in the *DSM*. Proponents who support this inclusion state that the ability to concretely identify the subset of bereaved individuals who are at risk for the complications that may occur as a result of PGD (Prigerson et al., 2009) could lead to earlier and more effective treatment for these individuals, preventing further long-term sequelae. In addition, the ability to cite a defined diagnosis and code from the *DSM* may open the door for these individuals to have access to additional resources and supports, including reimbursement by third-party payers for these services.

Many clinicians oppose the inclusion of grief into the mental disorders section of the *DSM*, concerned that doing so will cause further stigma to be attached to all bereaved individuals. These clinicians also express concern that the clinical language and "jargon" that often accompany the medical model of assessment and diagnosis of disorder may lead to the objectification of individuals through diagnostic labels rather than the empowerment of an individual to identify choices and the range of possible responses to loss. Words such as *dysfunctional, disordered, impaired, pathological,* or identifying a person with a *diagnosis* may reinforce the social vulnerability that an individual experiences after a life-altering loss event (Dietz, 2000). Given the tendency for diagnoses to be utilized as a dividing line between those who are "healthy" and those who are mentally ill, great care must be taken when associating a client's distress and pain with a reified set of criteria in a diagnosis code.

STAYING CURRENT IN THE FIELD

In a study of grief counselor's descriptions of their work with clients, Breen (2010–2011) interviewed clinicians who currently had counseling practices that specialized in the area of grief. In her study, most of the grief counselors who were interviewed were not informed of current best practices in grief counseling, with many citing adherence to stage theories of grief and a continued belief in the "grief work" hypothesis for all their clients, emphasizing the need for *all* bereaved individuals to talk about their loss and their emotions in order to "recover" from their grief. Earlier in this chapter, we discussed the lack of empirical and anecdotal relevance of stage theories of grief to the actual experience of most bereaved individuals. The grief work hypothesis, which we discussed in an earlier chapter, emphasizes that bereaved individuals must confront and express their feelings after the death of a loved one. This way of viewing grief has not been proven applicable to many bereaved individuals in empirical studies (Stroebe & Stroebe, 1991).

However, many clinicians have not availed themselves of this current research in bereavement and will still insist upon the necessity of emotional catharsis and confrontation with the loss for bereaved individuals to "recover" from a significant loss.

This type of theory-bound, cookie-cutter approach to grief counseling can cause more harm than good, completely undermining the unique needs and personal characteristics of the bereaved individual who may seek assistance through grief counseling. Some studies have identified that some individuals actually fare better by not talking about their feelings or the loss itself (Coifman et al., 2007; Stroebe, Schut, & Stroebe, 2005). Probably what is most important in this discussion is the need to recognize that there are many variables that affect the experience and needs of bereaved individuals, and an effective grief counselor will assist clients to find ways to recognize and cope with loss that are congruent with the individual client's personality, strengths, and needs as they are identified and stated by the client.

The need to stay current in the field of grief counseling is of paramount importance, as there is a great deal of research and writing about when grief counseling is and is not helpful, what approaches may or may not be indicated for which groups, and when further referrals for other professionals to be involved are indicated. Many counselors cite problems with accessing research findings because of their not being affiliated with institutions that carry scholarly journals that would report the most current findings in the field, and lack of time to read published research as problematic (Altmaier, 2011; Breen, 2010–2011). Recently, the Association for Death Education and Counseling (ADEC) negotiated with publishers to be able to include subscriptions to several of the most well-known journals in thanatology as a benefit of membership in order to address this issue of difficulty in access to current literature and research that has been raised by clinicians who wished to have access to scholarly writings in the field. Many grief counselors have formed professional online networking groups to share and discuss current information and controversial issues that are relevant to practice. The availability of such online networking and sharing may be of benefit to counselors who might otherwise not have the time or availability of these resources in their everyday working hours.

CREDENTIALING AND TRAINING

Unlike any other field in counseling, grief counseling tends to draw people who have experienced significant losses in their lives to become "helpers" to others who are facing loss and grief. Indeed, the helper-therapy principle is a well-known phenomenon, and this personal experience by grief counselors may be of benefit for the cultivation of empathic connection between the counselor and a client (Reissman, 1965). However, it can also be fraught with many drawbacks. For instance, what actually qualifies someone to be a grief counselor? If you lost your child and attended a self-help or support group and then "graduated" from that group, are you now qualified to counsel other bereaved parents? When I (D.L.H.) took my first university course on the dynamics of grief support groups, I was taken aback when the instructor, a widow of 5 years, indicated that it was her belief that only another widow could truly understand what she went through when her husband suddenly died. I did some checking on the background and training of this "professor" for the course. She had a bachelor's degree in English and had taught high school until her husband died. She then quit her job with the school board and began running grief support groups for widows out of her home. Because she was recognized in the community as someone who worked with bereaved widows in a group format, she was asked to teach a university level course on this topical area. However, she was not familiar with the current research or literature on group dynamics and had no formal training in counseling or group work. She did not know of the writings of some of the main scholars or clinicians in the field.

This instructor's experience was valuable for us to hear and understand, but we left that course with a very limited understanding of the ways that grief could be expressed (based upon a feminine view of a widow's experience), and a sense of despair that if we had not experienced the same loss as a client, we would be completely unable to be fully effective with that client—a view that is certainly not supported in the literature in counseling practice, nor upon accounts of clients' descriptions of what they found most helpful in their counseling sessions (Altmaier, 2011; Norcross, Beutler, & Levant, 2005).

We are frequently asked about what credentials and training are appropriate for someone to provide grief counseling. The first issue to be addressed is for someone to check into their locale for laws and restrictions that apply to individuals who are counselors. The requirements for someone to practice counseling and/or therapy will vary from state to state and province to province. Most states will specify a minimum level of education (usually involving a certain minimum number of clinically supervised hours in a counseling setting) that is necessary for practice. Another issue pertains to the recognition of credentials by insurance companies to qualify for reimbursement for services. This recognition usually includes affiliation and/or licensure with a regulatory body of some type (i.e., College of Therapists, American Counseling Association, American Psychological Association, etc.), and as part of your membership with this regulatory body, minimum standards for licensure are usually specified. These standards would most likely include level and type of education and preparation, continuing education and compliance with ongoing standards of current practice, and adherence to ethical standards of practice that are developed from the membership. There are difficulties in standardizing credentials because some very rigorous clinical training programs are offered through institutes, and although they are the equivalent of postgraduate training, they are not recognized as equivalent to graduate training because they are not affiliated with a university setting. Programs that train in psychoanalysis and Gestalt are such examples. This can be a very tricky and controversial topic, as having an advanced degree does not necessarily mean you will be the most effective clinician to work with a certain population. However, the issue of protection of the public and the adherence to ethical standards of practice somehow needs to be addressed for individuals who have not gone through supervised training programs in counseling.

Because there are many different forms of education about grief, and the information that is offered can range from a weekend workshop on grief recovery to undergraduate and graduate degrees in thanatology, it is important to be informed about the requirements in the area where you plan to practice to know what educational process would be the best to provide you with the necessary training and experience to be a competent practitioner. Currently, most people who provide grief counseling have advanced degrees in fields that provide training in clinical work, such as nursing, psychology, pastoral care, social work, and medicine. Once this training is completed, these students usually then engage in another program of study that will immerse them into current theory, research, and practice related to death, dying, and bereavement, which provides a more specialized form of learning and training to focus on issues related to grief and loss.

There is much confusion over the titles and terms that are used to describe people who provide bereavement support. In her book, Konigsberg (2010) described the confusion with individuals who call themselves "grief specialists" and "grief facilitators," along with grief counselors and death educators. Generally, individuals who volunteer or who do not have formal education in counseling or bereavement theory provide peer support. These individuals may assist as lay volunteers in their faith communities to provide outreach and visitation to bereaved individuals whose needs focus mostly on activities of daily living, companionship, sharing, and faith-based support. These individuals are often the ones who have moved further down the road in their grief and use their experiences to assist in the organizing

224 Principles and Practice of Grief Counseling

and running of grass-roots support groups, with the self-help model in mind. It is our view that once someone is providing a service where there is a referral base, receiving a fee for service, and the focus is on a skilled helper model, the individual providing that service should have basic training in a counseling-related field, be affiliated with a regulatory body for ongoing competency requirements, and have some form of accountability with established ethical standards of practice. Psychotherapists typically have graduate-level training in a counseling-related field, along with a minimum number of supervised clinical hours while in training, in addition to affiliation with a regulatory body (usually in the form of licensure).

The ADEC has introduced a certification program to designate individuals who have demonstrated that they possess a foundational body of knowledge in the field of thanatology (identified as "Certified in Thanatology" with the initials "CT"). Individuals who apply for the CT credential with ADEC are required to have a minimum of a bachelor's degree, to have completed a minimum number of hours working in a relevant field in thanatology, to provide two letters of reference from individuals who have been in proximity to their work, and must pass a written examination to demonstrate proficiency with the current understandings and principles of practice within thanatology. Unfortunately, this credential is often misunderstood as the completion of a training program, an indication of clinical competence, or as a certification with a clinical component, and none of these assumptions is reflected in the designation or purpose behind the CT designation. The CT credential simply indicates that the individual has a specific educational background, worked in a relevant area for a minimum number of hours, and demonstrated that he or she has proficiency in a specialized body of knowledge related to thanatology.

CONCLUSION

The field of bereavement research and practice has experienced a great surge of interest in the last 20 years, adding to our knowledge of grief, while also engendering controversies regarding how to incorporate these new understandings into the current practice of grief counseling. Counselors who work primarily with bereaved individuals need to be aware of the issues that are raised by new research in the field, and to stay abreast with clinical practice implications and recommendations from the research and literature in the field in order to provide support to their clients that is informed, relevant, and responsive.

Glossary of Terms

Congruence an individual's ability to experience and express his or her grief in a way that feels consistent with his or her personality, beliefs, culture, and experiences.

"Macro practice" exploration of experiences from family systems, organizational systems, and social and political structures that have an influence upon the individual's interpretations of their experience.

"Micro practice" focus on an individual's personal reactions to a loss. The focus of most clinical work is upon the individual, either in private counseling or in small group work.

Resilience the ability to recover quickly from illness, change, or misfortune; buoyancy.

Stage theories of grief the notion that a natural psychological response to loss involves an orderly progression through distinct stages of bereavement.

Questions for Reflection

1. What are some of the social and political influences upon how an individual experiences loss and grief?

2. You are a grief counselor. List sources of information on practice and research in the field that you would regularly consult to stay current in the field. What might be the barriers to your being able to regularly access this information? What are possible ways that you could network and exchange information with other professionals in the field?

3. In this chapter, we discuss the possibility of certain aspects of grief being included in the upcoming version of the *DSM*. On the one hand, being identified with a *DSM* diagnosis code may help some bereaved individuals to access third-party funding for additional resources and support that may not otherwise be available to them. On the other side of the argument is the concern that the application of a *DSM* diagnosis may then identify a bereaved individual with a disorder and potential accompanying stigma. Explore the pros and cons of including complicated grief into the upcoming *DSM*.

4. What do you think should be the minimum level of education, training, and experience for individuals who assist bereaved individuals?

5. One of the current controversies in grief counseling is the argument that the focus on professional intervention for grief implies that normal grief needs professional intervention, despite the fact that most people do not require the assistance of a professional to successfully navigate through

their grief. When do you think people might need the assistance of a grief counselor? When might grief counseling be unnecessary, or even harmful?

References

Altmaier, E. M. (2011). Best practices in counseling grief and loss: Finding benefit from trauma. *Journal of Mental Health Counseling, 33*(1), 33–45.

Bonanno, G. A., & Keltner, D. (1997). Facial expressions of emotion and the course of conjugal bereavement. *Journal of Abnormal Psychology, 106*(1), 126–137.

Breen, L. J. (2010–2011). Professionals' experience of grief counseling: Implications for bridging the gap between research and practice. *Omega, 62*(3), 285–303.

Coifman, K. G., Bonanno, G. A., Ray, R. D., & Gross, J. J. (2007). Does repressive coping promote resilience? Affective-autonomic response discrepancy during bereavement. *Journal of Personality and Social Psychology, 92*(4), 745–758.

Dietz, C. A. (2000). Responding to oppression and abuse: A feminist challenge to clinical social work. *Affilia, 15*(3), 369–389.

Doka, K. J., & Martin, T. L. (2010). *Grieving beyond gender: Understanding the ways men and women mourn.* New York, NY: Routledge.

Golden, T. R. (2000). *Swallowed by a snake: The gift of the masculine side of healing* (2nd ed.). Kensington, MD: Golden Healing Publishing.

Kirst-Ashman, K. K., & Hull, G. H. (2009). *Understanding generalist practice* (5th ed.). Belmont, CA: Brooks/Cole.

Konigsberg, R. D. (2010). *The truth about grief: The myth of its five stages and the new science of loss.* New York, NY: Simon & Schuster.

Kulber-Ross, E. (1969). *On death and dying.* New York, NY: Macmillan.

Larson, D. G., & Hoyt, W. T. (2009). Grief counselling efficacy: What have we learned? *Bereavement Care, 28*(3), 14–19.

Lee, C. C., & Hipolito-Delgado, C. P. (2007). Introduction: Counselors as agents of social justice. In C. C. Lee (Ed.), *Counseling for social justice* (2nd ed., pp. xiii–xxviii). Alexandria, VA: American Counseling Association.

Lund, D. A. (2001). *Men coping with grief.* Amityville, NY: Baywood.

Morgan, J. D., & Laungani, P. (2002). *Death and bereavement around the world.* Amityville, NY: Baywood.

Norcross, J. C., Beutler, L. E., & Levant, R. E. (2005). *Evidence-based practices in mental health: Debate and dialogue on the fundamental questions.* Washington, DC: American Psychological Association.

Prigerson, H. G., Horowitz, M. J., Jacobs, S. C., Parkes, C. M., Aslan, M., Goodkin, K., . . . Maciejewski, P. K. (2009). Prolonged grief disorder: Psychometric validation of criteria proposed for *DSM-V* and *ICD-11*. *PLoS Medicine, 6*(8), e1000121.

Prigerson, H. G., & Maciejewski, P. K. (2008). Grief and acceptance as opposite sides of the same coin: Setting a research agenda to study peaceful acceptance of loss. *British Journal of Psychiatry, 193*, 435–437.

Reissman, F. (1965). The "helper" therapy principle. *Social Work, 10*, 27–37.

Schut, H. A., Stroebe, M. S., van den Bout, J., & Terheggen, M. (2001). The efficacy of bereavement interventions: Determining who benefits. In M. S. Stroebe,

R. O. Hanssen, W. Stroebe, & H. A. Schut (Eds.), *Handbook of bereavement research: Consequences, coping, and care* (pp. 705–738). Washington, DC: American Psychological Association.

Staudacher, C. (1991). *Men and grief: A guide for men surviving the death of a loved one: A resource for caregivers and mental health professionals.* Oakland, CA: New Harbinger.

Stroebe, M. S., & Stroebe, W. (1991). Does "grief work" work? *Journal of Consulting and Clinical Psychology, 59*(3), 479–482.

Stroebe, W., Schut, H., & Stroebe, M. S. (2005). Grief work, disclosure, and counseling: Do they help the bereaved? *Clinical Psychology Review, 25,* 395–414.

Wortman, C., & Silver, R. (1989). The myths of coping with loss. *Journal of Consulting and Clinical Psychology, 57*(3), 349–357.

Wronka, J. (2008). *Human rights and social justice.* Thousand Oaks, CA: Sage.

Afterword

NEXT STEPS

Cassandra was a 43-year-old woman who called to set up an appointment for counseling after the sudden death of her husband 3 months earlier. When she came for the appointment, she discussed feeling paralyzed by the images of the paramedics working on her husband in their home just before he died. She also felt angry that she had been left alone to handle so many financial issues regarding his business and was greatly concerned for their three children, aged 5, 8, and 11. She used the ensuing sessions to sort through the traumatic imagery that centered on her husband's death, and to prioritize her concerns about daily matters with the business, the family, and herself. She was very worried about her children and had placed each of them into grief counseling with a child therapist. However, they were resistant to attending the sessions and did not seem to be getting much out of them. She felt they needed grief counseling because she knew that losing their father was very difficult for them, and she worried about their ability to cope with such a huge loss.

In one of her sessions, Cassandra asked for ideas about how to overcome her children's resistance to their counseling sessions. It had never occurred to her that perhaps what her children needed most was her attention and presence, and not to attend counseling. Cassandra had been strongly influenced by the almost ubiquitous notion in North American society that grief is something that needs to be treated. When we reviewed possible signals that would indicate whether her children were coping well or not, it seemed that although each of them felt sad at times and would talk about missing their Dad or feeling that his death was unfair, they were all managing to cope with his loss by relying upon the supports they already had in place at the time. With some trepidation, Cassandra decided to cancel their grief counseling sessions and reported back that they seemed relieved to not feel pressured by her to attend them. We shared possible signals in the children that might point to the need for intervention by a professional in the future, and discussed the possible regrief phenomenon that they all might experience at special dates, occasions, and milestones when their Dad's absence might be highly prominent to them. After this discussion, Cassandra felt more empowered to care for her children in the midst of their grief. She continued to attend sessions for a couple months more, and then finished counseling after she began sleeping better and was ready to return to work.

Thinking back about what we have shared in this book, could you think about ways that you might have supported Cassandra in her loss? How about her concerns for her children? How would you have known what was most important to focus upon in her sessions? We hope that after reading the content of this book, you would feel more confident in your support of a client like Cassandra, and that you would be able to assist her to build upon her innate strengths and resilience as she continues to rebuild her world.

In this book, we have discussed many aspects of grief counseling. We have delineated how grief counseling is unique from other forms of counseling because the normal grieving process is not something that needs to be treated, but rather allowed to unfold in its own healthy and adaptive way. Whether you are a clinician with many years' experience or a novice to this field, hopefully you have gleaned a good, solid understanding of the grieving process and an appreciation for the importance of learning how to be fully present to the experiences of bereaved individuals, both as a professional and as a fellow traveler of life's path. We also hope that you will more readily recognize that experiences of significant loss and change can be akin to the grief that occurs after the death of a loved one. There does not need to be a "body" per se in order to realize that a death of something intangible or symbolic has occurred.

Grief counseling is really about honoring losses that occur as part of normal lived human experience. The grief response is often socially stigmatized because it reveals our vulnerability in the midst of a society that places such a high value upon productivity, efficiency, and rugged individualism. Human beings are social creatures, meant to form strong attachments to others as part of their existence and survival; however, the focus upon highly individualistic and materialistic goals makes this relational side of our being seem like a detriment instead of a gift. What we have often found in counseling individuals whose worlds have been shattered by loss is that the place of feeling broken and vulnerable can also be a time of great potential. In the painful process of having to rebuild your assumptions about the world after a significant loss, you might also begin to question priorities and goals that were previously taken for granted, or to see life in a way that you may never have seen it before.

After a while, it is common for our clients to begin to realize that they are much stronger and more resilient than they ever thought possible. With this recognition, there are new doors and possibilities that are present that may never have been considered before. When you journey alongside bereaved clients for a while and begin to see this type of pattern emerging from the despair, you begin to trust the process more, and you find the work nurturing a sense of hope and meaning rather than being depressing and morbid. Halifax (1993) referred to this type of journey as the "fruitful darkness," indicating that we often become more open to receiving and learning some of the most valuable lessons and insights about ourselves, others, and the world after we go through some of the darkest times in our lives.

It is our hope that as you embark in a practice with individuals who are grieving, you will also find these things to be true. You can learn more about your capacity to care and the depth of your ability to be fully present to others. You can also hold the hope for those who seek your assistance at this time, knowing that this painful journey has the potential to lead them to a place of greater compassion for themselves and others. But most of all, we hope you simply find a greater appreciation for life in all its diversity and experiences, and embrace the deep resilience and strengths that each of us may have.

Reference

Halifax, J. (1993). *The fruitful darkness: A journey through Buddhist practice and tribal wisdom.* New York, NY: Grove Press.

Index

Accommodation, 35, 87, 101, 136
Accurate empathy, 7, 11
Acute grief, 4
  meaning reconstruction therapy,
    143–144
  symptoms in complicated grief (CG),
    134, 135, 147
ADEC. *See* Association for Death
    Education and Counseling
    (ADEC)
Adults
  attachment behaviors/styles, 28
  sandtray therapy, 169–170
Advanced empathy, 68–69, 78
Advocacy, complicated grief (CG) in, 146
Ambiguous loss, 104–105, 111
  aspects of, 105–106
  chronic sorrow and nonfinite loss, 107
  effects of, 106
  identification, 105
  and nonfinite loss features, 106–107
Ambivalence normalization, 109–110
"America's Most Wanted" show, 146
Anger, 82, 127–128
Anxiety, 123, 135, 138, 142
  CG, control of anxiety, 137
  versus fear, 125
  with unsafe feeling, 139, 142
Assimilation, 35
Association for Death Education and
    Counseling (ADEC), 221, 224
Assumptive world, 15–17, 22
  challenges to, 35
  coping, 206

and loss, 98–99
  traumatic grief, 138, 147
  working environments, 200
Attachment relationship
  avoidant attachment patterns, 30
  behaviors, 22, 28–29
    of adults, 28
    defined, 27
    demonstration, 119
    in human, 27
    infants and mothers, 27–28
    older widows, research with, 28
    versus relational bonds, 26–27
  system, 140–141
    adult bereavement, 98
    and assumptive world relation, 99
    grief, 119, 140
    in infants, 27
  theory, 16–17, 27
    dual process model, 30
Attending skills, 78
  attentive body language, 61–62
  eye contact, 60
  SOLER model, 62
  verbal tracking, 61
  vocal qualities, 60–61
Attentive body language, 61–62
Avoidant attachment patterns, 30
Awareness exercise, 175–176, 207

Behaviors. *See also* Attachment
    relationship
  of bereaved individuals, 86